Pastoral Cosmopolitanism in Edith Wharton's Fiction

Pastoral Cosmopolitanism in Edith Wharton's Fiction

The World Is a Welter

Margarida Cadima

ANTHEM PRESS

Anthem Press
An imprint of Wimbledon Publishing Company
www.anthempress.com

This edition first published in UK and USA 2023
by ANTHEM PRESS
75–76 Blackfriars Road, London SE1 8HA, UK
or PO Box 9779, London SW19 7ZG, UK
and
244 Madison Ave #116, New York, NY 10016, USA

© 2023 Margarida Cadima

British Library Cataloguing-in-Publication Data
A catalogue record for this book is available from the British Library.

Library of Congress Control Number: 2023933115
A catalog record for this book has been requested.

ISBN-13: 978-1-83998-843-1 (Hbk)
ISBN-10: 1-83998-843-6 (Hbk)

Cover Credit: Edith Wharton Collection. Yale Collection of American
Literature, Beinecke Rare Book and Manuscript Library.

This title is also available as an e-book.

CONTENTS

"The world is a welter and has always been one; but though all the cranks and the theorists cannot master the old floundering monster, or force it for long into any of their neat plans of readjustment, here and there a saint or a genius suddenly sends a little ray through the fog, and helps humanity stumble on, and perhaps up."

Edith Wharton, *A Backward Glance* (1934)

ACKNOWLEDGMENTS

This book is the outcome of a lifelong passion for reading literature, which culminated in researching an author who has led an international life, Edith Wharton. I cannot fathom writing my book on anyone else's fiction.

It was at the 2016 Institute for World Literature at Harvard University, inspired by the seminar on "Cosmopolitanism and Its Discontents," that I had the primordial notions for the concept of "pastoral cosmopolitanism" found in this thesis. I am grateful to Prof. Mariano Siskind, with whom I first shared my ideas and consequently motivated me to pursue them further.

My most heartfelt thanks go to my doctoral supervisor Dr. Andrew Radford, at the University of Glasgow without whom this book could not have happened at all. Thank you for the unconditional support and brilliant feedback on my writing and for continually encouraging my ideas, my research and my pursuit of academic opportunities to present my doctoral work. These past four years you have always been promptly available to read my drafts, to clarify my queries and to recognize the stakes of my research project. My PhD thesis is the result of your nurturing and rigorous supervision.

It is not easy to secure access to resources during this pandemic. I would like to thank Prof. Francis Morrone for the Central Park reading suggestions. They were invaluable. Moreover, I am very grateful to Prof. Carol Singley and Prof. Frederick Wegener for the copies of the two typescript gardening articles that can be found in the Appendices of this book.

Finally, I would like to thank my parents. Thank you for giving me an international upbringing and for encouraging my intellectual curiosity from a young age. I would like to thank my father for funding my doctoral studies which allowed me to pursue my love for literature thus far. I dedicate this book to my mother, without whose love, support and unwavering faith in me I could not have made it this far. Mãezinha, isto é para ti.

INTRODUCTION

In her 1934 autobiography *A Backward Glance*, Edith Wharton proposes that the "world is a welter and has always been one."[1] Apprehending the "world" as little more than a mass of sensations, opinions and beliefs reminds us of Nietzsche's famous conception of advanced industrial "modernity," its white noise, bewildering complexities and civic pathologies in *The Will to Power*. For Nietzsche, the sheer "abundance of disparate impressions" is "greater than ever […] The tempo of this influx *prestissimo*."[2] Does Wharton find relief from, or even a partial panacea for this "welter"—Nietzsche describes it as a hectic "flood of impressions"—in the improved, idyllic or pristine forms of nature synonymous with pastoral? Could this literary, social and cultural phenomenon be viewed as a storehouse of utopian ideas, at a time when many cultural commentators saw the "frontier" ending, cities expanding and rural communities dwindling? Might the pastoral illuminate alternative values to an audience grown weary of the mantras and watchwords synonymous with an American expansionist agenda: ceaseless and explosive growth, "development, size (bigness), and—by extension—change, novelty, innovation, wealth, and power."[3] These questions are not only central to my book but acquire greater urgency given Lawrence Buell's recent claim that pastoral is a type of "cultural equipment that Western thought has for more than two millennia been unable to do without."[4]

My research situates Wharton as an author who is acutely responsive to pastoral tropes and terrain, among other species of spaces. She addresses the affective and geographical resonances of such sites, especially sparsely populated localities, and landforms—voguish mountain resorts, private ornamental gardens, lush public parks, monumental and "sham" ruins—which offered pampered American socialites a brief escape from the "welter." In a letter to Anna Bahlmann from May 3, 1893, Wharton recounts her travels through Brittany, France:

The drive took us through a lovely rolling country with hedges of hawthorn & broom, & on arriving we found a most beautiful old château, placed on a high plateau overlooking a wide expanse of woods & meadows—a beautiful pastoral landscape, such as one would never tire of.[5]

The beauty of this "pastoral landscape" is mirrored and enacted in mellifluous and witty effects of rhyme ("château [...] plateau") and alliteration. Wharton's writerly agency and artfulness is apparent in how she orchestrates as well as records a natural world of "woods and meadows." Her graceful stylistic flourishes play to our culturally ingrained expectations and assumptions, the ways in which we conceive of the serene bucolic "expanse"—a restorative retreat of which we, like Wharton, never seem to "tire." Describing her move to The Mount, her house in the Berkshires of Massachusetts, Wharton averred that "life in the country is the only state which has completely satisfied me, and I had never been allowed to gratify it, even for a few weeks at a time."[6]

When portraying her visit to "La Palazzina (Villa Gori), Siena" in the 1904 nonfiction study *Italian Villas and Their Gardens*, Wharton noted that "the remembrance of this leafy stage will lend new life to the reading of the Italian pastorals."[7] Wharton's tone here is less rapt than in the letter above, but equally intriguing. "New life" implies that "pastorals" can be employed to open up and complicate the ways in which we register and construe our physical surroundings; that it is a flexible and reflexive mode, morphing to process increasingly challenging environmental and political conditions at the dawn of the twentieth century. However, "remembrance"—with its hint of communal nostalgia and idealization—and "reading" draws attention to the mannered artifice and *backward glance* of pastoral itself, how it is frequently performed and promoted via "stage" or page. Is it perhaps, a sad tribute act to a world that no longer exists, utterly divorced from the feelings of embodied situatedness that contemporary place writers aspire to distil? To what extent are pastoral ideals reliant on a fantasized rather than palpable geographical milieu? Wharton's phrasing, such as "*leafy* stage" (my emphasis), evokes a keen desire for an innocent link with a locus of mountain wilds, green altars and the ancient Greek god of shepherds and flocks who features in Robert Frost's early poem "Pan with Us" (1902). Such yearning is shot through by an anxious sense that in our everyday transactions and movements—for example travelling overseas by plane or train—we have irretrievably damaged the *prospect* of such innocent immersion.[8] Wharton's reference to "pastorals" in *Italian Villas* makes us reassess a mode that often voices topographical and socio-economic unease, utilizing tropes of estrangement and sought-after reconciliation. "Pastorals" appeal, on some basic level then, to a vision of "lovely rolling country" that may only be savored through the stylizations of verse or frozen and framed on a painter's canvas. Wharton's "leafy stage" implies that composing work in this mode is as much about daydreaming as it is about methodical and mature documentation.

These brief examples are only—to borrow from William Empson—some versions of pastoral found in Wharton's oeuvre.[9] As Paul Alpers rightly observes, weighing the myriad scholarly endeavors to pin down the core facets of this mode, and thus, "delimit" its scope, "there are as many versions of pastoral as critics who write about it."[10] Indeed, Alpers's own effort to capture the essence of the mode—"pastoral's defining characteristics: idyllic landscape, landscape as a setting for song, an atmosphere of *otium,* a conscious attention to art and nature, herdsmen as singers, and [...] herdsmen as herdsmen"—comically slides into vagueness and generalization.[11] "[I]n all probability," according to T. G. Rosenmeyer, "a tidy definition of what is pastoral about the pastoral tradition is beyond our reach."[12] For Peter Marinelli, pastoral is "the most all-embracing" of literary terms, while Bryan Loughrey posits that its multifarious legacy contributes towards its interpretation as a bitterly contested label.[13] Arguably one of the most perceptive recent scholars in this field, Terry Gifford, explains how some readers still view pastoral as "a deeply suspect" aesthetic phenomenon in an epoch of ecological crisis. Martha Hale Shackford goes further than Gifford: "pastoral has, in many cases, justly been a word of reproach and ridicule [...] Pastoral, idyll, eclogue, bucolic" are "used interchangeably for productions that range from exquisite poetry to sustained doggerel."[14]

These definitional difficulties do not deter Wharton from brooding over the aesthetic and political connotations of pastoral in her fiction—far from it. She is rather energized and liberated by Alpers's overriding notion that pastoral is a capacious category "that includes, but is not confined to, a number of identifiable genres."[15] What is curious here is how, at the very moment when the stoical and doughty precapitalist yeoman farmer seemed ancillary to twentieth-century America's self-perception, pastoral tropes continued to shape the cultural imaginary, especially "New World" notations of citizenship, democratic empowerment and (the literary) marketplace.[16] This trend has been variously acknowledged by Mathilde Skoie and Sonia Bjornstad Velaquez's *Pastoral and the Humanities: Arcadia Re-Inscribed,* William Barillas' *The Midwestern Pastoral: Place and Landscape in Literature of the American Heartland,* as well as Ann Marie Mikkelsen's *Pastoral, Pragmatism, and Twentieth-Century American Poetry.*[17] Mikkelsen's shrewdly angled and historicized account charts how white male poets like Robert Frost, Wallace Stevens and John Ashbery radically remodeled pastoral imagery, showing how verse could keep pace with a modern political economy and debates about the defects of a purely fiscal and proprietary relation to land.

These critically nimble studies do not, regrettably, shed much light on how Wharton, impelled by a sense of the malleability of pastoral at the turn of the twentieth century, portrays her protagonists' sensory enquiries, encounters and explorations in the "non-metropolitan." I employ the term "non-metropolitan" pointedly here. I wish to complicate popular perceptions of "Wharton's world"—reinforced by numerous handsomely produced cinematic and television adaptations of her novels—as one rooted in often opulent domestic interiors with their waspish social cliques, strict rules of politesse and elaborate hierarchies. Virginia Woolf, in a 1925 *Saturday Review of Literature* essay on "American Fiction" famously—or notoriously?—sketched a picture of Wharton driven by the "obsession with surface distinctions—the age of old houses, the glamour of great names."[18] While acknowledging that this is an aspect of Wharton's mainstream appeal, I prioritize her aesthetic representations of more panoramic vistas, especially the imbrication of gendered subjectivity and external nature. As Janet Beer states: "Throughout her writing life," Wharton "sought to communicate her sense of the importance of place, of literal terrain, but also the landscape of the imagination, her own powers of invention and expression being most freely exercised in the Old but on the subject of the New World."[19]

Beer's stress on "the importance of place" has proven prescient given how scholars in the environmental humanities like Lawrence Buell and Terry Gifford seek to pinpoint, dissect and quantify the pastoral mode, how its cardinal features harmonize (or clash) with current ecological enquiries. That such scholarly debate is rich in possibilities for reappraising Wharton's work is apparent in Nancy Von Rosk's 2001 essay "Spectacular Homes and Pastoral Theatres: Gender, Urbanity and Domesticity in *The House of Mirth*." Unfortunately, Von Rosk's article only discusses a single primary text, but her conclusion warrants repeating: "What makes Wharton's work so compelling is the extent to which it embodies the psychic and cultural shifts of her time."[20] In Von Rosk's account, the pastoral conveys these shifts—it is not a static, monolithic or obsolescent poetic phenomenon. Subsequent pundits have taken Von Rosk's remarks as an invitation to explore the pastoral in other fictional texts by Wharton. The results have not been entirely satisfying. This is because critics tend to focus on supplying a historically nuanced case for how Wharton's twentieth century "American pastoral" is distinct from earlier fictional articulations of the "school." The problem here of course is that Wharton's familiarity with and use of the mode comprises a unique fusion of "Old" and "New World" tropes. Judith Fryer, in the chapter devoted to Wharton in *Felicitous Space: The Imaginative Structures of Edith Wharton and Willa Cather*, proposes that "Wharton created an 'urban pastoral', I mean 'pastoral' in a particular way."[21] Fryer goes on to clarify that Wharton "neither attributed healing qualities to nature nor urged a withdrawal from society."[22] This argument, however, is not fully developed. Nevertheless, Fryer's lively critical approach—scrutinizing how narrative form and lexis refreshes extant conceptions of the bustling American city and the rustic sanctuary—invites us to weigh Wharton's aesthetic articulation of topographical experiences, issues and imaginaries *across* her oeuvre. Meredith L. Goldstein and Emily J. Orlando's *Edith Wharton and Cosmopolitanism* (2016) takes up this challenge to a limited degree. Annette Benert also probes these ideas in her chapter entitled "The Romance of Nature" from *The Architectural Imagination of Edith Wharton*, published in 2007. Benert is fascinated by how Wharton's shifting attitudes, fictional tropes and philosophies are mirrored in her meticulous portrayal of the material environment. Ultimately her discerning analysis says more to gender theorists than to commentators operating under the disciplinary banner of ecocriticism. However, there is a great deal we can add to Benert's key finding: "the traditional American paradigm that identifies the natural world with freedom of all sorts and juxtaposes it to culture, to the social world, identified with restraint, artifice and inauthenticity."[23]

By paying scrupulous attention to Wharton's fictional landscapes, we can bring into sharper focus how her texts chart intricate, dynamic and evolving interactions between history, "the social world" and what Wharton's friend Vernon Lee called the *genius loci* or spirit-of-place.[24] Lee's evocative term serves as an apt and salutary reminder that Wharton's narratives of the "Old" and "New World" are deeply entwined with the "afterlives" of the leitmotifs and techniques of nature writing in general and the pastoral mode specifically.[25]

Past/oral, Present and Future

As I have suggested, pastoral is a flexible term and Wharton's usage reveals sophisticated (and at times slippery) habits of thought and expression. My emphasis on Wharton's lifelong interest in and engagement with pastoral, how she refines fresh critical and creative applications for its tropes, owes a major debt to Lawrence Buell and those whose research he has influenced, like Ken Hiltner. In the "General Introduction" to *Ecocriticism: The Essential Reader* Hiltner appeals for the "humanities, such as literary study," to play a more active and inventive "role" in "our shared challenge of forging an environmentally better future."[26] Buell's 1995 book *The Environmental Imagination* explains that "Nature has long been reckoned a crucial ingredient of the American national ego. Ever since an American literary canon began to crystallize, American literature has been considered preoccupied with country and wilderness." This is not a dazzling or audacious intervention. What makes Buell's project notable is its thoughtful response to Leo Marx's ground-breaking *The Machine in the Garden: Technology and the Pastoral Ideal in America* (1964) which Buell calls "the best book ever written about the place of nature in American literary thought."

Marx describes a North America impelled to subordinate natural land-scapes to industrial and entrepreneurial imperatives. Marx's closing pages challenge future scholars to make pastoral relevant again, as a means of guiding readers onto a less ecologically damaging path. Buell responds to *The Machine in the Garden* by positing that pastoral has always possessed this public, socially conscious, even inspiring energy—it does not sidestep or evade but rather validates a "green agenda" in often surprising ways. Buell opines that since Virgil pastoral has privileged the class and ethical obsessions of the pilgrim-poet, who also grasps and surveys scenarios beyond his own circum-scribed "emotional horizon." Of course, Buell is mindful of the peculiarly problematic issues associated with these claims. He registers that the "ambig-uous legacy of Western pastoralism" offers up "some major stumbling blocks in the way of developing a mature environmental aesthetics."[27] For African American authors, as Paul Outka notes, the pastoral carries a profoundly sinister affective charge given how the rustic hinterland is inextricably linked with a history of racist violence, oppression and slavery.[28] However, these fac-tors should not derail, in Buell's opinion, our efforts to gauge the literary and political possibilities, as well as frustrations, of pastoral writing in relation to ecological themes like sustainability, waste/lands, overconsumption and resource conservation. His case is anchored in a confident grasp of the lon-gevity and elasticity of pastoral's cultural applications—shapeshifting is both vital to and inherent in the mode's aesthetic DNA.

Buell's published research does not address in granular detail how Wharton explicitly made American and European facets of pastoral core to her imaginative mapping of place over the course of her career. However, Buell furnishes a critical lens through which to investigate how she bolsters the modern pastoral by confronting turn-of-the-century socio-economic convulsions and the ever more intricate divisions among reading commu-nities that they fostered.[29] Moreover, novels such as *The House of Mirth* and *The Custom of the Country* are especially alert to "the hidden interdependencies between areas of life usually seen as opposites: nature and artifice, pastoral and nature, leisure and work, fantasy and reality."[30]

Before we embrace Buell's scholarly campaign wholeheartedly—especially his stress on "the ecocentric repossession of pastoral"—it is worth weighing what other, more skeptical critics like Greg Garrard and Terry Gifford parse at the conceptual blind spots, obfuscations and naiveties of the tradition.[31] Gifford recognizes the surprising dearth of cutting-edge research on mod-ern American pastoral and welcomes Buell's nuanced contribution. However,

Gifford concludes, "we cannot ignore the evidence of the anti-pastoral and the development" even prevalence, of "the pejorative use of the term."[32] Such generic shortcomings are implicit in Kevin R. McNamara and Timothy Gray's identification of "Some Versions of Urban Pastoral" for *The Cambridge Companion to the City in Literature*: "*Pastoral* conjures fantasies of rural freedom: shepherds lounging in meadows piping on oaten flutes, as they often do in Theocritus' *Idylls* and Virgil's *Eclogues*, or professing undying love for their coy mistresses, a common pastime" of the "early modern pastoral."[33] As these scholars variously imply, Buell's energetic appeal for readers of American literature to reassess the "luminous ideal" of pastoral and the potency of its politically progressive, even "oppositional forms," fails fully to answer the charges of rival pundits who subject the mode, its guiding principles and cultural legitimacy, to trenchant and sometimes scathing critique.[34]

As early as 1974, John Barrell and John Bull foresaw, in their *Penguin Book of English Pastoral Verse*, a remarkable "revival of interest in the Pastoral" alongside "the current concern with ecology."[35] However, they were far from convinced that such an alignment could be affirmed or defended. For Barrell and Bull, pastoral furnishes "Industrial Man" with an opportunity to "[look] away from his technological wasteland to an older and better world," thus softening the psychological impact of widespread environmental damage in a democratic but deeply unequal society.[36] Their phrasing here deliberately evokes the affective appeal of Tityrus' farmstead in Virgil's first eclogue, an origin story for the mode that measures pastoral satisfactions like material simplicity against the luxury, venal ambitions and unsavory political rifts of an urbanized world beyond. Wharton's fiction both indulges and interrogates this craving for escapist solace and greater affective spontaneity, as a protagonist like Lily Bart attempts to swap New York's gilded cage for a golden age of fresh green terrain. Lily's visit to Bellomont in *The House of Mirth* casts an acerbic sidelight on the temptation to "manufacture" a feeling of umbilical attachment to unspoiled American nature, as recompense for its apparent absence from "the world" of "welter" outlined in *A Backward Glance*. For Friedrich Schiller, "our feeling for Nature is like that of an Invalid for Health." Lily resembles Schiller's restive and "sentimental poet," embarking on a quest for "nature but as an idea and in a perfection in which it never existed."[37] As Lily learns to her chagrin, in the words of critic Joseph Meeker, retreat "into fantasies is not a workable solution to urban and existential ills."[38] Lily's pastoral reveries can do nothing to improve a polity that, in Virginia Woolf's very Wharton-esque lexis, "forbade any natural feeling" and functioned as "a very competent machine. It was convinced that girls must be changed into married women. It had no doubts, no mercy."[39]

As a necessary (and sobering) riposte to Buell's influential thesis, Barrell and Bull posit that the affective comfort of pastoral drifts dangerously into the realm of outright denial—the mode looks back in languor so that harsh, desensitizing present-day facts are blotted out. This is why, Barrell and Bull conclude, "the pastoral vision simply will not do"—it is hardly designed to tell us compelling and urgent stories of "today." Pastoral is composed from an unassailable position of metropolitan ease and erudition; it does not imply, as William Empson claimed, a "beautiful relation between rich and poor," the "high" and "low."[40] At best, Barrell and Buell observe, the pastoral registers environmental crisis by willfully sketching an agreeable parallel universe, without the need to depict or dissect the heedless human behaviors which triggered that crisis in the first place.[41] In T.G. Rosenmeyer's view, we savor "pastoral because it enables us to live, on our own terms, with a nature we have abandoned; pastoral relieves our sense of loss without forcing us to give up on our new gains as beneficiaries of the industrial age."[42]

Barrell and Bull's stern sense of a pastoral "vision that will not do" relies on an overly narrow reading of the mode as irresponsible, jejune and self-centered. There is not much room in their reading for my sense of a Wharton who documents myriad "rustic," "regional" or "natural" landscapes in order to interrogate not just the source and social function of her own novelistic practice, but also the *correct relationship* between a North American woman writer and the material terrain she surveys. Barrell and Bull's thesis implies that the environmental humanities will be hamstrung if it overcommits to pastoral as a subject of extended critical analysis or as model for ecological awakening. This is because, Barrell and Bull aver, the pastoral is wedded to the testimony of cosseted, detached and overwhelmingly male spectators. Reappraising Barrell and Bull's volume nowadays gives the impression that the pastoral actually facilitates environmental abuse by partitioning the domains of ecology and economy. However, their forthright assessment tells us little of the intricate links between pastoral form and content. The following chapters will demonstrate that Wharton's writing identifies and illustrates the perils synonymous with Barrell and Bull's version of pastoral. However, Wharton also perceives complicating ironies and a more refined, riddling and self-conscious energy at play, which is woven into the aesthetic fabric of the earliest examples of the mode. Kathryn Gutzwiller's research, admirably attentive to questions about caste power and patronage, gendered subjectivity, ethnicity and sexual orientation, shows us that what is missing from Barrell and Bull's critique is a fully realized feeling for how, say, Theocritus's pastorals are canny "representations." Such texts, she contends, are anchored in a productive "tension between what is being represented and the act of representation."[43]

Leo Marx, in the foundational *The Machine in the Garden* (1964) and later essays such as "Pastoralism in America" (1986) and "Does Pastoralism Have a Future?" (1992) revisits these issues. He asks—and this is especially pertinent when reflecting on Wharton—that we excavate imaginatively the real-world affect and actualities buried beneath the slick surface effects of the mode. Moreover, the drive toward "idealization" might be construed, Marx declares, "not as a failed attempt to transcribe reality, but rather as a vehicle for quasi-utopian aspirations without which no critique of existing culture can be effective or complete."[44] If, as Renato Poggioli claims in a seminal account, the "psychological root of the pastoral is a double longing after innocence and happiness, to be recovered not through conversion or regeneration but merely through a retreat," then we need to discount how Tityrus' farmstead in Virgil's first eclogue not only affords a still center in a turning world but also provides coded political commentary on the reasons why the farm is cherished—as a safe house from cruel political forces that make victims out of the virtuous.[45] This is helpful in addressing those Wharton characters who "take flight," often overseas, into the gardens, parks and icy peaks of Europe. These patterns of mobility and migration not only expose the privileged standpoint of affluent wayfarers. Such movements also imply the interpretive potential of what Scott Hess terms the pastoral's "perspective by incongruity." So, Lily Bart's search for a rustic retreat clarifies what is scorned or left behind, albeit briefly—a cheerless urban arena where the interplay of money and marriage reduces potentially decent people to mere bodies for barter. For Hess, the concealments of pastoral that Barrell and Bull deplore can be "re-angled" as (self-)critical components, motivating us to parse the representation of "escape" from various viewpoints, to foster new academic insights.[46]

This more positive attitude to pastoral tropes in art and literature is certainly attractive when turning to Wharton's many fictional episodes involving the imbrication of self and the organic plenitude of nature. Buell expands and nuances this scholarly standpoint to sketch a viable future for pastoral writing in the twenty-first century. However, Terry Gifford's book *Pastoral*, part of the "New Critical Idiom" series and recently updated in 2019, indicates that the mode's integrity, objectivity and interrogative impact is diluted by its entanglement within a web of aesthetic, commercial and political laws. Gifford, like Leo Marx, notes the "convincing testimony to the continuing appeal of the bucolic [...] supplied by advertising copywriters."[47] Marx's phrasing carries a faint echo of American philosopher John Dewey's sardonic conception, in *Art as Experience* (1934), of the prosperous, complacent "city man who lived in the country when he was a boy" and indulges a taste for "purchasing pictures of green meadows with grazing cattle or purling brooks."[48] Scott Hess's notion of "postmodern pastoral," for all its conceptual verve, is not blind to the glib, highly selective and compensatory tactics described by Gifford, Marx and Dewey. Hess understands why so many commentators see pastoral as "no longer set against" the ferment and disarray of "modern society" but rather furnishes "a consumer-friendly interface with that society."[49] In my chapter on Wharton's fictional summits we find a complex commentary on this "rebranding" of pastoral as a desirable commodity and upmarket tourist destination. Wharton's incisive depictions of modish hillside hotels and chalets or grand rural estates like Bellomont recall Raymond Williams' seminal *The Country and the City*, especially his conception of the "enameled" world of pastoral, whose regal splendor is made possible and perpetuated by hard-headed political and economic activity: "it is not easy to forget that Sidney's *Arcadia* [...] is written in a park which had been made by enclosing a whole village and evicting the tenants."[50]

As this necessarily brisk survey of criticism demonstrates, the ethical provocations and "alternative set of values" that Lawrence Buell locates and lauds in pastoral stock-in-trade must themselves be subjected to suspicious close reading. Through such rigorous scrutiny we can get a better handle on how Wharton's fiction reacts to Terry Gifford's recent query: "Can there really be no twentieth-century continuations of the pastoral form?"[51] At a time when New York City was transforming into the metropolis we know today and Paris had just undergone Haussmann's radical renovations, Wharton pushes against John Barrell's impatient dismissal of a hopelessly dated, exclusionary and elitist mode. Rather she sees pastoral as bracingly open-ended, ideologically intricate and ecologically inquisitive—capable of expressing the intellectual labors, aesthetic tastes and political convictions of those like herself who had been historically marginalized because of gender. Here she demonstrates that "pastoral" authors are "inescapably of their own culture," its preoccupations, traumas and tensions. Indeed, Dominic Head concludes that "each generation" will thoroughly test "the relevance of pastoral writing"—as "human needs change, so does the function of pastoral evolve."[52]

The Book Chapters

Although it has long been debated how the pastoral seems to stand in vexed (and critically vexing) relation to metropolitan values, codes and energies, it is time to acknowledge that the mode stages a much more involved "conversation" with the urban, at least in Wharton's published texts. My first chapter– "The Pastoral Cosmopolitanism of the (not so) Secret Garden"— pays tribute to Marx's *The Machine in the Garden* as well as those now very familiar accounts of American history that rely on catchwords like Edenic frontier, nature's nation and virgin land to limn the distinct components of

"New World" pastoral.[53] Marx's searching account of the confounding and
contradictory relationship with nature epitomized by modern American pastoralism—whereby Wharton's affluent countrymen waxed lyrical about rural
standards and yet pursued ecologically destructive commercial ploys to realize a bucolic paradise—has been rightly extolled by recent spatial theorists
such as Peter Cannavo.[54] My following chapters' principal concern is with
Wharton's fictional gardens and parks, and how they vouchsafe examples of
what Terry Gifford calls the pastoral tendency to portray "borderland spaces
of activity which can be seen through a number of frames."[55] I prefer Gifford's
"borderland" to the concept of the "frontier" that once dominated academic
discussions of a uniquely American pastoral mode.[56] In my view, Gifford's
"borderland" is a better term for identifying those nebulous physical sites
which not only subvert fixed and unchanging conceptions of place but also
reveal where culture and nature, the interloper and the indigene, meet and
negotiate. The ornamental gardens and public parks in Wharton's novels and
short stories are such intricately liminal localities. Moreover, her elaborate
descriptions of pastoral design in a country estate reflects—in often mischievous or self-conscious ways—our contemporary concerns about city living.
By focusing on these zones, we gain a more nuanced grasp of how Wharton's
pastoral is brought into bolder relief at that very moment when it seems to
be engulfed by the forces synonymous with a different type of "frontiering"
gusto—one more invested in industrial and commercial "development" than
territorial acquisition or enlargement. Wharton's fictional borderlands are
places where the traditional tropes of Anglo-Saxon farmers clearing and
toiling upon the soil are replaced by weirdly immaculate country estates in
which "adventuring" figures like Lily Bart find themselves surrounded by
new threats and enemies from the metropolitan glitterati.

    In order to reinforce these arguments, I employ the term "pastoral cos-
mopolitanism"—joining two concepts that seem to be at odds or profoundly
divergent, when, in fact, they are not. The "return to nature" or the potency
of the countryside that some of Wharton's jaded, frontier-crossing characters crave—to enjoy the tranquillizing sights and sounds of a secluded nook
or bower—is a cosmopolitan form of displacement. This is illustrated by
Wharton's "garden plots" in novels such as *The Age of Innocence*, where the
retreat from a sterile and snobbish urban culture is all too brief. Wharton
indicates that her characters' desire to seek out new fields of experience and
revel in an Arcadian elsewhere allows us to reappraise "cosmopolitanism" as
a critical category. We can also ponder how the social self—and the values
and virtues of travel—are culturally constructed. A crucial research question
in my first chapter is whether curiosity about the garden refuge—or what
is termed in *The House of Mirth* a special "spot of earth"—can be reconciled

with, and even enrich, an intrepid globe-trotting tendency.[57] I suggest that a
number of Wharton's protagonists are well placed to address this issue, given
how they are caught *between* overcrowded city and undisturbed hinterland,
urbanized Europe and American wilderness, nostalgic fancy and utopian
hope, progress and the primitive, modest homeland *roots* and glamorous foreign *routes*.[58]

In Part I, I also contend that when Wharton's narrators evoke localized
green retreats, we must practice a different form of reading, one attuned to
the palimpsests of place. The Bellomont episode in *The House of Mirth* provides a vital opportunity to refine this close/r reading. I indicate that Lily
Bart's vexation during her stay at this lavishly appointed country house derive
from her failure to construe her organic surroundings precisely. Bellomont
seems to promise a refreshing rustic "getaway" when in fact its neat gravel
walks, parterres and picturesque vistas conceal a history of violence—waged
by patrician men against their "property" (women, slaves, soil), and by watchful women against each other. *The House of Mirth*, like *The Age of Innocence* and
Twilight Sleep, remind us of what Leo Marx terms precarious and "complex
pastorals": "Most literary works called pastorals" do not "finally permit us
to come away with anything like the simple, affirmative attitude we adopt
toward pleasing rural scenery." Marx believes that "in one way or another"
such texts "manage to qualify, or call into question, or bring irony to bear
against the illusion of peace and harmony in a green pasture."[59] Lily Bart's
and Newland Archer's inability to secure any lasting "peace" and stability
evidences a lack of topographical literacy, even a failure to *translate* the runic
inscriptions of public parks and gardens.

My fourth chapter then moves on to weigh a series of haunted or Gothic
gardens. The short story "Kerfol" is a striking text in this regard. The narrative is memorable not only for the consummate skill with which Wharton
evokes the uncanny experience of place. "Kerfol" also exploits the semantic
ambiguities of *possession*. The next chapters are an enquiry into Wharton's
fascination with North American and European gardens designed on a much
more ambitious scale, for example New York's Central Park and the Parisian
Tuileries.

Chapter Eight gauges "Endless Plays of Mountain Forms." Here I start by
mapping the "sublime" European summits and peaks depicted in Wharton's
work. This is a chance to scrutinize "edgelands at an altitude." I borrow the
term "edgelands" from the British landscape historian Marion Shoard, who
is credited with being the first to designate these mysterious and marginal
zones in *Remaking the Landscape* (2002), although the cultural geographer
Richard Mabey had documented comparable "in-between" zones decades
before in *The Unofficial Countryside* (1974). Shoard defines the "edgelands" as

those "interfacial areas between town and country and are sites where essential but despised functions are located."[60] What I find suggestive in Shoard's conception—and also in subsequent work by poets Paul Farley and Michael Symmons Roberts—is the sense of the "unobserved parts of our shared landscape" that are unaccounted for in "the duality of rural and urban writing." For these contemporary writer-pilgrims of place, "edgelands" represent amorphous, oddly entrancing and "untranslated landscape," thus raising urgent questions about "the contested ground between pastoral and ecology," as well as the myriad bequests of "pastoral idealization."[61]

We might think that there is barely anything "edgy" about the stylish hillside hotels and chalets depicted in, say, *The Custom of the Country*. There is, I propose, scope to modify the meaning of Shoard's "edgelands" to address how Wharton's high-altitude resorts mix and merge urban comforts and the ambience of remote rurality. After examining Wharton's portrayals of European peaks, I move on to the stark New England community depicted in *Ethan Frome*, and the austere "Mountain" from *Summer*. This latter novella provides a stinging contrast to the Kantian conception of "man [living] an Arcadian, pastoral existence of perfect concord, self-sufficiency and mutual love."[62] I propose that the indigent Mountain folk of *Summer* embody the American "countryside" at its most chaotic, disturbing and unruly. The Mountain community in *Summer* occupy a version of "edgelands" that "makes a great deal of our official wilderness seem like the enshrined, ecologically arrested, controlled garden space it really is."[63] The abject, shadowy and "drink-dazed creatures" who scratch out the meanest existence on the Mountain also make a mockery of those pleasing, picturesque wanderers of the wilderness synonymous with James Fenimore Cooper's oeuvre. *Summer* closes this chapter because Wharton's Mountain, with its "strange lands," barren "stony fields" and perilous "granite ledges," comprehensively scrambles figurations of a resource-rich New Eden, or the soothing cultivated countryside synonymous with Bellomont's manicured lawns in *The House of Mirth*. Wharton's gloomy Mountain exposes the grievous limitations of classifying species of space by way of their marks of connection to recognizable sub/urban or rustic enclaves.

Chapter Thirteen—"Romantic Ruins? Edith Wharton's Sedimented Vision"—exploits the notion that her fictional green zones operate as an accrual—or even better—a stratification of cultural meaning. Wharton's narrators are tireless imaginative excavators, uncovering in layered terrain the rubble of a long forgotten, and in the case of her first piece of published prose fiction "Mrs. Manstey's View," a much more recent past.[64] In this chapter the presence of a material ruin shows how the search for pastoral ease of life, solitude or serenity is *haunted* by fraught feelings of unhomeliness, even cultural oblivion. Wharton's engagement with her admired predecessor John Ruskin's poignant evocations of the "ruin" supplies a conceptual scaffold for my early sub-sections, which examine the august Coliseum of "Roman Fever" and the damaged North African fortress in "A Bottle of Perrier." What makes "A Bottle of Perrier" especially resonant in this part is how it challenges that delight in the spectacle of ruin/ation which signals the privileged standpoint of a moneyed capitalist-traveler who can "afford" the luxury of sketching "quaint" crumbling sites from a cozy distance. However, there is nothing quaint or anodyne about the fortress in "A Bottle of Perrier." Wharton's vivid depiction of the battered structure compels us to ponder how abandoned sites in the desert may be the outcome of forced migration, bitter internecine strife or political ferment. Wharton employs this ruin as a narrative and "conceptual *topos*" that calls our cherished ideas of locality "and our aesthetics of the world into question."[65]

Chapter Fifteen also confronts issues of dissolution and economic displacement caused by urban expansion in "Mrs. Manstey's View." This early story focuses on "people and places left behind." Mrs. Manstey is a case study in what sociologists and cultural geographers nowadays call "place-attachment": the "positively experienced bonds, sometimes occurring without awareness, that are developed over time from the behavioral, affective and cognitive ties between individuals and/or groups and their socio-physical environment."[66] Wharton's short story documents how people in straitened circumstances craft a sense of selfhood embedded in an apparently unpromising milieu. What Mrs. Manstey has to realize is that treasured homes and neighborhoods can suddenly become mere "waste" —what Brian Thill describes as "every object, plus time."[67]

I close this chapter by addressing Wharton's delineations of sham ruins as well as the abandoned, forlorn physical structures of *Summer*. This novella again proves fruitful since it meditates on how all tangible sites are, at some level, reminders, remainders and remnants.[68] Wharton wonders what happens to humble localities left behind by the "welter" of the "world," like the threadbare township of North Dormer; or on a more intimate level, the tumbledown cottage where Charity Royall makes decisions that will irrevocably change the course of her life. That this ramshackle building seems to be the true specter of the novella is suggested by the way it is empty yet so expressive; on the brink of collapse yet undoubtedly, eerily, still "there." It is another example of an "edgeland," in-between existence and non-existence, the garden plot and the unfenced wild, the decorous and the feral. Muted in tone and modest in length *Summer* may be—yet it furnishes a memorable fictional framework around the patterns, rhythms and results of abandonment in place. That Wharton's narrator carefully portrays dereliction in this text—the almost-unperceived, the already residual, the slow inexorable sinking-into-soil—is part of a move to theorize how such zones operate as a troubling counterpoint to an overpopulated and rapidly expanding New York City. Following Caitlin DeSilvey's argument that "the disintegration of structural integrity does not necessarily lead to the evacuation of meaning," it is crucial we evaluate the significance of *Summer*'s "ruins" in the mapping of the discarded, the perished or "left behind." Throughout this final chapter the ruin/ed is a locus of physical and subliminal interaction, a partially readable cultural text that throws into relief a version of pastoral much more profound that the mere absence of inhabitants or background noise.[69]

My Conclusion revisits and extends some of the key findings of my core chapters. I also sketch future directions for ecocritical scholarship on Wharton. In the Appendix two typescript unpublished gardening article dating from the 1930s can be found: "Spring in the French Riviera Garden" and "December in the French Riviera Garden."[70]

Notes

1   Edith Wharton, *A Backward Glance*. Simon & Schuster, 1998, 379.
2   Friedrich Nietzsche, *The Will to Power*. Translated by Walter Kaufmann, Random House, 1967, 47.
3   Leo Marx, "American Literary Culture and the Fatalistic View of Technology.," *The Pilot and the Passenger: Essays on Literature, Technology, and Culture in the United States*, edited by Marx Leo. Oxford University Press, 1988, 179–207.
4   Lawrence Buell, *The Environmental Imagination: Thoreau, Nature Writing and the Formation of American Culture*. Harvard University Press, 1995, 11. More recently Greg Garrard has suggested that "pastoral has decidedly shaped our constructions of nature. Even the science of ecology may have been shaped by pastoral in its early stages of development." See Greg Garrard, *Ecocriticism*. The New Critical Idiom. Routledge, 2010, 33.
5   Edith Wharton, *My Dear Governess: The Letters of Edith Wharton to Anna Bahlmann*. Edited by Irene Goldman-Price. Yale University Press, 2012, 115.
6   Wharton, *A Backward Glance*, 124.
7   Edith Wharton, *Italian Villas and Their Gardens*. The Century, 1905, 123.
8   On pastoral as a reaction to a compromised and "unacceptable world," written when "an ideal or at least more innocent world is felt to be lost" see Joseph Meeker, *The Comedy of Survival: Literary Ecology and a Play Ethic*. 3rd ed., University of Arizona Press, 1980, 50; Peter V. Marinelli, *Pastoral*. Methuen & Co, 1971, 9. Marinelli's concise text affords a vivid sense of how pastoral is "in search of the original splendour, but the different ways in which it conceives of that splendour are the ground of its fertility and multiple variations," 11.
9   See William Empson, *Some Versions of Pastoral*. New Directions, 1974.
10 See Paul Alpers, "What Is Pastoral?" *Critical Inquiry*, vol. 8, no. 3, 1982, 437–60. *JSTOR*, www.jstor.org/stable/1343259. Accessed May 24, 2021.
11 Paul Alpers, *What is Pastoral?* University of Chicago Press, 1996, 23.
12 T. G. Rosenmeyer, *The Green Cabinet: Theocritus and the European Pastoral Lyric*. University of California Press, 1969, 3. See also Harold E. Toliver, *Pastoral Forms and Attitudes*. University of California Press, 1971.

13 Marinelli, *Pastoral*. The Critical Idiom, 8.

14 Bryan Loughrey, *The Pastoral Mode: A Casebook*. Macmillan, 1984, 8; Terry Gifford, *Pastoral*. Routledge, 1999, 147; Martha Hale Shackford, "A Definition of the Pastoral Idyll." *PMLA*, vol. 19, no. 4, 1904, 583–92. *JSTOR*, www.jstor.org/stable/456511. Accessed May 27, 2021, 583.

15 Alpers, *What is Pastoral?*, 44.

16 On eighteenth century American pastoralism and its link to republican ideals of "righteous" citizenship see the work of J. Hector St. John de Crèvecoeur. For Crèvecoeur, the yeoman farmer's connection to the soil he tends is economically and legally sound, as well as morally certified: "the instant I enter on my own land, the bright idea of property, of exclusive right, of independence, exalt my mind." He continues: "What should we American farmers be without the distinct possession of that soil? [...] This formerly rude soil has been converted by my father into a pleas-ant farm, and in return, it has established all our rights." See J. Hector St. John Crèvecoeur, *Letters from an American Farmer and Sketches of Eighteenth Century America*. 1782. Penguin Classics, 1981, 54.

17 Mathilde Skoie and Sonia Bjornstad Velaquez, *Pastoral and the Humanities: Arcadia Re- Inscribed*. Bristol Phoenix, 2006; William Barillas, *The Midwestern Pastoral: Place and Landscape in Literature of the American Heartland*. Ohio University Press, 2006; Ann Marie Mikkelsen, *Pastoral, Pragmatism, and Twentieth-Century American Poetry*. Palgrave Macmillan, 2011.

18 Virginia Woolf, "American Fiction.," *The Moment and Other Essays*. Harcourt, 1948, 113–27.

19 Janet Beer, *Edith Wharton*. Liverpool University Press, 2001, 7. "That Edith Wharton felt herself out of sympathy with her native land did not mean" according to Beer, "that she did not understand it: her discomfort was perhaps one of the chief sources of inspiration for her work as writer both of fiction and of cultural criticism." For Pamela Knights, it is not possible to separate the two, but rather to look at Wharton's fiction as a transatlantic corpus: "In her texts, simple oppositions are rare, and Europe and America, as with other narratives of encounter and contact, fuse and intertwine, to generate newer, hybrid cultures." Pamela Knights, *The Cambridge Introduction to Edith Wharton*. Cambridge University Press, 2009, 24.

20 Nancy Von Rosk, "Spectacular Homes and Pastoral Theatres: Gender, Urbanity and Domesticity in *The House of Mirth*.," *Studies in the Novel*, vol. 33, no. 3, 2001, 322–50. *JSTOR*, www.jstor.org/stable/29533458. Accessed May 24, 2021, 323.

21 Judith Fryer, "Book II: Edith Wharton.," *Felicitous Space: The Imaginative Structures of Edith Wharton and Willa Cather*. University of North Carolina Press, 1986, 54–199, 106.

22 Fryer, *Felicitous Space*, 106.

23 Annette Benert, "The Romance of Nature." *The Architectural Imagination of Edith Wharton: Gender, Class, and Power in the Progressive Era*. Fairleigh Dickinson University Press, 2007, 140–65, 140. Benert argues that "Ideologically, and sometimes actu-ally, Wharton identifies natural landscapes with men, and the built environment — houses, cultural institutions, gardens — with women," 143. See also Gary Totten who addresses how "Wharton's work encourages us to consider positive continuities of nature and culture." Gary Totten, "Women, Art, and the Natural World in Edith Wharton's Works." *The New Edith Wharton Studies*, edited by Jennifer Haytock and Laura Rattray. Cambridge University Press, 2019, 175–88. Twenty-First-Century Critical Revisions, 187.

24 See Vernon Lee, *Genius Loci: Notes on Places.* Leopold Classic Library, 1898.

25 I am conscious here of Ken Hiltner's argument that pastoral "perception of forests and mountains (what we sometimes broadly refer to as 'nature') is, to a large degree, historically and culturally dependent." See Ken Hiltner, "General Introduction.," *Ecocriticism: The Essential Reader,* edited by Ken Hiltner. Routledge, 2015, xii–xvi, xv.

26 Hiltner, *Ecocriticism: The Essential Reader,* xii.

27 See Buell, *The Environmental Imagination,* 11, 33, 22, 34–36.

28 Paul Outka, *Race and Nature from Transcendentalism to the Harlem Renaissance.* Palgrave Macmillan, 2008.

29 Buell, *The Environmental Imagination,* 32–33. On the longevity of literary pastoral, which "first appeared in classical antiquity" and "had an enormous vogue in the Renaissance" see Alpers, *What is Pastoral?,* 8.

30 Richard Kerridge, "Ecothrillers: Environmental Cliffhangers.," *The Green Studies Reader: From Romanticism to Ecocriticism,* edite by Laurence Coupe. Routledge, 2000, 242–52, 242.

31 Buell, *The Environmental Imagination,* 52; Greg Garrard, "Radical Pastoral?" *Studies in Romanticism,* vol. 35, no. 3, 1996, 449–65. JSTOR, www.jstor.org/stable/25601184. Accessed May 27, 2021, 459.

32 Gifford, *Pastoral,* 147.

33 Kevin R. McNamara and Timothy Gray, "Some Versions of Urban Pastoral." *The Cambridge Companion to the City in Literature,* edited by Kevin R. McNamara. New York: Cambridge University Press, 2014, 245–60, 245. McNamara and Gray conclude that pastoral desires "are most often suffused with an awareness of loss or sense of longing because the green world has always already vanished."

34 Buell, *The Environmental Imagination,* 51.

35 John Barrell and John Bull, eds., *The Penguin Book of Pastoral Verse.* Penguin, 1974, 432.

36 Barrell and Bull, *The Penguin Book of Pastoral Verse.*

37 Friedrich Schiller, *On the Naive and Sentimental in Literature.* Carcanet New Press, 1981, 35–42.

38 Joseph Meeker, *The Comedy of Survival: Literary Ecology and a Play Ethic.* University of Arizona Press, 1997, 73.

39 Jeanne Skulkind, ed., *Moments of Being: Virginia Woolf, Unpublished Autobiographical Writings.* Harcourt, 1976, 134–35.

40 William Empson, *Some Versions of Pastoral.* Chatto & Windus, 1935, 11.

41 Barrell and Bull, *The Penguin Book of Pastoral Verse,* 432.

42 Rosenmeyer, *The Green Cabinet,* 17. Rosenmeyer's study is alert to how environmentally-oriented literary pastoral updates Alexander Pope's reflections upon the idealizing and indirect patterns of the mode. Pope writes that "we must therefore use some illusion to render a pastoral delightful; and this consists in exposing the best side only of a shepherd's life, and concealing its miseries." See Alexander Pope, "Discourse on Pastoral Poetry." *Essays on Poetry and Criticism,* edited by E. Aubrey Williams. Methuen & Co., 1961, 27–30.

43 Kathryn J. Gutzwiller, *Theocritus' Pastoral Analogies: The Formation of a Genre.* Wisconsin University Press, 1991, 5.

44 Leo Marx, "Does Pastoralism Have a Future?," *The Pastoral Landscape,* edited by John Dixon Hunt. Washington National Gallery of Art, 1992, 223.

45 Renato Poggioli, *The Oaten Flute: Essays on Pastoral Poetry and the Pastoral Ideal.* Harvard University Press, 1975, 1. See also W. W. Greg, *Pastoral Poetry and Pastoral Drama.* Russell & Russell, 1959, 4.

46 Scott Hess, "Postmodern Pastoral, Advertising, and the Masque of Technology." *Interdisciplinary Studies in Literature and Environment*, vol. 11, no. 1, 2004, 71–100. *JSTOR*, www.jstor.org/stable/44086226. Accessed May 24, 2021. Hess's account shares some common traits with Frank Kermode's thesis that it is pastoral which greatly "complicates the simple town-country contrast with serious reflections upon that contrast; which cultivates simplicity in decorated language; and which uses the country scene and rustic episode for allegorical purposes." See Frank Kermode, *English Pastoral Poetry: From the Beginnings to Marvell*. George G. Harrap, 1952, 25; see also Andrew V. Ettin, *Literature and the Pastoral*. Yale University Press, 1984, 12.

47 Marx, "Does Pastoralism Have a Future?" 6; see also Roger Sales, *English Literature in History 1780-1830: Pastoral and Politics*. St. Martin's Press, 1983, 17.

48 John Dewey, *Art as Experience* [1934]. Perigree Books, 1980, 113. See also Dewey, *Experience and Nature*. [1929]. Dover Publications, 1958.

49 Hess, "Postmodern Pastoral, Advertising, and the Masque of Technology," 89, 80.

50 Raymond Williams, *The Country & The City*. Chatto & Windus, 1973, 22. See also Gerald Maclean, Donna Landry, and Joseph P. Ward, eds., *The Country and the City Revisited: England and the Politics of Culture, 1550-1850*. Cambridge University Press, 1999.

51 Terry Gifford, *Pastoral*. Routledge, 2019. The New Critical Idiom, 3. In order to answer this question adequately, we must be aware that pastorals "demand alert readings that are capable of making critical judgements about their inner tensions, their contextual functions, their multiple layers of contradictions," 12.

52 Gifford, *Pastoral*, 52; Dominic Head, *An Introduction to Modern British Fiction 1950-2000*. Cambridge University Press, 2002, 190. For Peter Marinelli, "if pastoral lives for us at all at the present time, it lives by a capacity to move out of its old haunts in the Arcadian pastures and to inhabit the ordinary country landscapes of the modern world, daily contracted by the encroachment of civilization and as a consequence daily more precious as a projection of our desires for simplicity." See Marinelli, *Pastoral*, 3.

53 See, for example, Henry Nash Smith, *Virgin Land: The American West as Symbol and Myth*. Harvard University Press, 1950; Perry Miller, *Nature's Nation*. Harvard University Press, 1967; Myra Jehlen, *American Incarnation: The Individual, the Nation, the Continent*. Harvard University Press, 1986.

54 Peter F. Cannavo, "American Contradictions and Pastoral Visions: An Appraisal of Leo Marx, *The Machine in the Garden*," *Organization & Environment*, vol. 14, no. 1, 2001, p. 74–92. JSTOR, www.jstor.org/stable/26161714. Accessed May 27, 2021; Tony Hiss, *The Experience of Place: A New Way of Looking and Dealing with Our Radically Changing Cities and Countryside*. Random House, 1990.

55 Gifford, *Pastoral*, 12.

56 See Louis Slotkin, *Regeneration through Violence: The Mythology of the American Frontier, 1600-1860*. Harper Perennial, 1996.

57 Edith Wharton, *The House of Mirth*. Edited by Elizabeth Ammons. W. W. Norton & Company, Inc, 1990, 314.

58 For Barbara Bender, these tensions—such as between the particular and the universal—can be felt in the natural world: "to force a recognition of the multiplicity of experience through time and space, and at any given moment of time and place; to relativise 'our' own experiences and to recognise both their particularity and that they are part of a process and therefore continually open to change; and, finally, to

permit an exploration of the ways in which people, differentially engaged and differentially empowered, appropriate and contest their landscapes." See Barbara Bender. "Introduction: Landscape - Meaning and Action." *Landscape, Politics and Perspectives*, edited by Barbara Bender. Berg, 1993, 1–17.

59 Leo Marx, *The Machine in the Garden: Technology and the Pastoral Ideal in America*. Oxford University Press, 1967, 15.

60 Marion Shoard in Jennifer Jenkins, ed., *Remaking the Landscape: The Changing Face of Britain*. Profile Books, 2002, 192. "Waste landscapes" or "drosscape" have also been used by environmental scholars to specify these tricky-to-describe areas. See Alan Berger, *Drosscape: Wasting Land in Urban America*. Princeton Architectural Press, 2007. The architect Ignasi Solà-Morales Rubio favors the phrase *terrain vague* to pinpoint the evacuated, forlorn or dilapidated sites scattered across and around a modern city.

61 Paul Farley and Michael Symmons Roberts, *Edgelands: Journeys into England's True Wildernesses*. Jonathan Cape, 2011, 6.

62 Immanuel Kant, *Political Writings*. Translated by H. B. Nisbet. Edited by Hans Reiss. Cambridge University Press, 1991, 44–45.

63 Farley and Roberts, *Edgelands*, 7–8.

64 This concept of the narrator-excavator can be seen in the astonishing depictions of blasted landscapes in Wharton's Great War texts, especially *Fighting France* (1915). In "The Look of Paris," the war is imaged as a "monstrous landslide, […] burying under a heap of senseless ruin the patiently and painfully wrought machinery of civilization." Wharton frequently relies on anthropomorphic lexis to delineate an Ypres, "bombarded to death" and "a disembowelled corpse," with shattered houses in whose "exposed interiors the poor little household gods shiver and blink like owls surprised in a hollow tree." See Edith Wharton, *Fighting France*. Scribner's 1915, 9, 152–53, 173.

65 See Aidan Tynan, *The Desert in Modern Literature and Philosophy: Wasteland Aesthetics*. Edinburgh University Press, 2020, 4–5, 9.

66 Barbara Brown and Douglas D. Perkins, *Place Attachment*. Plenum Press, 1992, 284.

67 Brian Thill, *Waste*. Bloomsbury Academic, 2015, 8–9.

68 For more on this idea see Thill, *Waste*, 15–37.

69 See Caitlin DeSilvey, *Curated Decay: Heritage Beyond Saving*. University of Minnesota Press, 2017, 5.

70 Please see Appendix I and II. The original sources can be found in the Edith Wharton Archive at the Beinecke Library, Yale University in New Haven, CT.

Part I
GARDENS

Chapter 1

THE PASTORAL COSMOPOLITANISM
OF THE (NOT SO) SECRET GARDEN

In her 1934 autobiography *A Backward Glance*, Edith Wharton refers to her own literary production as her "secret garden": "Therefore I shall try to depict the growth and unfolding of the plants in my secret garden, from the seed to the shrub-top—for I have no intention of magnifying my vegetation into trees!"[1] It is a striking choice of metaphor, but not a surprising one: Wharton was passionate about the arts of writing and gardening.[2] Parkland, subsistence plots and ornamental gardens feature conspicuously in her life and work. Indeed, Renée Somers contends that Wharton dedicated so much of her time to studying "the complex relationships that exist between people and their built environments," as well as shifting conceptions of the garden's cultural meaning, scope and worth, that we should view her as a "spatial activist." Somers rightly prioritizes Wharton as an author for whom the garden or park was an "imagined" as well as a "material" zone; and to get a better purchase on that imagined zone she became fluent in, and savvy about, the socio-economic discourses in which that imagining was expressed.[3] Somers has proven useful in reminding scholars to look at Wharton's fictional gardens not only in terms of her deep knowledge of environmental history, or her appreciation of certain large-scale landscape designers. We should also consider how her characters, especially female protagonists, *use* these areas—to anchor themselves socially (in a world of money, marriage and fashion), emotionally, morally, even spiritually.[4]

Wharton embraced the chance to develop ambitious estate designs for her myriad properties: The Mount in Lenox, Massachusetts; the Pavilion Colombe and Castel Sainte-Claire in France.[5] Her library contained work by the Michigan-born Liberty Hyde Bailey, one of the most industrious and eloquent horticulturalists, rural journalists and botanists in the early years of the twentieth century.[6] Hyde Bailey's avowed ambition was to help America arrive on the world stage as a self-assured and robust civilization. This would be attained, he averred, by pushing gardening into the realm of a national art form: constructing "great pictures out-of-doors."[7] Wharton, like Hyde Bailey and Sarah Orne Jewett, saw intriguing links and contrasts between horticultural labor and cultivating unexpected configurations of narrative pathways.[8]

Wharton used her thorough knowledge of interior design as well as landscape history—evidenced by the publication of *The Decoration of Houses* (1897) and *Italian Villas and Their Gardens* (1904)—to think through an array of narrative concerns, among which: mimesis, the laws and limits of genre, relations between form and content. In a letter dated from July 3, 1911, to Morton Fullerton she remarked: "I am amazed at the success of my efforts. Decidedly, I'm a better landscape gardener than novelist, and this place, every line of which is my own work, far surpasses *The House of Mirth*."[9] These terms remind us how "borders" emerge in Wharton's work not just as ways of maintaining caste hierarchies or as "lines" slicing a garden's soil into pleasing shapes of self-contained flora. They also reveal where narrative tracks intersect. Moreover, in her "Secret Garden" chapter from her autobiography, she opens with an epigraph from Walter Scott's diary that evokes the writing process as a "wielding of the unreal trowel." Jacqueline Wilson-Jordan weighs the significance of this intertext: Wharton's "metaphor of the trowel is doubly rich, paying homage to her love of gardening while calling attention, in the realm of the unreal, to her view of writing as a metaphorical dig."[10] Wharton's narrative practice can be interpreted here as imaginative archaeology, excavating her personal experience to capture "something beyond the usual range of her vision."[11] Wharton thus plays a pivotal role in American literature's development of novelistic form, refined as part of an ongoing theoretical conversation with the realm of garden and landscape design that she also addresses at length in her nonfiction texts.[12]

Wharton is widely feted for her tales of the city in which sophisticated cosmopolites take center stage, like Newland Archer in *The Age of Innocence* who speaks fondly of "European scenes," of "Granada and the Alhambra."[13] Often, at pivotal moments, these characters—many with untrammeled access to the *global* due to inherited and/or earned wealth—seek out, or wander into the intensely *local*, specifically a private garden or a public park. For Wharton a garden epitomizes that beguiling space *between* the unfenced and the enclosed, the unfarmed wild and the artificer's agency, where, according to critic Michael Pollan, "nature and culture can be wedded in a way that can benefit both."[14] The "betweenness" of a garden or park—exposing tensions between bustling metropolis and the retired sociability of country estate, industrial and agrarian toil, the machine and the manicured lawn—is significant because it reminds us of Elaine Showalter's influential argument that "the literary history of American women writers" is defined "by the spatial images of the father's library and the mother's garden."[15] Showalter explains that Wharton's position is anomalous, neither in one space nor the other:

> While the standard pattern for nineteenth-century American women writers was a strong allegiance to the maternal line and the female community, Wharton belonged to the more troubled and more gifted countertradition of women writers who were *torn between* the literary world of their fathers and the wordless sensual world of their mothers.[16]

Such tension informs Wharton's fictional scheme and is evident in garden and parkland scenes that deserve more sustained scrutiny. Because of this liminal or "torn between" quality, the novelistic terrain exemplifies what I call in this part of the book "pastoral cosmopolitanism."[17]

Cosmopolitanism has been extensively canvassed, by, among others, Meredith L. Goldstein and Emily J. Orlando in *Edith Wharton and Cosmopolitanism* (2016). However, scholars have frequently underestimated how her literary works map and tap what Showalter calls above a more "sensual world," which I connect with pastoral ambience. Pastoral itself occupies a curious "in-between" zone, as it has done since the *Idylls* of Theocritus and Virgil's *Eclogues*. The pastoral speaks of the semi-primitive and the unvarnished. It is regulated by the two neighboring conditions of a genteel urban culture and unimproved wilderness. Wharton is fascinated by how pastoral appeals to reveries of a rustic Golden Age, unsullied both by the challenges of grueling outdoors labor as well as the commotion of city living. This is a twee and unrealizable fantasy. However, pastoral design in an ornamental garden or public park confronts and processes—in frequently impish, ironic, or highly self-conscious ways—some of the dislocating complexities of our modern experience. This version of pastoral emerges and evolves at the very moment when it is hampered or stifled by the potencies of urban and technological expansion.

My argument in this part of the book is that "pastoral cosmopolitanism" is the unlikely and unpredictable pairing of two concepts that seem to be contradictory opposites when, in fact, they are not. A "return to nature"—or at least an eagerness to savor the pastoral imaginary via the physical arrangement of, say, a public park—is a cosmopolitan form of displacement and not a reaction against cosmopolitanism. This is apparent in Wharton's many "garden plots," where the escape from inhospitable social codes, or the dreary rituals of a patrician urban clique, is fleeting, fragile, and often symbolic. What I propose here is that cosmopolitanism reveals a habit of mind, whereby a déraciné or a moneyed citizen of the world, perhaps wearied by globe-trotting, craves the pleasurable frisson of local attachment, the slower pace of bucolic life, a purgative encounter with native leaves of grass, mountainous heights and deep gorges. For the Scottish American environmental philosopher John Muir, "tired, nerve-shaken, over-civilized people" should learn that "going to the mountains is going home; that wildness is a necessity."[18] This desire to inhabit—if only briefly—a lush, Arcadian hideaway permits us to reflect upon and reassess "cosmopolitanism" as an analytic construct. Here a crucial question arises: can a curiosity about the culturally specific, the pleasing materiality of a modest patch of earth or the garden nook, be reconciled with an enlightened, transnational, frontier-crossing impulse? Many of Wharton's protagonists are uniquely situated to weigh this issue, caught as they are *between* center and periphery, near and far, the endemic and the exotic, homeland *roots* and foreign *routes*.

In Renaissance Italy, which saw a notable burgeoning of interest in land-scape aesthetics as well as innovations in horticultural skill according to Claudia Lazarro, gardens were defined as "third nature." For Cicero and his followers, untamed wilderness is "first nature," while terrain modified by human ingenuity is "second nature." The "third" shows how a garden might be very different from, and elevated above, other modes of landscape modifi-cation, such as growing produce and raising animals, arduous outdoors tasks memorialized in a georgic literary tradition.[19] "Nature and art are united into an indistinguishable whole, in which nature becomes the creator of art and shares the essence of art. Together they produce something that is neither one nor the other, and is created equally by each."[20] This is akin to pastoral cosmopolitanism, in the sense that two separate terms, frequently construed as counterparts, come together to form a fresh, vital experience.[21] Lazzaro argues that the "idea of a third nature grew out of established notions of art and nature, and recalled specifically a related concept of a second, or another, nature."[22] Lazarro is enthralled by how a garden cross-pollinates nature and art in a generative, sometimes unrestrained, interaction. Her key terms will prove fruitful in approaching Wharton's fiction, especially the ostentatious, out-of-town Bellomont estate of *The House of Mirth*.

Although the Garden of Eden is the archetypal garden in the Judeo-Christian tradition, and signifies, in the terms of Karen R. Jones and John Wills, "the most prominent vision of a park-like landscape in early Western civilization,"[23] allusions to it are conspicuously absent not only from Wharton's fiction, but also her personal writings and erudite pieces on horti-culture. There is one reference to a biblical garden in an early novella, pub-lished in 1903, entitled *Sanctuary*.[24] In it, the female protagonist Kate muses about her relationship with Denis thus: "Their affection had been the *garden enclosed* of the Canticles, where they were to walk forever in a delicate isolation of bliss. But now love appeared to her as something more than this—something wider, deeper, more enduring than the selfish passion of a man and a woman."[25] What is striking is how this passage implies complicated ties and contrasts between human geography and human affect. "Garden enclosed" conjures set demarcation lines, captivating borders of choreographed care and beauty. However, "passion" signals dangerous disorders of feeling that threaten to erode those lines. As we will see in this chapter, the notion of a rarefied romantic attachment ("something wider, deeper") played out in the arena of a sun-dappled idyll, is one to which Wharton returns and revises, time and again in her published texts.

The first part of the book is divided into seven chapters. The first two chapters treats Wharton's depiction of "Private Gardens," enjoyed in the main by New York socialites.[26] The third chapter also explores the haunting or haunted garden and how uncanny affect extends beyond her much-admired ghost stories. The last three chapters consider "Public Parks" on both sides of the Atlantic; it not only ponders the function of Central Park in Wharton's fiction in the fifth chapter, but also, in chapters six and seven, French parks and how they express the cultural reach and kudos of a sovereign state that Wharton deemed the very "land of letters."

Notes

1 Wharton, *A Backward Glance*, 198.
2 A separate and lengthy chapter could be written on Wharton's detailed awareness of Italian and French formalist gardens, and how she packaged this knowledge to trigger a revitalized public interest in horticultural pursuits.
3 Renée Somers, *Edith Wharton as Spatial Activist and Analyst*. Routledge, 2005, 2–4. See also Malcolm Andrews, *Landscape and Modern Art*. Oxford University Press, 1999; Jane Brown, *The Pursuit of Paradise: A Social History of Gardens and Gardening*. HarperCollins, 2000; Dan O'Brien, ed., *Gardening: Philosophy for Everyone*. Wiley-Blackwell, 2010; Dorri Beam, *Style, Gender, and Fantasy in Nineteenth-Century American Women's Writing*. Cambridge University Press, 2010.
4 See Robert Pogue Harrison, *Gardens: An Essay on the Human Condition*. University of Chicago Press, 2008.
5 In the last two decades, incisive research has been published on this aspect of Wharton's life and career. See Somers, *Edith Wharton as Spatial Activist and Analyst*. Wharton's niece, Beatrix Farrand, was a gifted garden designer. On their discussions regarding landscape theory and practice see Mia Manzulli, "'Garden Talks': The Correspondence of Edith Wharton and Beatrix Farrand.," *A Forward Glance: New Essays on Edith Wharton*, edited by Clare Colquitt, Susan Goodman, and Candace Waid. Associated University Presses, 1999, 35–48.
6 Wharton's library contained an impressive array of garden-related texts, such as histories of English horticulture by Reginald Blomfield, Charles Holme and Inigo F. Thomas; Aubrey Le Blond's *The Old Gardens of Italy* (1912); garden theory by Gertrude

Jekyll; and substantial botanical works by luminaries such as Hugo De Vries and Asa Gray. See George Ramsden, *Edith Wharton's Library: A Catalogue.* Stone Trough Books, 1999.

7 American gardens and parks have the potential to be "some of the greatest works of art that man can make." See Liberty Hyde Bailey, *The Outlook to Nature.* The Macmillan Company, 1905, 87–89; see also Richard Heinberg, *Memories and Visions of Paradise: Exploring the Universal Myth of a Lost Golden Age.* Quest Books, 1995.

8 See William Conlogue, *Working the Garden: American Writers and the Industrialization of Agriculture.* University of North Carolina Press, 2001.

9 Edith Wharton, *The Letters of Edith Wharton.* Edited by Richard Warrington Baldwin Lewis and Nancy Lewis. Collier Books, 1988, 242.

10 Jacqueline Wilson-Jordan, "Materializing the Word: The Woman Writer and the Struggle for Authority in 'Mr. Jones.'" *Memorial Boxes and Guarded Interiors: Edith Wharton and Material Culture,* edited by Gary Totten. University of Alabama Press, 2007, 63–82. Studies in American Realism and Naturalism, 67.

11 Edith Wharton, *The Age of Innocence.* Edited by Candace Waid. W. W. Norton & Company, Inc, 2003, 189.

12 The first book Wharton published, with Ogden Codman, was the interior design manual *The Decoration of Houses.* She later focused specifically on landscape in *Italian Villas and Their Gardens* and wrote multiple gardening articles which have not been published. Beyond her love for gardens and gardening, Wharton writes about enjoying life in the country, when describing her move to The Mount, her house in the Berkshires of Massachusetts. See *A Backward Glance,* 124.

13 Wharton, *The Age of Innocence,* 91.

14 Michael Pollan, *Second Nature: A Gardener's Education.* Grove Press, 1991, 5.

15 Elaine Showalter, "The Death of the Lady (Novelist): Wharton's *House of Mirth.*" *Representations,* no. 9, 1985, 133–49. *JSTOR,* www.jstor.org/stable/3043768. Accessed Apr. 1, 2020, 145.

16 Showalter, "The Death of the Lady (Novelist): Wharton's *House of Mirth,*" 145–46, my emphasis.

17 This oxymoron evokes both Homi Babha's concept of "vernacular cosmopolitanism" and Angali Gera Roy's "pastoral cosmopolitanism." See Homi Bhabha, "Unsatisfied: Notes on Vernacular Cosmopolitanism.", *Text and Nation,* edited by Laura Garcia-Morena and Peter C. Pfeifer. Camden House, 1996, 191–207; Angali Gera Roy, *Imperialism and Sikh Migration: The Komagata Maru Incident.* Routledge, 2017.

18 John Muir, *Our National Parks.* University of California Press, 1991, 59.

19 See Lewis Holloway and Moya Kneafsey, eds. *Geographies of Rural Cultures and Societies.* Ashgate, 2004.

20 Claudia Lazzaro, *The Italian Renaissance Garden: From the Conventions of Planting, Design, and Ornament to the Grand Gardens of Sixteenth-Century Central Italy.* Yale University Press, 1990. See also Yrjo Haila and Chuck Dyke, eds., *How Nature Speaks: The Dynamics of the Human Ecological Condition.* Duke University Press, 2006.

21 See John Dixon Hunt, *Greater Perfections: The Practice of Garden Theory.* University of Pennsylvania Press, 2000; Martin Hoyles, *The Story of Gardening.* Journeyman Press, 1991; Kathryn Cornell Dolan, *Beyond the Fruited Plain: Food and Agriculture in U. S. Literature, 1850-1905.* University of Nebraska Press, 2014.

22 Lazzaro, *The Italian Renaissance Garden,* 9.

23 Karen R. Jones and John Wills, *The Invention of the Park: Recreational Landscapes from the Garden of Eden to Disney's Magic Kingdom.* Polity Press, 2005, 11; see also Evan Eisenberg, *Ecology of Eden.* Vintage Books, 1999.

24 Here Wharton alludes to the following Biblical text: "You are a garden locked up, my sister, my bride; milk and honey are under your tongue." (*Song of Songs* 4:12). *The Holy Bible: New International Version.* Hodder & Stoughton, 2000, 756.

25 "Sanctuary." *Madame de Treymes and Three Novellas,* by Edith Wharton. Scribner & Schuster, 1995, 119–210, 151.

26 Jones and Wills, *The Invention of the Park*, 11; see also Thomas Mickey, *America's Romance with the English Garden.* Ohio University Press, 2013.

Chapter 2

AMERICAN BACK GROUNDS

Bellomont

In "The Background," the opening chapter of *A Backward Glance*, Wharton ties her ecological awakening to a specific moment in her childhood: "I cannot remember when the grasses first spoke to me, though I think it was when, a few years later, one of my uncles took me with some little cousins, to spend a long spring day in some marshy woods near Mamaroneck."[1] It is especially notable that she connects this awakening to the Hudson Valley, an area that features prominently in some of her novels. As an adult writing about an event that took place many decades before, Wharton includes vivid tangible detail regarding blossoms and sward. Westchester county was "where the earth was starred with pink trailing arbutus, where pouch-like white and rosy flowers grew in a swamp, and leafless branches against the sky were netted with buds of mother-of pearl."[2]

I propose here that Wharton's literary narratives restage and reassess this ecological awakening or moment of being through "garden plots." She indicates how her creative faculty flows from a heightened consciousness of this natural terrain:

> My imagination lay there, coiled and sleeping, a mute hibernating creature, and at the least touch of common things—flowers, animals, words, especially the sound of words, apart from their meaning—it already stirred in its sleep, and then sank back into its own rich dream[3]

Wharton's conception of a "coiled" imagination—implying a living organism—invites comparison with Katherine Mansfield's "love" for a type of artistic "mind" that "must have wild places, a tangled orchard where dark damsons drop in the grass, an overgrown little wood, the *chance of a snake or two*" and "paths threaded with flowers planted by the mind".[4] For Wharton, as for Mansfield, gardens comprise "such a subtle combination of the artificial and the natural—that is, partly, the secret of their charm."[5] Wharton's garden imagery shows how she tunes her own aesthetic gifts to the frequency of "things" that make visible the point where domesticated (human) nature and the wild (psychic) hinterlands contend, negotiate and converge. Wharton crafts her own version of "negative capability" here—an acute responsiveness to "dream," fancies, native auras and subliminal potencies that emanate from local soil. It is this ability which allows her to show the strange, unearthly power of "common" things such as "flowers" and "animals."

In the chapter "Life and Letters" from *A Backward Glance,* Wharton goes back to ponder this impactful, even epiphanic, moment in her felt experience: "Now I know the joys of six or seven months a year among the fields and woods of my own, and the childish extasy of that first spring outing at Mamaroneck swept away all the restlessness in the deep joy of communion with the earth."[6]Wharton sought to renew this ecological awakening throughout her life by spending extended periods of time in the countryside, at home and abroad. What I suggest here is that such "renewal" also takes place in the imaginative patterns of her fiction, with often complex results. It is through literature that she is able to voice and reappraise what she terms "my secret sensitiveness to the landscape—something in me quite incommunicable to others, that was trembling and inarticulately awake to every detail of wind-warped fern and wide-eyed briar rose."[7] The intensity and duration of her imaginative gaze is sharpened by "a unifying magic beneath the diversities of the visible scene—a power with which I was in deep and solitary communion whenever I was alone with nature."[8] This stress on "communion"— hinting at elation and embeddedness—echoes a Wordsworthian mysticism and conjures an image of a priestess worshipping at green altars.[9] It prompts us to gauge how this multiplied perception—a sense sublime—is changed (or diluted) when Wharton's rapt observing gaze shifts from so-called wild untamed nature, to the grounds of the palatial "houses on the Hudson River" with their groves, shrubberies and well-groomed edges.[10] Wharton both participates in and probes what Carolyn Merchant calls "a counternarrative of wilderness appreciation" that was "emerging among elites" and "would be expressed through poetry, art, literature, and landscape architecture."[11] This "wilderness appreciation" resonates through three novels that operate here as case studies; starting with Bellomont in *The House of Mirth* in this chapter, followed by the Skuytercliff encounter in *The Age of Innocence* and the Cedarledge retreat in *Twilight Sleep* in the next chapter.

Early in Wharton's 1905 novel *The House of Mirth*, the female protagonist Lily Bart is conceived of thus: "Selden reflected that it was the same streak of sylvan freedom that lent such savor to her artificiality."[12] Despite, or perhaps because of his location in a well-appointed Manhattan apartment at the Benedick, Lawrence Selden associates Lily with woodland haunts. His stress on "sylvan" evokes a poeticized domain of frolicking nymphs, fauns and satyrs. Of course, Selden's notion of a spirited—or uninhibited—femininity in terms of "sylvan freedom" is itself "artificial"—a hint of the male *cultivation* that relies on hackneyed mythic allusions and other learned reference to maintain gendered hierarchies. Selden's fanciful conception of Lily is tested during their meeting in the Hudson Valley, at the Trenors' house, Bellomont Park during a Sunday stroll. Gary Totten contends that "Bellomont's artificiality is emphasized by the way in which its rural nature has been manufactured."[13] As Totten notes, there is a sense that Bellomont, much like Selden's "republic of the spirit"[14] is a piece of theatre that offers a methodically structured snapshot of countryside manners and mores. This is apparent in Bellomont's library, the "only surviving portion of the old manor-house," whose "pleasantly shabby books" are simply stage props rather than precious reading matter that offers intellectual nourishment. Lily is acutely aware that Bellomont is a different kind of space, whose owners have left stories layered on top of one another in the form of wood, glass and stone. Plus, she is conscious of the highly contrived natural beauty encircled within somebody's else's property. She can look and linger, but how close can she get to the blossoms to appreciate their hues and organic texture? Can she claim Bellomont's abundant cultural resources as her own, or do they simply throw into relief the "meagreness of her own opportunities" as an interloper?[15] The estate is not hers and so to stroll in it, by permission, is to register a pronounced spatial difference.[16] A welcomed guest can so easily become an upstart trespasser. However, the palpable details of this site, on a cursory view, suggest a languorous, even paradisical milieu:

> Everything in her surroundings ministered to feelings of ease and amenity. The windows stood open to the sparkling freshness of the September morning, and between the yellow boughs she caught a perspective of hedges and parterres leading by degrees of lessening formality to the free undulations of the park.[17]

This external effect ("ease") gives little hint of the "brutal and self-engrossed" hangers-on and social parasites who occupy the lofty hall within. The outward, surface splendor camouflages perhaps a fraught history of class struggle and animosity. This tension is hinted at by the etymological associations of the name "Bellomont" ("beauty" and "battle") as well as the décor of the mansion's main stairway and flesh-colored "crimson carpet." The weathering that lends the imposing Bellomont masonry its "beauty" contrasts with the youthful "freshness" that the high society ladies indoors must cultivate if they are to retain "value" and desirability as major players in the cut-throat marriage market.

The phrasing of the extract above also makes us ask: who pays for Lily's "feelings" of "amenity"? Her pastoral pleasure focuses our attention on the invisible, exacting manual labor (such as weeding and cleaning) that makes it possible. The *"garden enclosed* of the Canticles"[18] in *Sanctuary* contrasts with the enclosure portrayed here—not just the "great gilt cage" of Bellomont but the reduction of public rights of way, even a land grab of the commons. The "ease and amenity" of this planned outdoor space is tied to a sense of Bellomont as a mixture of naturalist and formalist styles of garden design, which, based on the evidence of Wharton's horticultural writings, is peculiarly problematic. Bellomont's visual variety shows that it looks overseas for frameworks of inspiration, collecting and melding signs from obscure, archaic and defunct garden languages but without quite arriving at a distinctive and self-confident American style. Wharton's *Italian Gardens and their Villas* celebrates the "purity" and rigor of garden formalism, its sober divisions, clipped geometries, and framed views of distant prospects—not the ecumenical "mix and match" of landscaping strategies that Lily's view of Bellomont implies. Garden formalism—whose aesthetic credos affirm the operations of human creativity—had regained popularity in the final two decades of the nineteenth century. For the landscape historian and theorist John Dixon Hunt this type of park is "third nature" because it is, fundamentally, an "expression of human experience"—a place as "art object" enriched by an infectious eclecticism.[19] However, Wharton's narrator suggests that the Bellomont "park," with its "parterres" and "hedges," instead of manifesting the "exquisite suitability" of, say, the Cedarledge estate in *Twilight Sleep*, makes only modish gestures towards the Italian-inspired baroque pleasure gardens of eighteenth- and nineteenth-century France, with their witty, not-completely natural orchestration of finished borders, gravel walks, luxuriant topiaries, fountains and sculptural elements.

There is a droll irony in how the "sparkling freshness" and "free undulations" that Lily notes here has been precisely—and no doubt expensively—crafted by teams of professional landscapers well-drilled in the structuring of "perspectival projections."[20] Plus there is a hint of the absurd in how the owners of Bellomont—who might like to proclaim in public that they espouse egalitarian republicanism—craft their garden along aristocratic lines. The "yellow boughs" become a framing device, tempting Lily to assume that the park's notable features (the ostensibly haphazard, natural disorder of "free undulations") somehow mirrors her emancipated and hidden self—a self that deserves better than the stale manners of the New York glitterati and seeks instead romantic adventure with male companions on winding woodland footpaths.

Such horticultural prowess in designing agreeable, eye-catching tensions between the "formal" and the "free" at Bellomont, the calculated and the seemingly spontaneous, speaks insistently to Lily. After all, she is adept at staging a stylish femininity with—as Selden remarks—a piquant "streak of sylvan freedom." Selden unwittingly associates Lily with the country estate when he muses in the first chapter: "she must have cost a great deal to make."[21] The text even implies Lily herself is a kind of gardener whose body must be presented in the most graceful manner: "the modelling" of her "little ear, the crisp upward wave of her hair—was it ever so slightly brightened by art?—and the *thick planting* of her straight black lashes" (my emphasis). Such pointed terms remind us that Lily's "work"—securing an affluent spouse— might be made easier by a terrace overlooking "sunken gardens" whose ambience is "propitious" to her "scheme of courtship."[22] The green retreat and the woman within it become, in Selden's eyes at least, artistic commodities.[23] However, Bellomont's grounds represent a tantalizing space, whose aesthetic and romantic associations can lead the unwary (female) visitor to ruin. The terraces hold out a promise of amorous fulfilment for Lily, foreshadowing the pleasant afternoon she will spend with Selden soon thereafter. As Wharton's narrator makes explicit, Bellomont's design offers too much scope for Lily to indulge her romantic thought-adventures. For all her self-belief and apparent poise, she is ill-equipped to navigate the affective and moral dilemmas synonymous with the parkland. Lily lacks the emotional equipment to "commune" with organic forms in the manner set forth by Wharton's *A Backward Glance*:

> The terrace at Bellomont on a September afternoon was a spot propitious to sentimental musings, and as Miss Bart stood leaning against the balustrade above the sunken garden, at a little distance from the animated group about the tea-table, she might have been lost in the mazes of an inarticulate happiness.[24]

The "terrace" here becomes a stage not for full and frank self-analysis. Rather it allows for "sentimental musing," a pose which connotes a willful distancing from the wellspring of honest affect. This again reminds us of a garden as a chic object—for Lily the ornamental lawns cannot be a "living creation that never stands still." Instead, it must offer a static platform for her *plotting* about potential partners, which seems closer to high society "performance art."[25] Long before Bertha Dorset casts Lily out from her refined social circle, Lily yearns for an alternative, less rule-bound and hidebound space. However, the pastoral and affective solace that Lily craves is forever on the other side of that maze of "inarticulate happiness"—suggesting her restiveness, estrangement and fear of passing time.

Whereas in "high society" episodes Lily stands out as an economic anomaly, unwilling or unable, to behave in the measured, modest fashion that is expected of her, against a verdant backdrop she tries to explore a different side to her temperament: "Seating herself on the upper step of the terrace, Lily leaned her head against the honeysuckles wreathing the balustrade. The fragrance of the late blossoms seemed an emanation of the tranquil scene, a landscape tutored to the last degree of rural elegance."[26] The narrator's terms here indicate that while the composition of Bellomont might proclaim a productive and pleasing *communion* between human and natural energies, the formal garden also reveals a history of human pruning and interference (not collaboration) with, even dominion over, the organic environment—hence "*tutored* to the last degree." If, in the words of poet R. S. Thomas, a garden is "a gesture against the wild, / The ungovernable sea of grass" then Bellomont shows how that gesture can turn belligerent.[27] The garden flowers have been "trimmed" to the point where they have lost the natural element of wonder perhaps—and what about the threat to biodiversity in such acts? For Wharton maybe, the apogee of such "tutoring"—horticultural splendor reliant on obvious deployment of manmade features—might have been the austere, even forbidding formality of the baroque spaces at Versailles.[28]

The striking descriptions of Bellomont raise a key question: does Lily intuit in this domestication and disciplining of private grounds—hiding defects and imposing "elegance" as a cultural touchstone—a force that oddly mirrors the constraints under which she chafes in her smart set? In this parkland is concretized an image of the policing instincts that fuel and perpetuate gender oppression. This might explain the affective impact of an incisive short sentence: "Lily did not want to join the circle about the tea-table."[29] A seemingly "tranquil" expanse invites us to ponder the human effort—or conquest and clearance—needed to create and sustain a regimented vista where forest becomes homestead, in whose "foreground glowed the warm tints of the gardens. Beyond the lawn, with its pyramidal pale-gold maples and velvety firs, sloped pastures dotted with cattle; and through a long glade the river widened like a lake under the silver light of September."[30] The adjectives "pyramidal pale-*gold*," "silver" (an echo of the earlier "breakfast tray, with its harmonious porcelain and silver") and "velvety" (my emphasis), bring a troubling hint of the hubristic, the commercial and the synthetic into this organic scene—a worry that the techniques of formal gardening reveals a distortion, not a judicious exercise of, human will. And it is this exercise (where cash trumps high art?), that threatens to smother, subdue, even decimate, the very thing it seeks to laud—the unrivalled, luxuriant beauty of native soil. For the sociologist Thorstein Veblen in 1899, the landscaping of Bellomont by the "well-to-do classes" would no doubt have signaled "a superior expensiveness or futility"[31]—conspicuous consumption that Fitzgerald's *The Great Gatsby* also targets with unerring accuracy. One of the founding fathers of North American landscape gardening, Andrew Jackson Downing, deplored—and this is apparent in his lexis—the profit-driven "[s]ymmetrical uniformity" that "governed with despotic power even the trees and foliage" of some east coast parks.[32] For the horticulturalist Robert Morris Copeland writing in the 1860s, this would have been a grave concern. We must admit, he concluded, "that nature far excels man in producing beautiful effects with earth, grass, trees, and water."[33]

When Lily misses the church service and happens upon Selden conversing with Bertha, she leaves that encounter to enter the park: "with a bright nod to the couple on whom she had intruded, Miss Bart strolled through the glass doors and carried her rustling grace down the long perspective of the garden walk."[34] What is suggested here of the connection between Lily's personal allure and her palpable locale, which represents a mediated and manufactured version of nature ("long perspective")? Again, "carried" indicates Lily's self-conscious awareness of creating a pose, playing a part, in a garden that conveniently broadcasts, rather than masks, artificiality. According to Alice Morse Earle, an early twentieth century landscape theorist, a "garden artilizes Nature"[35]—and Wharton's "long perspectives" also serve to frame and underscore Lily's *artful* performance of feminine "grace." Through this performance she tries to project adventurous independence of mind and body, a readiness to query demarcations, to break patterns and overstep borders: "At length, having passed from the gardens to the wood-path beyond, so far forgot her intention as to sink into a rustic seat at a bend of the walk."[36] As much as Lily's acts of self-fashioning try to question, resist and reject high society norms of "breeding" and gender (and its gatekeepers assert class solidarity by eventually rejecting her), she cannot cope by herself. She ends up in a kind of topographical and affective limbo. The narrator remarks with sly irony: "The spot was charming, and Lily was not insensible to the charm, or to the fact that her presence enhanced it; but she was not accustomed to taste the joys of solitude except in company, and the combination of a handsome girl and a romantic scene struck her as too good to be wasted."[37] Lily's self-placement as an eligible and "handsome girl" reveals how she converts—in a manner that prompts comparison with formalist landscape designers—the natural into "a scene," one that follows an organized script. For Lily, this scene should play out as an encounter rich in romantic possibilities. However, the role of melancholic recluse is one she cannot inhabit, and Lily is no happier here than she is in the terrible "company" indoors: "She felt a stealing sense of fatigue as she walked; the sparkle had died out of her, and the taste of life was stale on her lips."[38] This misery is crystallized by a "vague sense of failure, of an inner isolation deeper than the loneliness about her."[39]

That this key episode plays out in September, a transitional month between summer and autumn, adds a complex dimension to the portrayal of Lily and Selden's surroundings—"a zone of lingering summer": "through the light quiver of ash-leaves, the country unrolled itself in pastoral distances."[40] These "pastoral" sensuous effects are underlined by the lane showing "thickening tufts of fern and of the creeping glossy verdure of shaded slopes":

> The landscape outspread below her seemed an enlargement of her present mood, and she found something of herself in its calmness, its breadth, its long free reaches. On the nearer slopes the sugar-maples wavered like pyres of light; lower down was a massing of grey orchards, and here and there the lingering green of an oak-grove.[41]

The narrator's phrasing directs our attention to the quality of Lily's affective "enlargement" in this "landscape" of "sugar-maples." Does this moment really leave her energized, her "present mood" improved? The "long free reaches" seem to echo Bellomont's "free undulations." The problem here, of course, is that "Lily had no real intimacy with nature"—and little curiosity about the ideas and assumptions behind estate management. What she has instead is "a passion for the appropriate and could be keenly sensitive to a scene which was the fitting background of her own sensations."[42] Here the garden exposes one of her weaknesses—her habit of switching between social masks to proclaim a stable subjectivity. Her "passion" signals a readiness to be displayed under the right conditions; like flowers in full bloom, she can be ornamental, bright, eye-catching and fragrant. She contrives a winning artificial image to secure a niche among a New York patrician coterie she both envies and deplores. However, she cannot indulge masquerade and maintain her individual agency. This is the pathos that the Bellomont episode catches through the myriad references to flora—and even in Lily's own name.

It is tempting here to interpret Bellomont, with all its lavish, ersatz beauty chiseled by social ambition and riches, as a means of drawing out Lily's psychic frailties—caught as she is between the promptings of sensual *appetite* and rarefied *taste*. Lily confronts some of the core cultural narratives with which early twentieth-century American "high society" sought to define itself.[43] What separates, for example, old money from new, established social tribes from pushy ascendant ones? However, this would be to miss the point of the elaborate depictions of the estate. Lily's unease in this locality flows from her position as an incautious and inexpert reader of the garden's runic clues— what architectural historian John Vlach calls "articulated" space, a strategically devised visual "show" that discloses vital details about class hierarchy and links to European styles.[44] Bellomont is public to a limited degree, but it is a large-scale private project, a reflection of its owner's cultural cachet and fondness for display, an opportunity to consolidate the political sway of a lei-sured (if not really educated) elite.

Crucially, Bellomont is an ideological as well as environmental arena in which one will be surveyed, ruthlessly "valued" and appraised—and in Lily's case found wanting. Though she gambles on being able to manipulate people so as to clinch a prosperous future, she cannot quite grasp spatial semiotics. In contrast to Wharton, who in *A Backward Glance* can pinpoint, and learn from, that moment "when the grasses first spoke to" her, Lily is not able to apprehend those earth sacraments or "voices" from the soil. Furthermore, as she discovers to her chagrin, the realm of the "natural" is as much about deep pockets, social one-upmanship, surveillance and sexual politics as it is about sunlight and shadow, "sugar-maples" and "a massing of grey orchards." She does not, perhaps, take seriously enough, the rigid rules, expectations and especially the grievous costs synonymous with "the woman in a garden."[45] These expectations have little to do with botany and horticulture. Rather they touch upon the gendered narratives of men and women's *roles* in a country estate; how the orthodox rhetoric of gardening equates men with landowning prowess, daring design, inordinate wealth, and erudition, while the New York wives are demure and decorative entities, at best. The expanse whose terraces and parterres seem to supply "ease and amenity" is—presumably—the work of men serving the dominant structures of American landowning. Bellomont emerges then, for Lily at least, as a source of misleading and unhappy sensory affect, wrong turns and trickeries. It is far from the walled garden where out-side worries and upheavals cannot enter. Bellomont's "undulations" indicate how the landscape of "pastoral," promising the unbridled joys of a green retreat, can blur into a region of dread and disgrace.

Skuytercliff

Wharton's Pulitzer-winning 1920 novel *The Age of Innocence* also features a sig-nificant episode set in the Hudson Valley. Skuytercliff is the Van der Luydens' country house, and its name bears a telling assonance with Wyndclyffe, the Rhinecliff mansion of Elizabeth Schermerhorn Jones, Wharton's aunt. Wharton reminisces about playing "on the lawns of Rhinecliff" as a child in *A Backward Glance*.[46] However, it is also true that Aunt Elizabeth's mansion is recalled in the memoir as a locus of "terror" because of its "intolerable ugli-ness": "I can still remember hating everything at Rhinecliff," an "expansive but dour specimen of Hudson River Gothic." Wharton evokes the locality as the very antithesis of a rural idyll: "from the first I was obscurely conscious of a queer resemblance between the granite exterior of Aunt Elizabeth and her grimly comfortable" and "turreted home."[47] It is tempting to speculate that some of these sense-impressions color the Hudson Valley in her fictional writings.

As with *The House of Mirth*'s Bellomont which, instead of offering Lily an aesthetic, recreational or meditative balm, exposes her perceptual shortcomings as a reader of nature, so Newland Archer crucially fails to grasp the full extent of his future spouse's awareness during "the garden episode" of *Faust* at "the sociable old Academy,"[48] and later the Mission Garden in St. Augustine. Such personal lapses, frailties and blind spots in these crucial encounters mean that he is unable to disentangle himself from high society's gilded cage. What lends Skuytercliff its misleading power is how it awakens in Archer a responsiveness to its landscape as a series of painterly flourishes: "coming down a footpath that crossed the highway, he [Archer] caught sight of a slight figure in a red cloak, with a big dog running ahead. He hurried forward, and Madame Olenska stopped short with a smile of welcome."[49] Archer and Ellen's meeting becomes another literary "staging" of the biblical "garden enclosed" from Wharton's earlier novella *Sanctuary*. In this instance, Archer and Ellen seem to occupy an idyllic pastoral space that cannot be: "For a moment Archer stood watching, his gaze delighted by the red meteor against the snow; then he started after her, and they met, panting and laughing, at a wicket that led into the park."[50] The contrast in temperature evidences this: Ellen is a "red meteor" in the midst of winter "snow," melting Archer's heart as he pursues her.

The descriptions of the winter landscape prompt, on a cursory reading, comparison with the chilly vistas in *Ethan Frome*: "The white glitter of the trees filled the air with its own mysterious brightness, and as they walked on over the snow the ground seemed to sing under their feet."[51] The narrator deploys the oxymoronic "mysterious brightness" to suggest the incongruence of Archer and Ellen's adulterous relationship. By strolling through the park, Archer and Ellen seamlessly transition from what they see as a pastoral retreat to what Elizabeth Bradley calls a "Knickerbocker landscape": "They were walking past the house of the old Patroon, with its squat walls and small square windows compactly grouped about a central chimney."[52] This is not only a reminder of Wharton's own Dutch ancestry,[53] but an elaborate historical framing that permits Archer and Ellen's relationship to exist briefly, before the interruption of Julius Beaufort's arrival. At this point, the Skuytercliff meeting already seems a vaguely realized episode from the past: "Archer, as the three strolled back through the park, was aware of this odd sense of disembodiment: and humbling as it was to his vanity it gave him ghostly advantage of observing unobserved."[54] Archer's "odd sense of disembodiment" here is intriguing. It conveys a sense that not only the fluctuations of human feeling, but the natural world itself—"the park" in this episode—is "ghostly," tricky to apprehend and specify. What terminology should Archer employ to account for his surroundings and the people within it?[55] Just as he associates May with St. Augustine in his memory, so he links Ellen with Skuytercliff:

> All through the night he pursued through those enchanted pages the vision of a woman who had the face of Ellen Olenska; but when he woke the next morning, and looked out at the brownstone houses across the street, and thought of his desk in Mr. Letterblair's office, and the family pew in Grace Church, his hour in the park of Skuytercliff became as far outside the pale of probability as the visions of the night.[56]

"Enchanted pages" not only reminds us of the staging of an "enchanted garden" in the earlier performance of *Faust* ("No expense had been spared on the setting").[57] It also evokes those weird intangibles, complex rhetorical formulations and wispy abstractions that Wharton relies on in the *Italian Villas* essays to describe "garden-magic." What is so striking about the passage above is how Archer's sense of the "magic" with Ellen cannot be entertained for long. As soon as he tries to dwell on the links between romantic passion and garden plots, he finds the whole encounter beyond "the pale of probability." "Pale" not only captures the whiteness of the winter snow. It also alerts us to the interplay between the boundaries of a park (the posts separating gardens from virgin wilderness) and what is judged "proper" or decent (beyond the pale) by the gatekeepers of moneyed metropolitan respectability.

The last mention of Skuytercliff is as the location of Newland and May's honeymoon. The cruel irony is apparent: "The Van der Luydens show it to so few people. But they opened it to Ellen, it seems, and she told me what a darling little place it was: she says it's the only house she's been in America that she could imagine being perfectly happy in."[58] Archer has already shared this happiness with Ellen. The "magic" of Archer and Ellen's encounter, those "enchanted pages," are written over to become a partially effaced layer of a topographical palimpsest.

What is perhaps most arresting about the parks and country estates in *The House of Mirth* and *The Age of Innocence* is how Wharton's narrators seem to studiously avoid the brand of sardonic and spiky polemic, the politicized and historicized appraisal of "naturalist" versus "formalist" gardens which lends her nonfiction essays on landscape design their unusual tone. As we have seen, these two novels furnish often exact, even lyrical renderings of flora and fauna, and how parks mediate between myriad "oppositions that define human experience."[59] However, this is achieved without the overt, highly self-conscious, even combative theorizing of, say, *Italian Villas*, a text that leaves us in little doubt about Wharton's preference for (worthy) European garden design over (the aesthetically suspect), more naturalist or informal "English" style. The only trace we can find of Wharton's garden philosophy is through the professional gusto of Dallas Archer, Newland's adult son in *The Age of Innocence*. Clearly, Dallas has little time for the trappings of a "Colonial" style. Indeed, he is eager to undertake European travel so that he can sharpen his grasp of the classical form synonymous with Italian garden design and thus improve the aesthetic sensibilities of his wealthier countrymen.

Wharton's decision to eschew explicit conceptual commentary on the fictional gardens featured here—to construct certain "palings" between the novelistic and the horticultural—is, it turns out, a canny narrative strategy. We follow, and become increasingly absorbed by, Lily's and Archer's halting attempts to decipher structures of meaning in an ambiguous environmental "script." "To see another's garden," according to the American landscape architect Charles Downing Lay's 1924 *A Garden Book*, "may give us a keen perception of the richness and poverty of his personality, of his experiences and associations in life, and of his spiritual qualities."[60] However, Lily and Archer do not *see* clearly enough, they cannot construe the right stories in the fountains and flowers, the colorful borders and hedgerows, and so their "labors of love" yield paltry results. These romantic navigators of private gardens and parks must t/read carefully, locating those shrubs and broadleaf trees in the dense web of art, architecture, and socio-economic circumstances in which they are entrenched. As the fiery Carrie Fisher observes in *The House of Mirth*: "That's Lily all over [...] she works like a slave preparing the ground and sowing her seed; but the day she ought to be reaping the harvest" she "goes off on a picnic."[61] Like Lily, Newland Archer loses focus and mistranslates—he cannot resist converting coded warnings into buoyant signs of affective fulfilment. Their misperceptions suggest gardening is an innocent amusement, a gateway to Jonathan Bate's post-Romantic "recreational space in which we can walk and breathe and play."[62] However, Wharton shows the activity as a "making" of abiding human importance. The characters' failure directs our gaze to a profound, yet arcane idiom for some jaded habitués of country house great halls—what Wharton's friend Vernon Lee might call the "*lie* of the land" (my emphasis).[63]

Cedarledge

Although, as Hermione Lee notes, "Wharton did not write a novel about a gardener," it "might not be too fanciful to think that gardening and novel-writing have something in common."[64] This is not altogether accurate, because Pauline Manford, the female protagonist of the 1925 novel *Twilight Sleep*, is many things, including a keen recreational gardener: "She thought it a duty: it might help to spread the love of gardening (another of her hobbies); and besides it was undemocratic to refuse to share one's private privileges with the multitude."[65] Pauline's gardening project—with its sense of *noblesse oblige*—is the Manford's country estate Cedarledge in the Hudson Valley, which serves as a bucolic sanctuary from the "roar and menace" synonymous with New York City. Its tranquilizing effect is powerfully felt:

> And so it had come about that every year the Cedarledge estate had pushed the encircling landscape farther back, and substituted for its miles of golden-rod and birch and maple more acres of glossy lawn, and more specimen limes and oaks and cut-leaved beeches, domed over more and more windings of expensive shrubbery.[66]

This extract both reveals and conceals the economic tendencies and tactics of (male?) landowners—to dominate, consolidate and expand. Here it is the "Cedarledge estate" that "had pushed" the terrain "farther back," as if such growth is the *work* of organic nature itself as opposed to a large-scale enterprise funded by those with deep pockets and an irresistible need to proclaim social prestige through "more acres of glossy lawn." The invisible hand of inherited male privilege is contrasted with Pauline's status as a sensitive and pragmatic gardener, overseeing every detail of her estate—though she does not get her fingers overly green by weeding it. Unlike other thick descriptions of gardens in Wharton's oeuvre, Cedarledge is delineated in practical as well as botanical terms.[67] Cedarledge is less of an "in-between" space and more of a crisply specified modern site that requires watchful and scrupulous upkeep:

> To Pauline each tree, shrub, water-course, herbaceous border, meant not only itself, but the surveying of grades, transporting of soil, tunnelling for drainage, conducting of water, the business correspondence and paying of bills, which had preceded its existence; and she would have cared for it far less—perhaps not at all—had it sprung into being unassisted, like the random shadbushes and wild cherry trees beyond the gates.[68]

This evocation of "tree" and "shrub" implies Cedarledge looks forward to what Ursula Heise calls the ethical and empathetic project of "ecocosmopolitanism"—a situated mode of knowledge that links "experiences of local endangerment to a sense of planet that encompasses both human and nonhuman worlds." Heise is fascinated by the mutual entanglement of the "human" and "nonhuman" as well as the cultural standpoints and prejudices embedded in the natural world.[69] Cedarledge becomes an encompassing site for the "human"—in this case the Manford family—as well as for the "non-human," which includes both the endemic vegetation as well as the modern technological contrivances used to conserve and enhance the "glossy" green retreat.

In the first description of Cedarledge, both elements are included: "In the village, the glint of the gilt weathercock on the new half-timbered engine-house; under a rich slope of pasture-land the recently enlarged dairy-farm; then woods of hemlock and dogwood; acres of rhododendron, azalea and mountain laurel acclimatized about a hidden lake."[70] The "engine-house" coexists with the "pasture-land," a nascent, tentative form of eco-cosmopolitanism, that, as Heise proposes, "goes beyond environmentalist clichés regarding universal connectedness and the pastoral understanding of ecology that informed earlier kinds of modern environmentalist thinking."[71] By including both the advanced technology and the vegetation, eco-cosmopolitanism furnishes an intriguing vision of convergence. The design of Cedarledge also provides a vivid "glimpse" of:

Japanese water-gardens fringed with cherry bloom and catkins; open lawns, spreading trees, the long brick house-front and its terraces, and through a sculptured archway the Dutch garden with dwarf topiary work and endless files of bulbs about the commander's *baton* of a stately sundial.[72]

That the "Japanese water-gardens" and "Dutch garden" are all contained in the Hudson Valley, points to what Heise terms "an environmentally inflected cosmopolitanism" that "needs to combine sustained familiarity and fluency in more than one culture with a systemic understanding of global ecology."[73] Not only "global ecology"—we see that "global economy" and "culture" are accounted for: "The faint spring loveliness reached her somehow, in long washes of pale green, and the blurred mauve of budding vegetation; but her eyes could not linger on any particular beauty without its dissolving into soil, manure, nurserymen's catalogues, and bills again—bills."[74] "Beauty" (the serene life of a shepherdess in pastoral) and the necessary (exacting daily toil evoked by the georgic), the abstract and embodied experience, leisure and business, are woven through these verbal nuances. Wharton's narrator wittily balances "soil" and "manure" with "catalogues" and "bills." In a sly rhetorical flourish, touching "bills" is equated with handling "manure"—playing on the connotations of money as soiled paper, *filthy lucre*, etc.—to produce the same feelings of base disgust.[75] It is through this dense web of imagery that we grasp the cultural and economic significance of Cedarledge to its owners: "It had all cost a terrible lot of money; but she was proud of that too—to her it was part of the beauty, part of the exquisite order and suitability which reigned as much in the simulated wildness of the rhododendron glen as in the geometrical lines of the Dutch garden."[76] Does "exquisite order" point to the formal arrangement of a garden or the entrenched power of an emergent inter/national elite, linked by "lines" of shared fiscal and political interest? Wild/(er)ness is, of course, an intrinsically slippery and vexing category in any so-called nature writing, but the oxymoronic "simulated wildness" (anticipating an ever more commercialized or even virtual nature?) serves to exemplify the complexities of an environmentally oriented cosmopolitanism.

Pauline Manford has made Cedarledge what it is, however this version of the country estate is for her daughter Nona "simply the world of her childhood, and she could see it from no other angle, nor imagine it as ever having been different."[77] Unlike Pauline who relates to Cedarledge in a measured and no-nonsense fashion, Nona resorts to an idealizing tendency, or a mode of bourgeois escapism that has little time for the garden's relationship with industrial modernization: "To her it had always worn the *same enchantment*, stretched to the same remote distances. At nineteen it was almost the last illusion she had left" (my emphasis).[78] Like Brantwood for Ruskin, Cedarledge "answered every purpose of Paradise" to Nona.[79] We can compare Nona's "illusion" with the "enchanted pages" that Newland Archer associates with romantic and horticultural spaces in *The Age of Innocence*. Nona does not share her mother's acute concern with the practical challenges of maintaining Cedarledge, its woods and lake: she "knew nothing of what Cedarledge had cost, but little of the labor of its making."[80]

As the next part of this book will demonstrate, Nona shares with Charity Royall in *Summer* a passion for the natural world, albeit more toned down and tentative. When Nona reminisces about Cedarledge it is through the evocation of a specific flower: "She remembered mild spring nights at Cedarledge, when she was a little girl, and she and Jim used to [...] go to the lake, loose the canoe, and drift on a silver path among islets fringed with budding dogwood."[81] Dogwood is significantly included in the list of botanical specimens that a visitor might see upon first approaching Cedarledge, and it marks every memory of the estate. It is here that we find an echo of the biographical episode that comprises Wharton's ecological awakening as a child, that special day in the Hudson Valley woods: "It was the same tremor that had stirred in me in the spring woods of Mamaroneck when I heard the whisper of the arbutus and *the starry choir of dogwood*; and it has never since been still" (my emphasis).[82] Clearly dogwood has a potent affective resonance for Wharton both in her autobiographical texts and in *Twilight Sleep*. However, according to a couple of important nineteenth-century horticultural and conduct manuals it carries more tangled meanings. In Kate Greenaway's *Language of Flowers* (1884), dogwood is synonymous with "durability,"[83] an adjective that we might link with the resilient Pauline Manford. On the other hand, in John H. Young's *Our Deportment* (1879), dogwood prompts the question "Am I indifferent to you?"[84] This is a question that seems to be on Lita Wyant's lips, but it is never voiced. For Nona however, dogwood is a recollection—her very own Proustian madeleine—that is violently shattered by the end of *Twilight Sleep*.[85] The final reference to Cedarledge is a traumatic one: "The reminder of Cedarledge would once have doubled their beauty; now it made her shut her eyes sharply, in the inner recoil from all the name brought back."[86] When Gary Totten writes about this estate that "Nature's positive potential as a setting for women's introspection or renewal is apparent,"[87] this is not entirely convincing. By the end of the novel, it has, in fact, been completely undone. Nona is not revitalized but rather *haunted* by Cedarledge and the memory of what played out on the "leafy stage" of this country estate.

Notes

1 Wharton, *A Backward Glance*, 4.
2 Wharton, *A Backward Glance*, 4–5.
3 Wharton, *A Backward Glance*, 4.
4 Katherine Mansfield, *Katherine Mansfield Notebooks: Complete Edition*. Edited by Margaret Scott. University of Minnesota Press, 2002, 263, my emphasis.
5 Mansfield, *Notebooks*, 261.
6 Wharton, *A Backward Glance*, 124.
7 Wharton, *A Backward Glance*, 54.
8 Wharton, *A Backward Glance*, 54.
9 See Ralph Pite, "How Green Were the Romantics?" *Studies in Romanticism*, vol. 35, no. 3, 1996, 357–73. *JSTOR*, www.jstor.org/stable/25601179. Accessed May 25, 2021.
10 Hermione Lee, *Edith Wharton*. Vintage Books, 2008, 669.
11 Carolyn Merchant, *Reinventing Eden: The Fate of Nature in Western Culture*. 2nd ed., Routledge, 2013, 108.
12 Wharton, *The House of Mirth*, 12.
13 Totten, "Women, Art, and the Natural World in Edith Wharton's Works," 175–88. Twenty-First-Century Critical Revisions, 185.
14 Wharton, *The House of Mirth*, 55.
15 Wharton, *The House of Mirth*, 23.
16 See J. R. Watson, "Parkland in Literature." *Landscape Research*, vol. 7, no. 1, 1982, 9–13.
17 Wharton, *The House of Mirth*, 34.
18 Wharton, "Sanctuary," 151.
19 John Dixon Hunt, "Introduction: Reading and Writing the Site." *Gardens and the Picturesque: Studies in the History of Landscape Architecture*. MIT Press, 1992, 9–11.

20 See Allen Weiss, *Mirrors of Infinity: The French Formal Garden and 17th-Century Metaphysics*. Princeton Architectural Press, 1995, 14–16.

21 Wharton, *The House of Mirth*, 46, 4.

22 Wharton, *The House of Mirth*, 4–5.

23 Lily herself muses that her "beauty" was "not the mere ephemeral possession it might have been in the hands of inexperience: her skill in enhancing it […] seemed to give it a kind of permanence." See *The House of Mirth*, 49–50.

24 Wharton, *The House of Mirth*, 39.

25 Gordon Campbell, *A Short History of Gardens*. Oxford University Press, 2016, 6. On the garden as a complex art object see Mark Francis and Randolph T. Hester, eds., *The Meaning of Gardens: Idea, Place and Action*. MIT Press, 1990; George McKay, *Radical Gardening: Politics, Idealism and Rebellion in the Garden*. Frances Lincoln, 2011.

26 Wharton, *The House of Mirth*, 40. The expression "rural elegance" is akin to "rustic eminence," the words used by John Ruskin to describe his childhood country home. See John Ruskin, *Praeterita*. Vol. 1, George Allen, 1907, 35. See also Michael Conan, ed., *Perspectives on Garden Histories*. Dumbarton Oaks, 1991; U. P. Hedrick, *A History of Horticulture in America to 1860*. Timber Press, 1988.

27 Quoted in Cooper, *The Philosophy of Gardens*, 15.

28 The garden theorist Michael Pollan inveighs against the idea of the lawn as chemically controlled and aggressively tutored nature, or as he calls it "nature under totalitarian rule." See Michael Pollan, *Second Nature*. Grove Press, 1991.

29 Wharton, *The House of Mirth*, 40.

30 Wharton, *The House of Mirth*, 40.

31 Thorstein Veblen, *The Theory of the Leisure Class* [1899]. Oxford University Press, 2007, 81–83.

32 See Andrew Jackson Downing, *A Treatise on the Theory and Practice of Landscape Gardening Adapted to North America*. Wiley and Putnam, 1841, 90–93; see also Andrew Jackson Downing, *Rural Essays*. G. P. Putnam, 1853.

33 Robert Morris Copeland, *Country Life: A Handbook of Agriculture, Horticulture, and Landscape Gardening*. 2nd ed., Orange Judd and Co., 1867, 84–86.

34 Wharton, *The House of Mirth*, 49.

35 Alice Morse Earle, "Introduction" to Horace Walpole, *Essay on Modern Gardening* (reprint of 1785 edn). Kirgate Press, 1904, xx.

36 Wharton, *The House of Mirth*, 49.

37 Wharton, *The House of Mirth*, 49–50.

38 Wharton, *The House of Mirth*, 50.

39 Wharton, *The House of Mirth*, 50.

40 Wharton, *The House of Mirth*, 51.

41 Wharton, *The House of Mirth*, 51.

42 Wharton, *The House of Mirth*, 51.

43 See Gail Finney, *The Counterfeit Idyll: The Garden Ideal and Social Reality in Nineteenth-Century Fiction*. M. Niemeyer, 1984.

44 John Michael Vlach, *Back of the Big House: The Cultural Landscape of the Plantation*. exhibition, 1995; see also Christopher Thacker, *The History of Gardens*. University of California Press, 1985; Janet Fiskio, "Unsettling Ecocriticism: Rethinking Agrarianism, Place, and Citizenship." *American Literature*, vol. 84, no. 2, 2012, 301–25. Annette Giesecke and Naomi Jacobs, eds., *Earth Perfect? Nature, Utopia and the Garden*. Black Dog, 2012.

45 See David E. Cooper, *The Philosophy of Gardens*. Oxford University Press, 2006, 23.

46 Wharton, *A Backward Glance*, 28.
47 Wharton, *A Backward Glance*, 28.
48 Wharton, *The Age of Innocence*, 3.
49 Wharton, *The Age of Innocence*, 82.
50 Wharton, *The Age of Innocence*, 83.
51 Wharton, *The Age of Innocence*, 83.
52 See Elizabeth L. Bradley, "Dutch New York from Irving to Wharton." *The Cambridge Companion to the Literature of New York*, edited by Cyrus R. K. Patell and Bryan Waterman. Cambridge University Press, 2010, 27–41. Cambridge Companions to Literature, 38; Wharton, *The Age of Innocence*, 83.
53 Wharton writes that: "On both sides, our colonial ancestry goes back for nearly three hundred years, and on both sides the colonists in question seem to have been identified since early days with New York." Wharton, *A Backward Glance*, 9.
54 Wharton, *The Age of Innocence*, 85.
55 This is one of Lawrence Buell's core interests in, for example, *The Environmental Imagination*; Lawrence Buell, *The Future of Environmental Criticism*. Blackwell, 2005; Stacy Alaimo, *Bodily Natures: Science, Environment, and the Material Self*. Indiana University Press, 2001; Bill McKibben, *The End of Nature*. Viking, 1990; Roderick Nash, *Wilderness and the American Mind*. 3rd ed., Yale University Press, 1982.
56 Wharton, *The Age of Innocence*, 87.
57 Wharton, *The Age of Innocence*, 5.
58 Wharton, *The Age of Innocence*, 116.
59 Mara Miller, *The Garden as Art*. SUNY Press, 1993, 57.
60 Charles Downing Lay, *A Garden Book for Autumn and Winter*. Duffield & Co., 1924, 13.
61 Wharton, *The House of Mirth*, 190.
62 Jonathan Bate, *The Song of the Earth*. Picador, 2000, 64.
63 Lee, *Genius Loci: Notes on Place*, 5–6.
64 Lee, *Edith Wharton*, 563.
65 Edith Wharton, *Twilight Sleep*. Simon & Schuster, 2010, 103.
66 Wharton, *Twilight Sleep*, 213.
67 Wharton, *Twilight Sleep*, 213.
68 Wharton, *Twilight Sleep*, 213.
69 Ursula K. Heise, *Sense of Place and Sense of Planet: The Environmental Imagination of the Global*. Oxford University Press, 2008, 169.
70 Wharton, *Twilight Sleep*, 213.
71 Heise, *Sense of Place and Sense of Planet*, 159.
72 Wharton, *Twilight Sleep*, 213.
73 Heise, *Sense of Place and Sense of Planet*, 159.
74 Wharton, *Twilight Sleep*, 213–14.
75 This figuring of the monetary and the organic reminds us of Heise's argument that the "task of ecocriticism with a cosmopolitan perspective is to develop an understanding and critique of these mechanisms as they play themselves out in different cultural contexts so as to create a variety of ecological imaginations of the global." Heise, *Sense of Place and Sense of Planet*, 62.
76 Wharton, *Twilight Sleep*, 214.
77 Wharton, *Twilight Sleep*, 215.
78 Wharton, *Twilight Sleep*, 215.
79 Ruskin, *Praeterita*, 38.

80 Wharton, *Twilight Sleep*, 215.

81 Wharton, *Twilight Sleep*, 80.

82 Wharton, *A Backward Glance*, 54.

83 Kate Greenaway, *Language of Flowers*. Gramercy Publishing Company, 1978, 15.

84 John H. Young, *Our Deportment, or, The Manners, Conduct and Dress of the Most Refined Society: Including Forms for Letters, Invitations, Etc., Etc.: Also Valuable Suggestions on Home Culture and Training*. F. B. Dickerson & Co., 1879, 414.

85 Wharton evokes the same magical enchantment she felt as a child for dogwood, by having Lita's husband Jim Wyant say that: "There's the dogwood! Look! Never seen it in bloom here before, have you? It's one of our sights." The beauty of the dogwood is used to convince Lita to visit the country estate because she "had never seen the Cedarledge dogwood in bud, the woods trembling into green." Lita's presence at Cedarledge and her illicit, slightly incestuous affair with Dexter Manford, her mother-in-law's husband, is what will set in motion the unfortunate accident that plays out in this novel. Arthur Wyant shoots Nona Manford, who happens to walk in on her father and his mistress. When Pauline realizes what happened to her daughter, Powder the butler is instructed to tell the servants to "scour the gardens" for the culprit. Wharton, *Twilight Sleep*, 219, 108, 300.

86 Wharton, *Twilight Sleep*, 302.

87 Totten, "Women, Art, and the Natural World in Edith Wharton's Works," 175–88. Twenty-First-Century Critical Revisions, 175.

Chapter 3

GARDEN "HAUNTS"

In Wharton's 1924 novella *False Dawn*, the "Halston Raycie house overlooked a lawn sloping to the Sound." It seems to promise what Mark Francis and Randolph T. Hester call, in *The Meaning of Gardens* (1990), an "idealized order of nature and culture":[1]

> Below the verandah the turf was broken by three rounds of rose-geranium, heliotrope and Bengal roses, which Mrs. Raycie tended in gauntlet gloves, under a small-hinged sunshade that folded back on its carved ivory handle. [2]

In the very next sentence, the narrator swiftly undoes the blissful pastoral mood—melding a noble idea, a tranquil place and a less alienated mode of human labor—with the mention of a notorious traitor: "The house, remodeled and enlarged by Mr. Raycie on his marriage, had played a part in the Revolutionary war as the settler's cottage where Benedict Arnold had had his headquarters."[3] The country house is not haunted by Arnold's ghost in any trite sense. However, the pointed reference casts a long shadow over the scrupulous evocation of the estate.

As *False Dawn* implies, not all cultivated sites are serene green enclaves that point to biblical "gardens enclosed" in Wharton's oeuvre. These localities can be charged with foreboding and paranormal auras that *unsettle* the characters that seek to dwell in, or preside over, them. Some gardens, like Aunt Elizabeth's mansion in *A Backward Glance*, even inspire Gothic "terror." For critic Fred Botting, the "staples of the Gothic, are clearly identifiable in early Gothic texts," since the "tradition draws on medieval romances, supernatural, Faustian and fairy tales, Renaissance drama, sentimental, picaresque and confessional narratives as well as the ruins, tombs and nocturnal speculations that fascinated Graveyard poets."[4] My final chapter will focus entirely on depictions of "ruins" in Wharton's oeuvre, and what Gothic elements seem to be woven into the very bricks and mortar of these crumbling structures.

Here I am more concerned with how Wharton's narrators evoke what we might term "Gothic gardens," using verbal strategies that both register and subvert the vivid, even lurid paraphernalia of earlier "supernatural romance." Wharton is especially adroit in selecting and stressing particular facets of the visible, concrete terrain—the unembellished, unremarked, borderless qualities of green spaces, bringing to mind poet Ian Hamilton Finlay's thesis that "certain gardens are described as retreats when they really are attacks."[5] A notable early example is her historical short story "The Duchess at Prayer" (1900): "I looked down on the gardens. An opulence of dahlias overran the box-borders, between cypresses that cut the sunshine like basalt shafts. Bees hung above the lavender; lizards sunned themselves on the benches and slipped through the cracks of the dry basins."[6] Like the parkland in *The House of Mirth*, this ostensibly restful environment is not what it seems. Here verbal flourishes are oddly violent: "overran," "cut" and especially "hung" carrying nuances of disarray, turmoil, execution and fatality. Reptiles that serve a practical purpose of eating insects hint at sinister subterranean and nocturnal movements—what survives, even thrives by slipping "through the cracks." All of this is underscored by a profound sense of cultural loss: "[e]verywhere were vanishing traces of that fantastic horticulture of which our dull age has lost its art."[7] "Fantastic" here signifies both admiration as well as a disruptive element reminiscent of the Gothic tropes in Nathaniel Hawthorne's "Rappaccini's Daughter": "Nor did he fail again to observe, or imagine, an analogy between the beautiful girl and the gorgeous shrub that hung its gemlike flowers over the fountain; a resemblance which Beatrice seemed to have indulged a *fantastic humor* in heightening" (my italics).[8]

The novella *Bunner Sisters* (1892), Wharton's earliest long work of narrative prose fiction, also exploits the *unsettling* qualities of place found in "The Duchess at Prayer." *Bunner Sisters* draws attention to Wharton's re-visioning of local color and Gothic imagery to tease out, in the terms of cultural theorist Mark Fisher's *The Weird and the Eerie* (2016), "what lies beyond standard perception, cognition and experience."[9] Hermione Lee regards the novella as "a haunting piece of American urban pastoral, unlike anything else in Wharton."[10] In this text Ramy convinces the sisters to go out to Hoboken to visit his friend, Mrs. Hochmuller. The incentive? "She's got a real garden, you know."[11] This emphasis on "real garden" asserts a reassuring, palpable actuality—a site shaped by weather patterns over time, by habitations and activities of the non/human, and so on. However, "real" also gestures at its opposite—the unhomely, the subliminal and the spectral—immanent in a tree, shed, path or some other facet of what appears to be a harmless, even humdrum social milieu. While the New York smart set journeys to the opulent estates in the Hudson Valley, working-class wayfarers in *Bunner Sisters* must make do

with a modest pastoral refuge in New Jersey. They pass through "a thinly settled district, past vacant lots and arrow brick houses standing in unsupported
solitude, till they finally reached an almost rural region of scattered cottages
and low wooden buildings that looked like village 'stores'."[12] The "almost
rural" implies an edgeland—that "debatable space where city and countryside fray"—as well as prompting comparison with the New England village
where Wharton sets *Ethan Frome, Summer* and a few of her short stories.[13] As
in "The Duchess at Prayer" botanic specificities carry unusual affective and
symbolic heft: "Clumps of dielytra and day-lilies bloomed behind the paling,
and a crooked elm hung romantically over the gable of the house."[14] First
of all, in a mischievous irony, the romantic "elm" evokes Thomas Higgins's
1858 text *The Crooked Elm; Or, Life by the Wayside*, which seeks to exercise "a
healthy moral influence on the mind of the reader, by inculcating virtue."[15]
However, it is precisely this "virtue"—what Higgins terms "the necessity of
upright, honorable conduct"—that Ramy lacks in Wharton's text, given his
resolve to swindle younger sister Evelina.[16]

These resonances imbue the description of Mrs. Hochmuller's garden:
"When dinner was over Mrs. Hochmuller invited her guests to step out of
the kitchen-door, and they found themselves in a green enclosure, half garden, half orchard." The "enclosure" suggests not the boundless freedom
that Lily savors in *The House of Mirth*, but a trammeled, even claustrophobic
green zone designed for subsistence as well as leisure: "Grey hens followed
by golden broods clucked under the twisted apple-boughs, a cat dozed on
the edge of an old well, and from tree to tree ran the network of clothes-
line that denoted Mrs. Hochmuller's calling."[17] Beyond these apple-trees
"on the farther side of a rough fence, the land dipped down, holding a bit
of woodland in its hollow."[18] Into this woodland Evelina voices a desire to
go. Even though she is accompanied by Ramy, we are not made privy to
what happens there, only a disconcerting hint that it was "all strangely sweet
and still on that hot Sunday afternoon."[19] The phrasing "strangely sweet"
conveys an ominous echo not only of American author Nathaniel Parker
Willis's narrative poem "The Leper" ("the voice was like the master-tone
/ Of a rich instrument,—most strangely sweet") but also Jacobean play-
wright and poet John Marston's lyric "O Love, How Strangely Sweet." In
sharp contrast to Marston's direct and concise style, Wharton's narrator
circles around but cannot fully register or acknowledge the event. Rather
the text points to another layer of memory and (transgressive?) action that
has been added to this "almost rural" locality on a Sunday afternoon. That
intimation of a *secret history* (of male violence? of a Nature utterly indifferent
to less wholesome pastoral impulses?) points to an in-between zone where
binaries—frightening absence and reassuring presence, subjective and

objective, seen and unseen—fuse to reveal the possibilities for enchantment in seemingly drab things, like coppices, grass or soil. Perhaps what we are striving for here is closer to Mark Fisher's recent conception of "the weird": that "which does not belong. The weird brings to the familiar something which ordinarily lies beyond it, and which cannot be reconciled with the 'homely.'"[20] More importantly, *Bunner Sisters* shows how Wharton's haunted and haunting gardens can be surveyed from an "ecogothic" perspective, as Dawn Keetley and Matthew Wynn Sivils explain: "Adopting a specifically gothic ecocritical lens illuminates the fear, anxiety, and dread" that shapes "our interactions with nonhuman ecologies."[21]

Ecogothic puts pressure on those conventional expectations and lyrical associations of the private, kitchen or ornamental garden—that it should vouchsafe a pleasing open vista or haven, a handsome prospect or sensory fulfilment.[22] Such associations are skillfully undermined in Wharton's 1916 short story "Kerfol," which offers a striking, self-reflexive experiment with *mis-en-scene* and the genre trappings synonymous with supernatural fiction by Hawthorne, Wilkie Collins and Sheridan Le Fanu. "Kerfol" not only addresses and triggers ecogothic affect, but also reveals a sharp sense of how this "house of fiction"—to recall Henry James's lexis—reverberates with the cadences of other texts and authors.[23]

"Kerfol" portrays a haunted chateau in Brittany as well as cultural representations of the woman in, as well as cut off from, the garden. Wharton travelled to this region with her husband Teddy in the spring of 1893. In a letter to Anna Bahlmann, dated 3rd May 1893, Wharton recorded passing through the town of Vitré: "There were many quaint old tumble-down houses, there was even a fortified castle as well preserved as Langrais, but the castle is used as a prison."[24] Such forbidding and decrepit sites, largely emptied of the human, may well have served as inspiration for this tale, which Hermione Lee avers is the "strangest piece of fiction to come out" of Wharton's "war years."[25] The French setting is crucial here, given Wharton's argument in *The Writing of Fiction*: "As the soil of France is of all soils the most weeded, tilled and ductile, so the field of art, wherever French culture extends, is the most worked-over and the most prepared for whatever seed is to be sown in it."[26]

"Kerfol" is a text about the historical experience of enforced retirement or withdrawal from the social world. The garden—as a place of romantic dalliance, aesthetic pleasure or fruitful diversion in earlier sections of my chapter—becomes one of severe punishment and trauma here. This is implied when the narrator remarks of the chateau grounds: "to sit there and *be penetrated by* the weight of *its silence*" (my emphasis).[27] Here the narrator is not only attuned to how we operate in physical space ("sit there") but also the manner in which we interrelate with materiality through sight, smell, touch and especially in this case (the absence of) sound, like birdsong. Wharton's rhetorical tactics in this text remind us of her friend Vernon Lee's notable conception of "haunted" terrain in her essay "Faustus and Helena: Notes on the Supernatural in Art." For Lee a ghost:

> is the damp, the darkness, *the silence,* the solitude: [...] a ghost is the bright moonlight against which the cypresses stand out like black hearse-plumes, in which the blasted grey olives and gnarled fig-trees stretch their branches over the broken walls [...] Each and all of these things [...] is a ghost, a vague feeling we can scarcely describe, a some-thing pleasing and terrible which invades our whole consciousness.[28]

What if, Lee conjectures, "the ghost" *is* the garden? To what extent does she ascribe agency to the impalpable, the inanimate, the nonhuman? Little attempt is made to partition the spectral from the environmental, the intangible from the concrete. Such a "feeling" for the eerie—flowing from, or through, the "olives" and "fig-trees"—implies links between non-contiguous epochs and places, invading (or in Wharton's terms penetrating) the very *grounds* of one's being. Lee's account supplies a critical lens through which to parse "Kerfol."[29] As cultural theorist Stephanie Ross argues, "gardens are at once parts of the real world—actual pieces of land—and also virtual worlds—coherent sets of possible sensory stimuli."[30] "Kerfol" shows that what we conceive of as a readily understood cultural artifact—its physical form and function for, say, growing things—is also a twilight zone crusted with myriad paranormal imprints, rhythms and pulsations. It compels us to address visions that apparently have no foundation in the physical locale, beyond the remit of a rational, measurable system of beliefs.[31] The original designers, architects, patrons, plant materials, pathways—are largely gone but still present at a subliminal level. What should be straightforward in "Kerfol"—a three-dimensional space within a defined boundary, whose foundation is soil, in which shrubs are deliberately cultivated for physical and/or aesthetic sustenance—is encrypted.

As in Wharton's knowingly constructed vampire story "Mr. Jones," an "unsettling" aura is triggered when a privileged unnamed narrator approaches an ancient "pile." This encounter reveals a layered landscape crusted with the remnants of an older, more *inhospitable* culture. The narrator concedes that "I knew nothing of the history of Kerfol" or its garden: "I was new to Brittany, and Lanrivain had never mentioned the name to me till the day before—but one couldn't as much as glance at that pile without feeling in it a long accumulation of history."[32] This "accumulation" suggests how objects acquire the patina of age. The reader, allied with the narrator, seeks to read not only the weathered stones but the trees as well: "the aspect of Kerfol suggested something more—a perspective of stern and cruel memories stretching away, like its own grey avenues, into a blur of darkness."[33] This "blur" points to something less congenial than the "sheer weight of many associated lives and deaths which gives a majesty to all old houses."[34] The "blur" also explains why the narrator confesses to a level of botanical ignorance in this otherworld: "I know most trees by name, but I haven't to this day been able to decide what those trees were": "They had the tall curves of elms, the tenuity of poplars, the ashen color of olives under a rainy sky; and they stretched ahead of me for half a mile or more without a break in their arch."[35] Before approaching the haunted chateau itself, "Kerfol" demonstrates the first facet of ecogothic, that is: "a repository of deep unease, fear, and even contempt as humans confront the natural world."[36]

Barbara White notes that "the remoteness of the events narrated adds to the eerie atmosphere"[37] because these incidents took place in the sixteenth century. However, she does not consider that images of physical distance and "remoteness" compound this eerie effect, which is heightened later in the text when the narrator "enters the deep twilight of a narrow and incredibly old box-walk."[38] The chateau is surrounded by a moat, "filled with wild shrubs and brambles" serving as a barrier that prevents easy approach.[39] The narrator's growing sense that the "whole place is a tomb" anticipates what White calls "the ghost dogs of Kerfol."[40] These nonhuman entities reveal how for Wharton the "experience of violence and muteness lies at the heart of the ghost story's meaning."[41] However, what this reading underplays is how Wharton's "ghost story" compels us to reimagine our links to the materiality of "foreign" place/s, and what this might entail for the refinement of terms such as Vernon Lee's *genius loci*.

The narrator remarks that the "main building faced me; and I now saw that one half was a mere ruined front, with gaping windows."[42] "Gaping" here hints at an open wound—allowing the past to flow into and permeate the modern moment. Indeed, the entire site, as the text will show, is a lesion upon the landscape that will never be entirely healed. The narrator does not actually enter these ruins, but always remains on the edge of the grounds. By keeping the narrator outside, Wharton upholds the second aspect of the ecogothic, that is: "a literary mode that uses an implacable external 'wilderness' to call attention to the crisis in practices of representation."[43] This does not prevent the narrator from noticing how a "few roses grew against the wall" and on an upper window-sill "a pot of fuchsias."[44] When the "remarkably beautiful little dog" appears, the narrator reacts with the same uncertainty as she did with the trees earlier: "I was not sure of the breed at the time."[45] She compares the dog to "a large tawny chrysanthemum"[46]—a flower widely associated with mortality. The narrator is able to traverse the moat and get closer to "the garden" by scrambling "over a wall smothered with brambles."[47] The vegetation is varied but sparse, rather than lush and verdant: a "few lean hydrangeas and geraniums pined in the flower-beds, and the ancient house looked down on them indifferently."[48] These terms make us question whether this is a garden at all, given the house resembles a "fortress-prison."[49] Here, Wharton's narrator hints at another key tenet of the ecogothic: "a terrain in which the contours of the body are mapped, contours that increasingly stray beyond the bounds of what might be considered properly 'human' ."[50]

Wharton, who devoted much intellectual energy to the question of why gardens appeal to so many communities and cultures across time, shows how the castle garden is bereft of any "appeal" and generates claustrophobia instead: "I walked around the farther wing, went up some disjointed steps, and entered the deep twilight of a narrow and incredibly old box-walk."[51] Landscape gardener Beatrix Farrand affirmed that with a "Box Walk" it is "important to have a tall-growing tree of somewhat 'romantic' type."[52] Wharton takes this image of the tall, romantic tree and offers a bizarre transformation: "It was like the ghost of a box-walk, its lustrous green all turning to the shadowy greyness of the avenues."[53] The trees are personified and become threatening, belligerent entities: "the branches hitting me in the face and springing back with a dry rattle."[54]

The "dry rattle" seems to announce the secret history of "Kerfol," in which refined femininity, trapped in marriage, finds further restriction and a familiar, unforgiving male hegemonic pattern: "Kerfol was a lonely place, and that when her husband was away on business at Bennes or Morlaix—whither she was never taken—she was not allowed so much as to walk in the park unaccompanied."[55] If gardens are specified, to a large extent, by the punctilious exercise of formal control and calculation—and we see this in *The House of Mirth* with its portrayal of Bellomont's wide expanse of lawn—then in "Kerfol" that discipline acquires grislier authoritarian resonances. An "order" of masculine power is enforced at every level, to the point where a wife becomes prisoner, with only a partial view of the surrounding flora.

There is then, a grimly relished irony at the close of this story. If Wharton, as self-appointed custodian of the lore of landscape history in nonfiction like *Italian Villas*, is alert to how gardens answer a deep-seated desire to revere and nurture life, then the chateau grounds in "Kerfol" epitomize a macabre counter-site or contrast, where desiccation ("dry rattle") is the first article of the former estate-owner's creed. With the intransigent otherness of the "Kerfol" grounds we are at the furthest remove from that joyous Renaissance conception of the garden expounded by Eugenio Battisti: "a place" of "feasts, entertainment of friends," unpunished "sexual and intellectual freedom."[56]

The wife in "Kerfol" is denied all of this felicity. The garden in this story opens a portal to an era where the woman experiences no spiritual renewal, little sense of structure and pattern to life provided by regular exercise, fresh air, instruction in the rhythms of the organic world, no hint of camaraderie with fellow gardeners. She is brought closer to God not by strolling in the fortress grounds, but by viewing it as a site/sight of torment through the bars of her domestic jail. Unable to respond fully both to the organization of the chateau grounds and the trees that grow there, the wife in "Kerfol" existed as a spectral presence even when alive. All of this points to how a garden bears the "patina" or residuum of a brutish atavistic past—a husband who murders his spouse's dogs and is then himself murdered by their ghosts—concealed beneath patrician mores and manners.[57] With its echoes of Perrault's "Blue Beard,"[58] Judith Saunders argues how in "Kerfol" Wharton melds "words and images from valued literary ancestors into her own imaginative constructions."[59]

Notes

1 Francis and Hester, *The Meaning of Gardens: Idea, Place and Action*, 2.
2 Edith Wharton, "False Dawn." *Old New York*. Simon & Schuster, 1995, 7–80, 10, 39.
3 Wharton, "False Dawn," 39.
4 Fred Botting, "Introduction: Gothic Excess and Transgressions." *Gothic*. Routledge, 1996, 1–13. The New Critical Idiom, 10.
5 Alec Finlay, ed., *Ian Hamilton Finlay Selections*. University of California Press, 2011, 56.
6 Wharton, "The Duchess at Prayer." *Ghost Stories of Edith Wharton*. Vintage, 2009, 110–27, 111.
7 Wharton, "The Duchess at Prayer," 111.
8 The gardens are one of the meeting places for the eponymous Duchess and her unfortunate paramour, the cavaliere: "They were always together [...] walking the gardens." The Cavaliere is walled into the chapel by the Duke and eventually dies. See Wharton, "The Duchess at Prayer," 116.
9 Mark Fisher, *The Weird and the Eerie*. Repeater Books, 2016, 8.
10 Lee, *Edith Wharton*, 185. See also Barbara Hochman, "The Good, the Bad, and the Literary: Edith Wharton's *Bunner Sisters* and the Social Contexts of Reading." *Studies in American Naturalism*, vol. 1, no. 1/2, 2006, 128–43. JSTOR, www.jstor.org /stable/23431279. Accessed May 28, 2021; Linda Kornasky, "On 'Listen[Ing] to Spectres Too': Wharton's *Bunner Sisters* and Ideologies of Sexual Selection." *American Literary Realism, 1870-1910*, vol. 30, no. 1, 1997, 47–58. JSTOR, www.jstor.org/stable /27746714. Accessed May 28, 2021.
11 Wharton, *Bunner Sisters*. In *"Ethan Frome"; "Summer"; "Bunner Sisters."* Alfred A. Knopf, 2008, 271–366. Everyman's Library, 308.
12 Wharton, *Bunner Sisters*, 309.
13 Paul Farley and Michael Symmons Roberts, *Edgelands: Journeys into England's True Wildernesses*. Jonathan Cape, 2011, 3.
14 Wharton, *Bunner Sisters*, 309.

15 Thomas Higgins, *The Crooked Elm, Or, Life by the Wayside*. Whittemore, Niles and Hall, 1858, 3.
16 Higgins, *The Crooked Elm*, 3.
17 Wharton, *Bunner Sisters,* 310.
18 Wharton, *Bunner Sisters,* 310–11.
19 Wharton, *Bunner Sisters,* 311.
20 Fisher, *The Weird and the Eerie*, 10–11.
21 Dawn Keetley and Matthew Wynn Sivils, "Introduction: Approaches to the Ecogothic." *Ecogothic in Nineteenth-Century American Literature*, edited by Dawn Keetley and Matthew Wynn Sivils. Routledge, 2018, 1–20, 1. See also Cooper, *A Philosophy of Gardens.*
22 See Jennifer Wren Atkinson, *Gardenland: Nature, Fantasy, and Everyday Practice*. University of Georgia Press, 2018, 1–10.
23 Even though the story takes place in France, it also casts a sidelight on "the dominant American relationship with nature." See Keetley and Sivils, "Introduction: Approaches to the Ecogothic," 1.
24 Wharton, *My Dear Governess*, 115.
25 Lee, *Edith Wharton*, 519.
26 Edith Wharton, *The Writing of Fiction*. Touchtone Book, 1997, 28–29.
27 Wharton, "Kerfol." *Ghost Stories of Edith Wharton*. Vintage, 2009, 69.
28 Vernon Lee, *Hauntings and Other Fantastic Tales*. Edited by Catherine Maxwell and Patricia Pulham. Broadview Press, 2006, 310, my emphasis.
29 On these uncanny resonances of "place" see Edward S. Casey, *Getting Back into Place: Toward a Renewed Understanding of the Place-World*. Indiana University Press, 2009.
30 Stephanie Ross, *What Gardens Mean*. University of Chicago Press, 1998, 176.
31 On these so-called "occult" or "haunted" geographies see David Matless, "Nature, the Modern and the Mystic: Tales from Early Twentieth Century Geography." *Transactions of the Institute of British Geographers*, vol. 16, no. 3, 1991, 272–86. JSTOR, www.jstor.org/stable/622948. Accessed May 28, 2021; Steve Pile, "Emotions and Affect in Recent Human Geography." *Transactions of the Institute of British Geographers*, vol. 35, no. 1, 2010, 5–20. JSTOR, www.jstor.org/stable/40647285. Accessed May 28, 2021; Sara MacKian, *Everyday Spirituality: Social and Spatial Worlds of Enchantment*. Palgrave Macmillan, 2012.
32 Wharton, "Kerfol," 69.
33 Wharton, "Kerfol," 69.
34 Wharton, "Kerfol," 69.
35 Wharton, "Kerfol," 68.
36 Keetley and Sivils, "Introduction: Approaches to the Ecogothic," 1.
37 Barbara A. White, "Young Gentlemen Narrators, Ghosts, and Married Couples in the Middle Stories." *Edith Wharton: A Study of the Short Fiction*. Twayne Publishers, 1991, 57–82. Twayne's Studies in Short Fiction, 64.
38 Wharton, "Kerfol," 71.
39 Wharton, "Kerfol," 69.
40 White, "Young Gentlemen Narrators, Ghosts, and Married Couples in the Middle Stories," 70.
41 Haytock, "The Dogs of 'Kerfol': Animals, Authorship, and Wharton," 182.
42 Wharton, "Kerfol," 70.
43 Keetley and Sivils, "Introduction: Approaches to the Ecogothic," 4.

44 Wharton, "Kerfol," 70.
45 Wharton, "Kerfol," 70.
46 Wharton, "Kerfol," 70.
47 Wharton, "Kerfol," 71.
48 Wharton, "Kerfol," 71.
49 Wharton, "Kerfol," 71.
50 Keetley and Sivils, "Introduction: Approaches to the Ecogothic," 4.
51 Wharton, "Kerfol," 71.
52 Beatrix Farrand, *Beatrix Farrand's Plant Book for Dumbarton Oaks*. Edited by Diane Kostial McGuire. Dumbarton Oaks, Trustees for Harvard University, 1980, 76.
53 Wharton, "Kerfol," 71.
54 Wharton, "Kerfol," 71–72. These trees exemplify what Keetley and Sivils call "the spectral presence of the nonhuman" which "haunts America's literary mind." See Keetley and Sivils, "Introduction: Approaches to the Ecogothic," 17.
55 Wharton, "Kerfol," 76.
56 Quoted in Roy Strong, *Garden Party: Collected Writings 1979-99*. Frances Lincoln, 2000, 14.
57 See Janet Beer and Avril Horner, "'This Isn't Exactly a Ghost Story': Edith Wharton and Parodic Gothic." *Journal of American Studies*, vol. 37, no. 2, 2003, 269–85. *JSTOR*, www.jstor.org/stable/27557331. Accessed Apr. 1, 2021.
58 In *A Backward Glance*, Wharton argues that "the Contes de Perrault, still left me inattentive and indifferent," but the similarity to "Kerfol" seems to prove otherwise. Wharton, *A Backward Glance*, 33.
59 See Judith Saunders, "Literary Influences." *Edith Wharton in Context*, edited by Laura Rattray. Cambridge University Press, 2012, 325–34, 327.

Chapter 4

CENTRAL PARK AS AN "ECOLOGICAL THRESHOLD"?

In *A Backward Glance* Wharton, weighing her own reactions to the stifling atmosphere of New York City, asks: "How could I understand that people who had seen Rome and Seville, Paris and London, could come back to live contentedly between Washington Square and the Central Park?"[1] Central Park, the green lung of New York City was designed in 1858 by Frederick Law Olmsted and Clavert Vaux. "The two envisioned" the 800 acres of uninterrupted rurality "as a pastoral retreat from the pressures and aesthetic monotony of a growing city, and historians and landscape architects have seen it reflected in their eyes, as a work of landscape art."[2] Central Park reveals a juxtaposition and tension between nature and the urban, pointing to a "threshold motif" in pastoral cosmopolitanism.[3] "I pause on its threshold"—as Wharton mused in *A Backward Glance*, regarding her father's library to which she was perpetually drawn.[4] We too, as readers, are invited to pause on New York City's green verge to assess how it resonates in her fiction. Rather than a permanent, immovable divider or partition, the park acts as a lush permeable membrane within the urban sprawl of imposing townhouses. What social contacts take place through it and despite it?

This chapter addresses how Central Park, which covers about six percent of Manhattan, becomes a vital site of environmental enquiry for Wharton. Pointed references to, and reflections upon, this serene area of woods, sweeping meadows and ponds are sprinkled throughout her novels, published journalism, novellas and short stories alike. In *The Age of Innocence*, set in the 1870s, the matriarch Mrs. Manson Mingott builds a house "in an inaccessible wilderness near the Central Park."[5] There is impish wit in Wharton's lexis. This brand of "wilderness" pokes fun at that specific mode of American exceptionalism that separates a "New World" synonymous with cultural-nationalist vigor and pride from the "Old" and tired green spaces of Western Europe. The phrasing also acknowledges, and pays tribute to, the artificiality of Central Park, an audacious facsimile of untrammeled nature bounded by busy streets—an ingenious man-made enclave of pristine lakes that pretends to be a zone largely uncorrupted by man.[6] Wharton is mindful that the terms for the competition set by the Park Commissioners for the design of this site in 1857 evoked a space that would merge city and country, including at least four roads stretching from East to West, with ample scope for a handsome concert hall and skating zone.[7]

Returning to the image of the Garden of Eden in Abrahamic lore, Terry Gifford posits that in "Eden nature was not wild, but a garden for the delight of Adam and Eve."[8] He adds that "American Arcadias are usually set, not in a garden, but in a wilderness that is presumed to be in an innocent, original state that is beyond 'the frontier' in both space and time."[9] For Wharton the "American Arcadia" seems to be set in a public park in the middle of New York City, and that it is a "frontier" where harried citizens from all creeds and social classes can cross and find solace: "Frederick Law Olmsted and others created the grand gardens of democracy (for the taxpaying public, rather than for aristocratic patrons)."[10] For this very reason though, the reactionary *New York Herald* lambasted the Park before it was even constructed: "It is folly to expect in this country to have parks like those in old aristocratic countries." The "great Central Park will be nothing but a great beer garden for the lowest denizens of the city, of which she shall yet pray litanies to be delivered."[11] At its very creation then, the Park prompted visitors to ponder, according to Morrison H. Heckscher, "the role of open space on the island of Manhattan: the dynamic tension between pavement and pasture, between private and public land, between city and state government; between city square and urban park."[12] The formation, naturalistic designs and diversions of Central Park contains that friction between pastoral idyll and urban spread—a problem that some contemporary editors of periodicals on landscape aesthetics judged as insurmountable: "a sylvan retreat fit for shepherds and their flocks" in a vast city, "when the roar of traffic through the transverse roads shall drown the singing of the birds."[13]

Wharton's nuanced portrayal of Central Park is colored by these cultural debates, which expose weightier caste and ideological controversies, involving manual graft versus mental craft, artistic versus monetary value, the drably functional versus the chic, the productive versus the picturesque. The Park also evolves throughout her fiction. As it becomes progressively more fleshed out, so we as readers are compelled to ask: what is this gigantic garden, alert to English landscape traditions and yet different from the statue- and fountain-filled sites of London's Hyde Park and Paris's Jardin des Tuileries, actually for? Should we utilize its soil for dedicated, practical, laudable activities like producing the necessities for diurnal existence, or is the soil itself chiefly an elaborate "invention," an artfully composed "product" to be savored by New Yorkers as a fund of visual delight? Wharton was no doubt aware that the Park was built on rough, swampy and uneven terrain utilized by poverty-stricken immigrants and free African Americans for myriad subsistence endeavors.[14] Though these issues do not trouble Lily Bart in *The House of Mirth*, whose desultory stroll through the City on a spring day takes her to the entrance of Central Park. What her reaction tellingly points to is the *consumption* of scenic landscape that "mitigated the ugliness of the long crowded thoroughfare, blurred the gaunt rooflines, threw a *mauve veil* over the discouraging perspectives of the side streets, and gave a touch of poetry to the delicate haze of green that marked the entrance to the park" (my emphasis).[15] Mauve reminds us of the color Lily associates with the Maritime Alps earlier in the novel—so the question of transatlanticism is always present, here at the level of verbal tactic and subtle echo. The "touch of poetry" suggests a ruminative engagement with the site that Olmstead and Vaux would have recommended: "the act of immersing oneself in the scenery" instead of "production or boisterous forms of play."[16] Even at the denouement, when Lily is shunned by the New York smart set and having lost her job at the millinery where she was employed, she can still appreciate, and find comfort in, the contours of this interlinked series of bucolic landscapes.

Other Wharton characters will not pause at the entrance of Central Park: they go in and out, seeking the mental clarity and physical refreshment that Olmstead and Vaux envisioned in their written declarations of intent. In the 1900 novella *The Touchstone*, the protagonist Stephen Glennard lives with the shame of having sold the love letters from famed writer Margaret Aubyn addressed to him after her death. Consumed by guilt and self-recrimination, "he fell into the habit, on Sunday afternoons, of solitary walks prolonged till after dusk […] his wanderings usually led him to the Park and its outlying regions."[17] In this extract, the Park is not separated from the cityscape, but rather it seems to be a porous layer, permitting unspecified comings and goings. One of these "outlying regions" is precisely where Glennard's secret will be unveiled to the one person he does not want it to be known. Perhaps that is why Wharton's narrator is deliberately vague and oblique here. Unlike other texts, we are not told exactly where Glennard takes his walk or where he exits the Park: "One Sunday, tired of aimless locomotion, he took a cab at the Park gates and let it carry him out to the Riverside Drive."[18] There are eighteen entrances to Central Park, but only five on the West side.[19] The cab takes Glennard to Riverside Drive, presumably down, where he will see his wife Alexa talking to Barton Flamel and also becoming aware of his reprehensible deception. Since Glennard then tells the cab to "Turn—drive back"[20], we may assume that he exited the Park at one of the north-western exits—possibly at the suggestively named Strangers' Gate—and then turned around to return to his Westchester home.

A similar turn away from the Park occurs in *Twilight Sleep*, when Nona's paramour Stan Heuston asks her: "A turn, first—just round the Park?"[21] She declines, preferring instead to visit a jazz club, the Housetop, where she will see her father: "Manford, the day after his daughter had caught sight of him at the Housetop, started out early for one of his long tramps around the Park."[22] An 1860s statement explaining the Park's use policy underlined the area's supreme "power to gratify by sight."[23] Like Glennard however, Dexter Manford feels that "walk[ing] himself tired" takes priority over the desire for visual splendor.[24] Although Manford cannot find relief through a long walk, he does achieve mental clarity. This also happens to the delusional Anson Warley in Wharton's 1928 short story "After Holbein": "He had felt a little confusion that morning, when he was doing his daily sprint round the Park (his exercise was reduced to that!); but it had only been a passing flurry."[25] In the Park, Warley finds that "Yes; his mind, at that moment, had been quite piercingly clear and perceptive; his eye had passed with a renovating glitter over every detail of the daily scene."[26] Then, Wharton delivers what is one of the most jarring passages in her fiction: "He stood still for a minute under the leafless trees of the Mall, and looking about him with the sudden insight of age, understood that he had reached the time of life when Alps and cathedrals become as transient as flowers."[27] The Mall is "a quarter-mile-long avenue"[28] and Warley's epiphany achieves the very purpose Olmsted intended in his eloquent written statements on the Park: "the emotion sought to be produced in the Mall and playgrounds region—rest, tranquility, deliberation and *maturity*" (my emphasis).[29]

If Warley attains what can be called "maturity" at the Mall, in *The Age of Innocence*, two characters gather in the same spot to a very different effect: "The day was delectable. The bare vaulting of trees along the Mall was ceiled with lapis lazuli, and arched above snow that shone like splintered crystals."[30] When Newland Archer and May Welland meet here, May's thoughts remain a mystery, but Newland seems to be in profound "deliberation." If he achieves his own form of "maturity," then it is imperfect (self-)awareness since he revels in a feeling of "possessorship," which hints at a familiar image of the trophy bride, or the decorative female appendage in the garden: "It was the weather to call out May's radiance, and she burned like a young maple in the frost. Archer was proud of the glances turned on her, and the simple joy of possessorship cleared away his underlying perplexities."[31]

Not all romantic encounters in Central Park are like May and Archer's. Undine Spragg, the protagonist of Wharton's 1913 novel *The Custom of the Country* has two illicit romantic assignations that could jeopardize her ascent into the New York glitterati that she so eagerly wishes to join. If Julius Beaufort's "horizon was bounded by the Battery and the Central Park,"[32] the Park is also what divides the Spragg clan from this New York social elite because "the width of the Central Park divided mother and daughter from their Olympian portals."[33] The Spragg family's outsider status is demonstrated by the mere fact that unlike native New Yorkers who refer to Central Park simply as "the Park," the Spraggs always call it *the* Central Park. For example, Undine's window was facing "the leafless tree-tops of the Central Park."[34] Such phrasing raises questions about social mobility, self-fashioning, status, and class anxiety for the Spraggs—a Midwestern family seeking access to far more genteel haunts.

Undine, however, is a reckless and risk-taking urban pioneer: "Ever since they had come to New York she had been on the verge of one or two perilous adventures, and there had been a moment during their first winter when she had actually engaged herself to the handsome Austrian riding-master who accompanied her in the Park."[35] Patrician New Yorkers, including Wharton herself, would often go riding in this locality, a reminder of the multi-purpose, versatile, accommodating quality of the site: "There are ingenious new arrangements to serve large groups of people: hills and tunnels separate vehicular traffic (carriage originally, automobiles since) from pedestrian and equestrian circulation."[36] Undine's trysts with the Austrian riding instructor are only hinted at, but her meeting with first and fourth husband, Elmer Moffatt is described in some detail: "Undine, late the next day, waited alone under the leafless trellising of a wistaria arbor on the west side of the Central Park."[37] Two incongruences are salient here, the first being that the "wistaria arbor" where Wharton situates this episode, is on the east side of the Park, not the west. It is tempting to speculate that for a highly focused writer like Wharton this is a deliberate narrative strategy, not a blunder—bringing into bolder relief Undine's insecure, "outsider" status, plus her maladroit navigation of her green milieu. The second is the fact that this setting was a meeting place for women and not for lovers.[38]

Central Park goes on to take a palimpsestuous quality that Undine herself nearly recognizes: "Even now" she was "disturbed not so much by the unlikely chance of an accidental encounter with Ralph Marvell as by the remembrance of similar meetings, far from accidental, with the romantic Aaronson." The site becomes, for Undine, a repository or storehouse of amorous affect. She returns to Central Park to revel in the attentions of Peter Van Degen: "The winter twilight was deliciously cold, and as they swept through Central Park, and gathered impetus for their northward flight along the darkening Boulevard, Undine felt the rush of physical joy that drowns scruples."[39] This episode with Peter Van Degen is merely another "layering" on Undine's imperfectly sketched mental map of Central Park. The shady glens and gently rolling grasslands become a "stage" for furtive, and exhilarating, dalliance.

She is not fundamentally changed, transformed, or "matured" by exploiting the Park's expertly crafted rustic diversions.

According to Beatrix Farrand, with the "pressure of modern living a reaction has come in the shape of a positive craving for the rest and beauty which can only be satisfied through contact with nature."[40] While Undine's romantic exploits in the Park suggest a need to push against this desire for "rest," the 1916 novella *Bunner Sisters* addresses that need for a still center in a world defined by breathless rush. The eponymous sister, Evelina, expresses "how I'd love to get away [...] somewhere where it was green and quiet."[41] This impulse was, in Farrand's opinion, "felt by all classes alike, but while the rich man can easily escape from the tyranny of bricks and mortar, noise and dust, the vast majority of a city's population must endure them as best they may."[42] Ann-Eliza and Evelina do not have sizeable Hudson Valley estates like other characters in Wharton's fiction, so their recreational options are, as this novella shows, circumscribed. Herbert Ramy suggests that: "I guess we might go to Cendral Park some Sunday."[43] Mispronouncing "Central" as "Cendral" resonates as an onomatopoeia to indicate Ramy's uncertain Teutonic origin. On the Sunday, they arrive at Central Park, with Ramy guiding the party of four "through the Mall and the Ramble."[44] As Frederick Law Olmsted explained:

> A district called the Ramble, which can only be entered on foot, consists of a series of walks carried, in constantly changing grades and directions, through 80 acres of ground of very diversified character, the aspect of natural arrangement being everywhere maintained, while the richness of cultivation is added.[45]

The horticultural details set forth in *Bunner Sisters* precisely follow the terms of Olmsted's "plot."[46] The reference to "the Ramble" also had personal significance for Wharton. In *A Backward Glance* she describes as a child going with her mother for "a walk in the Central Park, a hunt for violets and hepaticas in the secluded dells of the Ramble."[47] The narrator of *Bunner Sisters* remains faithful to the specificities that caught Wharton's attention as a child, "leaving Evelina to exclaim at the hepaticas under the shady ledges."[48] The vegetation however, also serves as a camouflage to hide Ramy's drug use, which only becomes apparent at the end of the text.

In retrospect, the Central Park walk in *Bunner Sisters* marks the beginning of the sisters' tragedy: "On Sundays they usually went for the whole afternoon to the Central Park, and Ann Eliza, from her seat in the mortal hush of the back room, followed step by step their long slow beatific walk."[49] The sound patterning here ("Park ... walk"), coupled with the Christian connotations of "beatific"—with its assonance to the word "beautiful"—afford a reminder that *Bunner Sisters* is invested in mapping those moments where the everyday and the numinous, the tranquillizing and the anguished, the decorous and the unlawful, converge. Central Park emerges here, not just as an "iconic site for integrating [...] pleasure and play,"[50] but more importantly as a "stage" for more riddling, border-zone affect.

Notes

1 Wharton, *A Backward Glance*, 86.
2 Roy Rosenzweig and Elizabeth Blackmar, *The Park and the People: A History of Central Park*. Cornell University Press, 1992, 3; see also Iain Borden et al., *The Unknown City: Contesting Architecture and Social Space*. MIT Press, 1998.
3 "Many have noted and written about the importance of the theme of thresholds in her life and work and of a related theme of two worlds." See Deanna Holtzman and Nancy Kulish, "Edith Wharton's Threshold Phobia and Two Worlds." *Journal of the American Psychoanalytic Association*, vol. 62, no. 4, 2014, 573–601, 574, doi:10.1177/0003065114545991.
4 Wharton, *A Backward Glance*, 64.
5 Wharton, *The Age of Innocence*, 9.
6 See David Warn and Oliver Zunz, eds., *The Landscape of Modernity: Essays on New York City, 1900-1940*. Russel Sage Foundation, 1992.
7 For more detail on these "terms" see Frederick Law Olmsted, Jr. and Theodora Kimball, *Forty Years of Landscape Architecture: Central Park*. MIT Press, 1973.
8 Terry Gifford. *Pastoral*. Routledge, 1999. The New Critical Idiom, 33.
9 Gifford, *Pastoral*, 33.
10 Charles W. Moore et al., *The Poetics of Gardens*. The MIT Press, 2000, 210.
11 Quoted in Susanna S. Zetzel, "The Garden in the Machine: The Construction of Nature in Olmsted's Central Park." *Prospects*, vol. 14, 1989, 291–339, 293–94, doi:10.1017/S0361233300005779.
12 Morrison H. Heckscher, *Creating Central Park*. Metropolitan Museum of Art, 2008, 7.
13 Quoted by David Schuyler, *New Urban Landscape: The Redefinition of City Form in Nineteenth-Century America*. Johns Hopkins University Press, 1988, 96.
14 "All such rogue gardening practices were criminalized in the Park thereafter." See Atkinson, *Gardenland*, 148–49; see also Peter H. Rossi, *Down and Out in America: The Origins of Homelessness*. University of Chicago Press, 1989; Rosenzweig and Blackmar, *The Park and the People*; Bill Brown, *A Sense of Things: The Object Matter of American Literature*. University of Chicago Press, 2004.
15 Wharton, *The House of Mirth*, 231.
16 See Dorceta Taylor, "Central Park as a Model for Social Control: Urban Parks, Social Class and Leisure Behaviour in Nineteenth-Century America." *Journal of Leisure Research*, vol. 16, no. 2, 1999, 420–77.
17 "The Touchstone." *Madame de Treymes and Three Novellas*, by Edith Wharton. Scribner & Schuster, 1995, 17–118, 97–98.
18 Wharton, "The Touchstone," 98.
19 Heckscher, *Creating Central Park*, 49.
20 Wharton, "The Touchstone," 98.
21 Wharton, *Twilight Sleep*, 145.

22 Wharton, *Twilight Sleep*, 161.
23 Quoted in Rosenzweig and Blackmar, *The Park and the People*, 251.
24 Wharton, *Twilight Sleep*, 161.
25 Edith Wharton, "After Holbein." *The New York Stories of Edith Wharton*. New York Review of Books, 2007, 356–80, 362.
26 Wharton, "After Holbein," 362.
27 Wharton, "After Holbein," 362.
28 Heckscher, *Creating Central Park*, 36.
29 This quote is from a letter to Central Park Head Gardener Ignaz Anton Pilat dated September 26, 1863. See Frederick Law Olmsted, *Writings on Landscape, Culture, and Society*. Edited by Charles E. Beveridge. Library of America, 2015, 652.
30 Wharton, *The Age of Innocence*, 51.
31 Wharton, *The Age of Innocence*, 51.
32 Wharton, *The Age of Innocence*, 86.
33 Wharton, *The Custom of the Country*. In *Three Novels of New York*. Penguin Classics, 2012, 267.
34 Wharton, *The Custom of the Country*, 270.
35 Wharton, *The Custom of the Country*, 273.
36 Moore et al., *The Poetics of Gardens*, 210.
37 Wharton, *The Custom of the Country*, 313.
38 Rosenzweig and Blackmar, *The Park and the People*, 220.
39 Wharton, *The Custom of the Country*, 361.
40 Beatrix Farrand, "City Parks." *Municipal Affairs, a Quarterly Magazine*, vol. III, 1899, 687–90, 687.
41 Wharton, *Bunner Sisters*, 300.
42 Farrand, "City Parks," 687.
43 Wharton, *Bunner Sisters*, 300.
44 Wharton, *Bunner Sisters*, 301.
45 Olmsted, *Writings on Landscape, Culture, and Society*, 373.
46 Wharton, *Bunner Sisters*, 301.
47 Wharton, *A Backward Glance*, 57.
48 Wharton, *Bunner Sisters*, 301.
49 Wharton, *Bunner Sisters*, 321–22.
50 See Atkinson, *Gardenland*, 21.

Chapter 5

FRENCH GARDENS AND THEIR MEANING

Lily Bart's Monte Carlo Casino Garden

In *Garden Plots* (2006), Shelley Saguaro notes that there are "many books of fiction, poetry, and prose over the centuries which, while not always obviously or even primarily about gardens, use them as a crucial and integral part of the whole."[1] *The House of Mirth*, as we have seen, exploits Bellomont to situate Lily as a rash and imperfect reader of American nature's signs. Her struggles to decipher accurately cultural and topographical designs are magnified by the sheer scale and ornamentation of overseas gardens, especially those synonymous with the Côte d'Azur. As critic Nancy Von Rosk points out, in the opening of Book II, Selden and Lily find each other in an idyllic landscape, one far removed from all activities relating to the humdrum business of the American frontier—the material provision of life.[2] "It came vividly to Selden on the Casino steps that Monte Carlo had, more than any other place he knew, the gift of accommodating itself to each man's humor."[3] This "gift" first of all implies the social and technical developments (improved roads, railway networks) that made this stretch of coastline more accessible and appealing to affluent overseas visitors. The "gift" of experiencing this region reminds us of Renato Poggioli's theory about the "psychological root of the pastoral," which is "a double longing after innocence and happiness, to be recovered not through conversion or regeneration but merely through a retreat."[4] The importance that Selden ascribes to the Monte Carlo Casino Gardens "retreat" is anchored in how the locality speaks to "the holiday vein in human nature"—it "struck refreshingly on a mind jaded by prolonged hard work in surroundings made for the discipline of the senses."[5] Selden's sense of escape from a dispiriting, even Puritanical American scene of "prolonged hard work" carries a faint echo of Nathaniel Hawthorne's famous denunciation of labor as "the curse of this world" because "nobody can meddle with it, without becoming proportionally brutified."[6] However, implicit in the Riviera episodes is a sense of how entitled, self-absorbed American travelers can become "brutified" through dogged adherence to inhuman snobberies, or hierarchies of value whose cruelty—seen in the lack of empathy for figures like Lily—is magnified by the glamorous foreign setting. The gardens here throw into sharper relief a spiteful underside of expatriate privilege and patronage. Such somber reflections do not vex Selden at this time. Indeed, to borrow terms from Hawthorne's 1852 novel *The Blithedale Romance*, Selden momentarily feels that Monte Carlo, and not the majestic American wilderness, is where one can inaugurate "the life of Paradise anew."[7] Even though this notion is short-lived it does serve to heighten his awareness of the opulent milieu and fine climate:

> As he surveyed the white square set in an exotic coquetry of architecture, the studied tropicality of the gardens, the groups loitering in the foreground against mauve mountains which suggested a sublime stage-setting forgotten in a hurried shifting of scenes—as he took in the whole outspread effect of light and leisure, he felt a movement of revulsion from the last few months of his life.[8]

Does this extract really evoke a stimulating, reposing and restorative place? Here "nature," in its "studied tropicality" has been tampered with and "tutored" way beyond anything found during Lily's gentle strolls through Bellomont. The "outspread effect of light" is misleading perhaps, causing not illumination or multiplied consciousness but rather partial blindness to the contaminating power of the wealth and kudos that Lily seeks. "Loitering" groups hints at how desperate sensation-seeking in glitzy foreign playgrounds can actually trigger forms of *displeasure*—impatience, carping, social fatigue and satiation. Such are the "afflictions" of Channel-hopping spendthrifts, as documented by Rebecca West in her 1936 novel *The Thinking Reed*, which takes a derisive look at prosperous visitors to the "pastoral" of a French Riviera.

The time of year—a lush spring, with flowers in bloom and reminders of Lily's name—is crucial to the rhetorical and emotional impact of this episode in *The House of Mirth*: "It was mid-April, and one felt that the revelry had reached its climax and that the desultory groups in the square and gardens would soon dissolve and re-form in other scenes."[9] The lily flower is traditionally associated with, and offered in France on May 1 since the Renaissance, the "muguet de mai." Lily's expulsion will take place in April, just before the French holiday that is celebrated with lilies of the valley. This hints at how—for a variety of reasons that begins with her expulsion from the yacht—Lily's life never reaches its full potential.

Wharton's narrator develops this intricate garden imagery by adapting lexis from both the theatre and the visual arts: "the exuberance of the flowers, the blue intensity of sea and sky, produced the effect of a closing *tableau*, when all the lights are turned on at once."[10] This is a "tableau vivant," a temporary representation of a painting, though the scene appears to be busier than the term implies:

> This impression was presently heightened by the way in which a con-
> sciously conspicuous group of people advanced to the middle front, and
> stood before Selden with the air of the chief performers gathered together
> by the exigencies of the final effect. Their appearance confirmed the
> impression that the show had been staged regardless of expense, and
> emphasized its resemblance to one of those 'costume-plays' in which the
> protagonists walk through the passions without displacing a drapery.
> The ladies stood in unrelated attitudes calculated to isolate their effects,
> and the men hung about them as irrelevantly as stage heroes whose
> tailors are named in the programme.[11]

According to J. C. Loudon's 1839 *Encyclopedia of Architecture*, a garden is land "laid out as a pleasure ground," with "a view to recreation and enjoyment, more than profit."[12] The mordant irony of the extract above is that for all the cash spent on this cultural production, what we see is a sad parody of "pleasure." Instead of a small-scale overseas Utopia we observe an awkward simulation of stimulation—plus the natural splendor of the region is utterly lost on such bored and self-centered "performers." Of course, this passionless ritual is no paean to ethno-cultural diversity and affective growth, a space where citizens of the world can gather, interact freely and learn from each other. Rather, it is peopled by the insipid and familiar faces of an American moneyed elite, with too much time on their hands and too little sense of responsibility to a wider community and the natural environment. These so-called "stage heroes" can only replicate the same type of high society engagement that prompted them to flee America in the first place. The sterile enactment points to "further enclaves of the rich (the characters view the world from their private railcar or luxury vessel); and when a 'foreign' setting (Monte Carlo or Nice) is directly represented, it features largely as an extension of the New York social stage."[13] Do the theatrical references suggest that these listless cosmopolites have lost all touch with the rhythms of everyday actuality? We are, of course, at a far remove from a quintessential wilderness novel; the frontier myth does not come into play here. It is not an American pastoral. What we observe instead through such stilted gestures is a unique European pastoral in which American figures try to "re-enact" some form of bucolic escape in a geographical crucible that is in-between the "Old" and "New" Worlds.

Lily's account of this milieu is clipped, watchful, more detached, but charged with meaning: she "leaned awhile over the side, giving herself up to a leisurely enjoyment of the spectacle before her. Unclouded sunlight enveloped sea and shore in a bath of purest radiancy."[14] The Monte Carlo Casino Gardens will be the setting for her social banishment, and when she finds herself at night alone with Selden, the locality is presented as drastically different from what was depicted at the start of Book II: "Outside, the sky was gusty and overcast, and as Lily and Selden moved toward the deserted gardens below the restaurant, [...] they walked on in silence, her hand on his arm, till the deeper shade of the gardens received them."[15] The phrase "deserted gardens" suggests its nightmarish other—a *garden become desert*, a cursed or blighted earth, to mirror Lily's psychological state and a glimpse of her future prospects. Where "unclouded sunlight" once poured over sand and sea there is now a glimpse of nature as obstacle in this somber scene. That Lily and Selden are "received" by "the deeper shade of the gardens" indicates how the showy materiality of Monte Carlo also points to a spectral hinterland ("shade" as revenant).

The imagery of a man and a woman alone in a garden carries an Edenic resonance. If Selden and Lily are Adam and Eve, then Bertha Dorset is the serpent who causes Lily's downfall. With Wharton having obtained the title for this novel from the Bible, she could also have drawn inspiration from the "Garden of God." However, this scene is a reversal of the "biblical paradise" enshrined "as an antediluvian utopia" and "duly venerated for generations of philosophers, writers and artists."[16] Unlike Adam and Eve who were ejected from the paradise garden because of Eve's sin, Selden and Lily find themselves in the casino gardens because of Bertha's malign scheming. As critic Joan Lidoff remarks: "As the glowing Edenic imagery of the first book fades, the novel's second book is progressively dominated by language of deprivation, anxiety, resentment and fear."[17] This Riviera episode marks the beginning of that fraught and uneasy lexis of the second half of *The House of Mirth*. This environment represents a "threshold pastoral," whose form and feel, captured by the "deeper shade" of the Casino gardens, points to Lily's gradual "descent" into an unfamiliar and inimical element.

"Will You Walk with Me? Let Us Cross the Tuileries"

Of all the illustrious public parks depicted in Wharton's fiction, the Tuileries was an "inherited" site. "Inherited" in the sense that she heard of it before she even saw it, because of a historical event her family witnessed: "on February 24, 1848, toward the hour of noon, incidentally witnessed, from the balcony of their hotel in the rue de Rivoli, the flight of Louis Philippe and Queen

Marie Amélie across the Tuileries gardens."[18] As Wharton recounts in *A Backward Glance*, it was fourteen years before she was even born. However, this scene so impressed her family that it eventually nourished Wharton's creative imagination. Wharton herself does not hide the disappointment that: "Though my mother often described this scene to me, I suspect that the study of the Paris fashions made a more vivid impression on her than the fall of monarchies."[19] Later in life, the Tuileries become significant in Wharton's private life—as one of the rendezvous for her affair with American journalist Morton Fullerton. Wharton herself never actually details her encounters with Fullerton besides her "Love Diary." However, she uses the Tuileries Gardens as a setting in her fiction, and it holds, as I will show here, a special resonance.

In order to better grasp the importance of this environment in Wharton's texts, it is worth retracing the history of the Tuileries. As Joan DeJean succinctly states, the site "had a modest start. In 1564, Henri II's widow, Queen Regent Catherine de Médicis, planted a small private garden hidden from the city behind a wall in front of the Tuileries Palace."[20] This palace garden, started by a foreign queen trying to make herself at home in the French capital, becomes a real-life example of the metaphor Wharton expounds in *French Ways and their Meaning:* the "deeper civilization of a country may to a great extent be measured by the care she gives to her flower-garden—the corner of her life where the supposedly 'useless' arts and graces flourish."[21] Moreover, Wharton suggests that in "the cultivating of that garden France has surpassed all modern nations; and one of the greatest of America's present opportunities is to find out why."[22] Wharton's scenes in the Tuileries Gardens invariably concern American characters, and so it becomes a "stage" on which to elaborate and experiment with her cultural theories.

The Tuileries Catherine de Medici created is not the one Wharton knew, as DeJean explains: "This garden was expanded and integrated into the cityscape over the decades, but it really came into its own only once Louis XIV had given landscape architect extraordinaire André Le Nôtre free rein."[23] Wharton was an admirer of Le Nôtre's work. She first writes about him in a letter to Anna Bahlmann dated 3rd May 1893, concerning a visit to the Chateau de Rochers-Sevigné near Rennes, that had a "beautiful formal garden designed by Le Notre & filled with Mme de Sévigné's orange-trees."[24] Moreover, Wharton cites examples of Le Nôtre's gardens in *Italian Villas and their Gardens*, measuring them against the venues that are her core concern: "In some of the great French gardens, at Vaux and Versailles for example, one is conscious, under all the beauty, of the immense effort expended, of the vast upheavals of earth, the forced creating of effects."[25] Wharton's locutions imply how French gardens reveal nature as ruthlessly regulated, domesticated and sculpted (or scalped) by humans, for humans. The "vast upheavals"—suggesting seismic convulsions, tsunamis or other extreme weather events—and "forced creating" makes us wonder how designing a garden (a new world in miniature, if you like) involves the wanton vandalism, even total desecration of the old one. Through such effort the Tuileries became a place of earthly delights made to be savored, that Parisians as well as foreigners could enjoy on their walks. This taste for the garden stroll is something they should take with them when they return to their home countries.[26] Thus, the "Tuileries became the first truly public Parisian garden and the prototype for public gardens all over Europe."[27] For Wharton it is also a theoretical template for how a garden ought to be appreciated.

The area features in the opening scene of Wharton's 1907 novella *Madame de Treymes*: "John Durham, while he waited for Madame de Malrive to draw on her gloves, stood in the hotel doorway looking out across the Rue de Rivoli in the afternoon brightness of the Tuileries gardens."[28] Wharton makes use of a "cinematic zoom" quality—the character is not in the garden, but rather contemplating from without what is, for critic William Blazek, "an ambiguous and multidimensional France."[29] It is at the prompting of Madame de Malrive (Fanny de Malrive, née Frisbee) that the action moves to the gardens: "Will you walk with me? Let us cross the Tuileries. I should like to sit a moment on the Terrace."[30] She displays, according to Janet Beer, that "gentle transatlanticism"[31] of a New Yorker at ease in a French setting with American company: "She spoke quite easily and naturally, as if it were the most commonplace thing in the world for them to be straying afoot together over Paris."[32] Wharton's narrator weaves this double identity into the imaginative fabric, with Durham making this comparison: if "Fanny Frisbee, from a brown-stone door-step, had proposed that they should take a walk in the Park the idea would have presented itself to her companion as agreeable but unimportant."[33] The pointed reference to Central Park here reminds us that Frederick Law Olmsted himself admired the design of this great Parisian site: "The garden of the Tuileries with the Champs Élysées forms the most magnificent urban or interior town promenade in the world."[34] The fact that Durham uses two names to describe the different facets of Madame de Malrive's personality reveals "the whole width of the civilization into which her marriage had absorbed her": "whereas Fanny Malrive's suggestion that they should stroll across the Tuileries was obviously fraught with unspecified possibilities."[35] For Beer, at the "heart of Wharton's writing in her French works, both fiction and non-fiction, is an idea of geographical specificity, a close identification between the individual and the dwelling place—either literally a house or a place in the sense of a role."[36] Madame de Malrive embodies this very notion: Durham "walked beside her without speaking down the length of the wide alley which follows the line of the Rue de Rivoli, suffering her even, when they reached its farthest end, to direct him in silence up the steps to the terrace of the Feuillants."[37] It is ironic that a convent once occupied the site on which this "terrace" stands.[38] Wharton's narrator is alert to these intricate historical resonances:

> The complicated beauty of this prospect, as they moved toward it between the symmetrically clipped limes of the lateral terrace, touched him anew through her nearness, as with the hint of some vast impersonal power, controlling and regulating her life in ways which he could not guess, putting between himself and her the whole width of the civilization into which her marriage had absorbed her.[39]

Unlike the scenes situated in New York's Central Park, here we are fully aware of Paris as a complex and sprawling geographical presence ("the verdant brightness of the Champs Elysées," the "Place de la Concorde").[40] Durham and Madame de Malrive are able to find a secluded spot in the garden to talk (and to reflect on lost times or places). In this isolation, the Tuileries gardens briefly transform into an Edenic site for the two figures. As with Lily Bart and Lawrence Selden, this couple can exist without fretfulness in the bounded sanctuary of a green space, but not outside it.[41] Crucially, this image of the *garden enclosed* is once again heightened by the narrator's reliance on dramatic nuance and associations. That Madame de Malrive can "*direct* him [Durham]"—as if he is a performer to be guided around a theatrical venue—hints at Wharton's readiness to mobilize the multiple functions of a garden through history, not just offering a splendid "prospect," but as a setting for masked balls, elaborate plays and costly entertainments. The scalding irony in the extract is that Madame de Malrive is herself *directed* by some "vast impersonal power." She is an actor who will not be permitted to improvise a satisfying role of her own in a hidebound and humorless French society. She must follow somebody else's tedious and enervating script. As is apparent in earlier sections of the chapter, Wharton's texts—such as *The House of Mirth*—capitalize on stage and garden as sibling arts, where lives are powerfully enacted and "framed" (in every sense of the word). [42]

Madame de Treymes is an early attempt to portray and explore the complex affective, historical, and cultural meanings of the Tuileries Gardens. Fifteen years later, in Wharton's 1922 novel *The Glimpses of the Moon*, another potential couple, Susy and Strefford, "sat on the terrace of the Tuileries above the Seine." About the terrace, Beatrix Farrand records that the "gardens of the Tuileries in their present form are also due to Le Nôtre. He made the terrace of the Cours de la Reine overlooking parterres which were close to the palace."[43] In *Madame de Treymes*, we are made conscious of the context of the park in a major European city. In this novel however, Wharton alerts us to other figures who frequent the site as part of their mundane, diurnal routine. The two characters "sat on a bench in the pale sunlight, discolored leaves heaped at their feet, and no one to share their solitude but a lame working-man and a haggard woman who were lunching together mournfully at the other end of the majestic vista."[44] The "discolored leaves" here remind us of the venerable "pages" of the New Testament, specifically *Luke* 14:13 and "The Parable of the Guests." If the Tuileries epitomize a "feast" for the stroller's senses, then it is only right that all communities should be invited to partake of this "majestic vista." Such sentiments provide a stark contrast to the disagreeable vision of a "private members club"—a cult of conspicuous consumption—in the Monte Carlo Garden episode from *The House of Mirth*. The presence of the "lame working-man" and "haggard woman" evokes the words of Christ: "But when you host a banquet, invite the poor, the crippled, *the lame*, and the blind, and you will be blessed" (my emphasis). This depiction of the Tuileries in *The Glimpses of the Moon* signals perhaps a cultural shift, according to Janet Beer:

> The cultural vocabulary of her [Wharton's] native land is now fully applicable to Europe, as the international scene is the "new world" and a new world which is as much a wilderness as the original because it presents again the conditions of geographical and personal dislocation which characterized American beginnings.[45]

Beer's argument allows us to view the "solitude" of this scene from a different angle. The gardens of Europe now imply those eerie, mysterious, even unfathomable green zones synonymous with the unfenced wilds of the "Old World."[46]

Wharton's Orangeries

In an early episode from *The Children*, the eponymous children's nanny Miss Scope, "unluckily, had found an old Baedeker on the steamer, and refreshing her mind with hazy reminiscences gleaned from former pupils, had rediscovered the name of a wonderful ducal garden containing ever so many acres of orange-trees always full of flowers and fruit."[47] The travel guidebook serves to revive her memory, one that dissolves into a pastoral daydream: "Her old pupils had gone there, she recalled, and been allowed by the gardeners to pick up from the ground as many oranges as they could carry away."[48] Here the garden, "the Giardino Aumale," is portrayed as a source of pleasure and plenitude for the scions of a leisured elite.[49] As this chapter has shown, the meticulous crafting of physical space ("a wonderful ducal garden") indicates how visionary landscape designers treat earth as a topographical "script," marking out a map of the human mind (of wealthy landowners, inquisitive sightseers), through a grammar and syntax of terraces, topiaries, gravel walkways and orchards. Such so-called "decorative," static elements frequently carry, in Wharton's oeuvre, traces of the political theories, romantic attitudes and scientific insights that mark any advanced industrialized society "on the move." This is not just the fanciful stuff of fiction, or the staple of poetic effusions anchored in an Arcadian elsewhere.

Wharton frequently roots this material in her own personal experience, blurring the lines between novelistic artifice and deeply felt sensation. On March 10, 1888, she recorded in *The Cruise of the Vanadis*: "we went down to the gardens of the Duc d'Aumale's Palace."[50] Wharton details her arrival, comparing the terrain to a seascape: "as we stepped out on the terrace at the back of the palace a veritable sea of foliage broke in waves of green at our feet."[51] With a typically assured sense of botanical specificity, she catalogues all the fruit trees that can be found there: "Orange and lemon, palm, bananas, bamboo, cypress and carouba."[52] Wharton also registers what she will later go on to write in a gardening article from the 1930s as "a rush of hurrying flower-feet [...] in the air!"[53] Such terms evokes a *genius loci* that seems divorced not only from metropolitan clamor but also the vicissitudes of physical nature itself. This environment offers Wharton and her myriad protagonists a peculiarly dense, on occasions contradictory, but nuanced mode of exploring—and indulging—the (secret) self.

These concerns imbue another "orange-garden" episode from Wharton's fiction. In *The Age of Innocence*, Newland Archer takes the train down to St. Augustine to meet May Welland and convince her to expedite their wedding. Wharton's narrator describes the beginning of the encounter thus:

> Early as it was, the main street was no place for any but formal greetings, and Archer longed to be alone with May, and to pour out all his tenderness and his impatience. It still lacked an hour to the late Welland breakfast-time, and instead of asking him to come in she proposed that they should walk out to an old orange-garden beyond the town.[54]

Under the stringent code of their patrician set, Newland and May cannot risk even the appearance of over-familiar talk in a "main street" synonymous with prying eyes. Alone in the garden, however, May and Newland can express their feelings for one another more freely:

To Archer's strained nerves the vision was as soothing as the sight of the blue sky and the lazy river. They sat down on a bench under the orange-trees and he put his arm about her and kissed her. [...] but his pressure may have been more vehement than he had intended, for the blood rose to her face and she drew back as if he had startled her.[55]

Despite the shaded intimacy of this restful garden setting, "beyond" a "town" overseen by ever-watchful custodians of genteel propriety, it is May (more so than Newland) who has internalized the exacting imperatives of an elite, unsmiling minority that specifies the rules for amorous dalliance. In the extract above Wharton's narrator measures Newland's ardent romantic and escapist feelings—activated by the tranquil, value-laden site under the "orange-trees" - against May's too *cultivated* state (a key term mentioned four times in the novel). If in the pastoral mode the act of "cultivation" suggests bringing out the very best via inspiring words and generous deeds, then *The Age of Innocence* details here how May has been cultivated—or thoroughly trained and tilled—into a pernicious politesse that thwarts not only spontaneous, uninhibited affect but any flicker of active imagination. Such demureness and *polish* in bourgeois manners, anxiously weighing the admissibility of certain courtship gestures, separate her from the material world of teeming ripeness that for Newland Archer seems to promise a loosening of social convention. Startled by his impulsive and *incorrect* action (indeed an infringement of her spatial expecta-tions?), May is constrained by the fact that the harsh metropolitan tribe expects more and forgives less of her than it does of Newland. Nevertheless, the couple meets once again, in another garden, this time in the town: "His only hope was to plead again with May, and on the day before his departure he walked with her to the ruinous garden of the Spanish Mission."[56] Newland's pleading is an indecorous act in the "hieroglyph world" of New York but a social per-formance that can be staged in the safer space of the Spanish Mission. This meeting acquires added significance because it triggers Newland's daydreams and longing for the "garden-magic" of a sensuous Old World haven, one that promotes impromptu displays of "vehement" feeling: "The background lent itself to allusions to European scenes; and May, who was looking her loveliest under a wide-brimmed hat that cast a shadow of mystery over her too-clear eyes, kindled into eagerness as he spoke of Granada and the Alhambra."[57] This desire for the pastoral idyll overseas acquires especial pathos because such emotion cannot take root in the sterile soil of a late nineteenth century New York where the edicts of "Taste" eclipse natural appetites.

Wharton has Newland recollect and mull over this scene throughout the novel: "It was wonderful that—as he had learned in the Mission garden at St. Augustine—such depths of feeling could coexist with such absence of imagination."[58] Their meeting in the garden becomes significant because Newland believes he has learned something crucial about May's temperament of which he was previously unaware. The garden is not only a place of illumination and bitter knowledge but also an arena in which competing concepts of what is "natural" (the carefully choreographed versus the defiantly unscripted, the socially decreed versus the instinctual) plays out. In fact, their "scene" in this garden tends to transform in Newland's memory to better suit his pastoral fantasies: "Archer, as he looked at her, was reminded of the glow which had suffused her face in the Mission Garden at St. Augustine."[59]

Newland clings to this memory until after May's death. At the end of the novel he looks at a photograph of her and is "transported" to that moment in the St. Augustine garden: "There she was, tall, round-bosomed and willowy, in her starched muslin and flapping Leghorn, as he had seen her under the orange-trees in the Mission garden."[60] As far as he is concerned, she is *rooted* in that garden plot, unchanged ("starched") and irradiated by fond recollection: "And as he had seen her that day, so she had remained; [...] faithful, unwearied; but so lacking in imagination, so incapable of growth, that the world of her youth had fallen into pieces and rebuilt itself without her ever being conscious of the change."[61] So "incapable of growth" undercuts an idealizing tendency by hinting at May's status as a strange flower trapped in the amber of social ordinances whose exact wording has long been forgotten.

In her biography of Wharton, Hermione Lee develops a comparison between gardening and writing:

> The mixture of disciplined structure and imaginative freedom, the reworking of traditions into a new idea, the ruthless elimination of dull, incongruous or surplus materials, and the creation of a dramatic narrative, all come to mind—not to mention patience, stamina, and attentiveness.[62]

Lee captures well here how Wharton portrays various geographies of "cultivation" throughout this chapter. Lee's "imaginative freedom" reminds us of the "sylvan freedom" that Lily Bart appears to personify in *The House of Mirth*. Lee's remarks also show us that a garden is as much figurative as it is palpable. Of course, Wharton's narrators are extraordinarily adept at conveying the sensuous immediacy of pastoral localities—the composition of lawns, shrubs and blossoms. Wharton's texts also prompt us to view this "species of space" as the locus for a complex of interlinked processes, practices and conditions that stretch from cheerless rustic seclusion, even enforced withdrawal, to conviviality, from the planning to the planting of Central Park, from sexual politics to unalloyed visual delight.

An imaginary colloquium in *The Poetics of Gardens* ascribes the following statement to Wharton: "This garden is (and in the tiny space has to
be) a setting, a place that can be seen and visited in the mind, serene and
evocative, dreamy and above all beautiful. It doesn't need any of your invo-
cations."[63] Her character concludes that: "I favor a garden structure cov-
ered with vines, perhaps hanging in the air for conjectural inhabitation."[64]
This book will now go on to *conjecturally inhabit* other geographical zones in
Wharton's fiction. First, the mountains in the next part, followed by ruins
in the last part.

Notes

1 Shelley Saguaro, "Introduction: The Politics and Poetics of Gardens." *Garden Plots:
   The Politics and Poetics of Gardens*. Ashgate Publishing, 2006, ix–xiii, ix–x.
2 Von Rosk, "Spectacular Homes and Pastoral Theatres," 344.
3 Wharton, *The House of Mirth*, 143.
4 Poggioli, *The Oaten Flute*, 1.
5 Wharton, *The House of Mirth*, 143.
6 Letter from Nathaniel Hawthorn to Sophia Peabody. In "Letters and Journals, 1841."
   The Blithedale Romance, edited by Seymour Gross and Rosalie Murphy. W. W. Norton,
   1978. Norton Critical Editions, 236.
7 Hawthorne, *The Blithedale Romance*, 9.
8 Wharton, *The House of Mirth*, 143.
9 Wharton, *The House of Mirth*, 144.
10 Wharton, *The House of Mirth*, 144.
11 Wharton, *The House of Mirth*, 144.
12 John Claudius Loudon, *Encyclopedia of Architecture*. Appleton & Co., 1839, 89.
13 Janet Beer et al., *Edith Wharton's 'The House of Mirth'*. Routledge, 2007, 8.
14 Wharton, *The House of Mirth*, 153.
15 Wharton, *The House of Mirth*, 170.
16 Jones and Wills, *The Invention of the Park*, 12. See also Wade Graham, *American Eden:
   From Monticello to Central Park to our Backyards*. HarperCollins, 2011.
17 Joan Lidoff, "Another Sleeping Beauty: Narcissism in *The House of Mirth*." *American
   Quarterly*, vol. 32, no. 5, 1980, 519–39, 525. JSTOR, www.jstor.org/stable/2712411.
   Accessed May 28, 2021.
18 Wharton, *A Backward Glance*, 19.
19 Wharton, *A Backward Glance*, 19–20.
20 Joan DeJean, *How Paris Became Paris: The Invention of the Modern City*. Bloomsbury USA,
   2014, 280.
21 Edith Wharton, *French Ways and Their Meaning*. D. Appleton and Company, 1919, 38.
22 Wharton, *French Ways and Their Meaning*, 38.
23 DeJean adds that: "Le Nôtre had the original garden torn up and replaced with
   the steps and the esplanade that still today connect the Tuileries and the Louvre."
   DeJean, *How Paris Became Paris*, 280.
24 Wharton, *My Dear Governess*, 115.
25 Wharton, *Italian Villas and Their Gardens*, 94.

26 Paraphrasing from this quote originally in French: "l'Etranger goûte enfin la promenade, & en fait usage lorsque il est de retour chez lui." Louis-Antoine de Caraccioli, *Paris, le modèle des nations étrangères, ou L'Europe françoise.* Veuve Duchesne, 1777, 231.

27 DeJean, *How Paris Became Paris*, 281.

28 Edith Wharton, "Madame de Treymes." *Madame de Treymes and Three Novellas*, by Edith Wharton. Scribner & Schuster, 1995, 211–82, 213.

29 William Blazek, "Wharton and France." *Edith Wharton in Context*, edited by Laura Rattray. Cambridge University Press, 2012, 275–84, 281.

30 Wharton, "Madame de Treymes," 214.

31 Janet Beer, *Edith Wharton: Traveller in the Land of Letters*. Palgrave Macmillan, 1990, 3.

32 Wharton, "Madame de Treymes," 214.

33 Wharton, "Madame de Treymes," 215.

34 Olmsted, *Writings on Landscape, Culture, and Society*, 364.

35 Wharton, "Madame de Treymes," 215.

36 Beer, *Edith Wharton: Traveller in the Land of Letters*, 30.

37 Wharton, "Madame de Treymes," 215.

38 In the entry about the Rue de Rivoli, there is a mention of the "couvent des Feuillants." Félix Lazare and Louis Lazare, *Dictionnaire Administratif et Historique des Rues de Paris et de ses Monuments*. Paris, 1844, 591.

39 Wharton, "Madame de Treymes," 215.

40 Wharton, "Madame de Treymes," 217.

41 "[T]heir walk would not have thus resolved itself, without excuse or pretext, into a tranquil session beneath the trees, for any purpose less important than that of giving him his opportunity." Wharton, "Madame de Treymes," 219.

42 Beatrix Farrand, "Le Nôtre and His Gardens." *Scribner's Magazine*, no. 38, July 1905, 43–55, 55.

43 Farrand, "Le Nôtre and His Gardens," 52.

44 Edith Wharton, *Glimpses of the Moon*. Pushkin Press, 2018, 146.

45 Beer, *Edith Wharton: Traveller in the Land of Letters*, 85.

46 Dianne L. Chambers proposes: *"The Glimpses of the Moon* highlights performance, staging, and notions of seeing and being seen both within the fictional world—where men and women continually fashion and refashion social selves—and in the narrative construction of that world." Dianne L. Chambers, "Gender and Performance in The Glimpses of the Moon." *Feminist Readings of Edith Wharton: from Silence to Speech*. Palgrave Macmillan, 2009, 125–50, 128.

47 Edith Wharton, *The Children*. Virago, 2010, 28–29.

48 Wharton, *The Children*, 29.

49 Wharton, *The Children*, 29.

50 Edith Wharton, *The Cruise of the Vanadis*. Rizzoli International, 2004, 68.

51 Wharton, *The Cruise of the Vanadis*, 68.

52 Wharton, *The Cruise of the Vanadis*, 68.

53 The gardening article is "Spring in a French Riviera Garden," and it dates back to the 1930s. It can be found at the Edith Wharton Collection in the Beinecke Library. Please see Appendix I.

54 Wharton, *The Age of Innocence*, 88.

55 Wharton, *The Age of Innocence*, 88.

56 Wharton, *The Age of Innocence*, 91.

57 Wharton, *The Age of Innocence*, 91.

58 Wharton, *The Age of Innocence*, 91.
59 Wharton, *The Age of Innocence*, 189.
60 Wharton, *The Age of Innocence*, 208.
61 Wharton, *The Age of Innocence*, 208.
62 Lee, *Edith Wharton*, 563.
63 Moore et al., *The Poetics of Gardens*, 227.
64 Moore et al., *The Poetics of Gardens*, 227.

Part II

MOUNTAINS

Chapter 6

"ENDLESS PLAYS OF MOUNTAIN FORMS": MAPPING THE MOUNTAINS

In a letter to Bernard Berenson's secretary Nicky Mariano on May 31, 1932, Wharton described the Sibylline mountains thus: "The run today was indescribably beautiful, with changing skies & such endless plays of mountain forms—."[1] Her response to the shape-shifting plasticity of this terrain is suggestive of the ways in which summits and peaks function in Wharton's fiction more broadly. Her writing project evinces an abiding and acute fascination with the metaphorical, aesthetic, and cultural aspects of mountains. Her eye-catching stress on "plays" here implies that these landforms become, in her oeuvre, much more than a source of creative inspiration. They operate as a "stage" for heroic striving or galling tragedy; a site of arduous, even transformative physical and emotional struggle; or a lyrical "performance" in which heightened states of feeling are converted into the sensuous particularities of narrative language. In the previous part of this book, Lily Bart saw the Maritime Alps from her window, as if it were a boundary, an unconscious demarcation of space.[2] This second part considers not only the Alpine milieu but other specific examples of mountainous nature on both sides of the Atlantic that feature in Wharton's fiction. Given the dense mesh of cultural, biographical and philosophical concerns that emerge through the conjunction of Wharton and mountains, the challenge facing the researcher is the imposition of some cogent structure on a topic that rings with so many resonances. It is vital to remember that, as Linda Costanzo Cahir proposes: "Wharton was born amid the dark and bright energies of American romanticism."[3] I will show that Wharton's subtle evocation of the varied phenomena found among the snowy peaks and precipices often confronts—and rethinks—two legacies of what we might call "Romantic" mountain affect: the attribution of moral qualities to wild nature and awe of "sublime" vastness.[4]

Astrid Bracke argues that "ecocriticism has long broadened beyond its original concern with wilderness and non-fiction writing to incorporate a wider variety of environments and texts."[5] The second part of this book construes key Wharton texts through this ecocritical lens, arguing that mountains and hills can be interpreted as "edgelands at an altitude." According to Marion Shoard, "edgelands" exist between "town and country" where "there has developed a new type of landscape different from either and endowed with distinctive characteristics of its own."[6] While Shoard depicts the "edgeland" as a strange, possibly artificial, recent, man-made area between suburbs and city, the mountain is a natural and geological formation evolved through many eons. As Sean Ireton and Caroline Shaumann explain, there is no exact designation of "mountain" according to gradient, volume or elevation. It is a "contingent" geological and ethnographic construct; what specifies it depends on "history, culture and language" through time.[7] This ambiguity, and the fact that through the active literary imagination, the mountain is "man-made" too, indicates an enticing yet threatening "in-between" zone ripe for ecocritical enquiry.

Wharton is widely feted for her tale of self-engrossed social climber Undine Spragg in *The Custom of the Country*. However, this part of this book prioritizes the mountain climber in Wharton's work. In the "Preface" to Vivienne De Watteville's travel book *Speak to the Earth*, Wharton admits that she was no mountaineer herself, in a way that wittily acknowledges more significant questions about sexual difference, gendered authorship and the interplay of stasis and mobility, the endemic and the exotic, the domestic nook and the foreign getaway. "I too, have lived that life and stammered that language, though my mountain tent was only the library lamp-shade, my wilderness a garden, my wildebeest stealing down to drink two astute and arrogant Pekingese."[8] Wharton's referencing of the private and the cozily genteel here ("library," "Pekingese") belies her status as a globe-trotter and an astute travel writer who examines, with self-assured authority, the cultural constraints faced by women writers at the turn of the twentieth century. Her travel narratives fueled her attempts to claim the role and responsibilities of a serious artist and literary professional, speaking to an educated, critical readership. As Sarah Bird Wright affirms: "her travel works embody a connoisseurship that may well have provided considerable cultural 'capital' for her fiction."[9] Wharton's *In Morocco*, published in 1920, portrays the Middle Atlas Mountains thus: "Range after range these translucent hills rose before us, all around the solitude was complete."[10] Fifteen years later when the short story "Looking Glass" is published, one hears a faint echo of this description in the masseuse Cora Attlee's reminiscences about "the Connemara hills" where her "mother" once "saw the leprechauns at dusk; and she said they smelt fine and high, too."[11] In such scenes, recording a sensation of "high" altitude is a means of engaging with, and challenging the power of masculine narrative tactics, moods and metaphors—since the experience of traversing the peaks, is inextricably linked, as first- and second-generation Romantic poetics implies, with male self-glorification and freedom from restraint.[12]

Shari Benstock proposes that "Edith Wharton's life breaks almost too easily into two parts: America and Europe."[13] While this is not the case for all of Wharton's literary production, it certainly applies to the depiction of mountainous terrain. Regardless of whether the summits are idealized as awesome summits or a "barbarous and inaccessible region, fitted only for savages and bears,"[14] there is a stark contrast between European and American peaks. This contrast enables us to identify and question the stylistic and intellectual procedures by which Wharton transmutes the mountains into an intricately textured mental space, as well as an image of pastoral cosmopolitanism.

The previous part of this book, on gardens, argued that pastoral cosmopolitanism indicates a crucial regard for the tangible world in all its variety – an attitude of intellectual curiosity and openness to vivid new experiences, yet anchored in a respect for bucolic hinterlands, country lore and seasonal rhythms. I demonstrated that Wharton's fictional public parks and private gardens offer scope to ponder pastoral cosmopolitanism; this chapter indicates how "edgelands at an altitude" furnish a similar opportunity. In order to do this, it is worth recalling how the mountain, before acquiring the status of aesthetic object, symbol of Romantic revelation or locus of secular pilgrimage, is an actual, geographical location. Bertrand Westphal's *Geocriticism* appraises these natural settings as "real referents":

> In their diversity, real referents abound: cities, islands, archipelagos, countries, mountains, rivers, lakes, seas, straits, peninsulas, deserts, continents, poles, and so forth. The variety of paradigms is considerable, such that geocriticism could devote all of its activity to any one of them. But the realeme is not always located in the sensory reality of the world, because the world is divided—at least in the universe of fiction—into a plurality of possible worlds in terms of representation. When transcribed in the literary text, the referent determines a particular world. [15]

Westphal notes here a "variety of paradigms," but he does not scrutinize any of them in searching detail. However, his fascination with literary cartography raises questions about *how* novelists like Wharton "move" the (imagined) material of "mountains" into the domain of the representational. As Robert T. Tally remarks, the fictional portrayal of "a seemingly real place is never the purely mimetic image of that space. In a sense, all writing partakes in a form of cartography, since even the most realistic map does not truly depict the space, but, like literature, figures it forth in a complex skein of imaginary relations."[16] Wharton not only evokes the cultural phenomenon of mountains and the people who flock to or reside near them. She is also, like Westphal and Tally, intrigued by how such landforms are subtly "changed" by each successive visit and each fresh aesthetic "representation." She delves into the genealogies of our feelings for the peaks and the processes by which, for example, an Alpine range is converted into an emblem of world physical geography—and how that emblem chimes with or challenges earlier textual figurations.[17] Through her unique transatlantic perspective of belonging to no specific land and finding herself in multiple settings throughout her lifetime, Wharton's European mountains are consistently shown more favorably than their American counterparts.

In *A Backward Glance*, Edith Wharton acknowledges that "I felt more at home with the gods and goddesses of Olympus, who behaved so much like the ladies and gentlemen who came to dine, whom I saw riding and driving in the Bois de Boulogne, and about whom I was forever weaving stories of my own."[18] The reference to Mount Olympus here is telling. Wharton's literary career is a metaphorical ascent, each text a step towards the summit. Myrto Drizou ties this notion to Wharton's keen fascination with "Greek mythology" in which she "found not only a source of inspiration but also a mode of connection to her contemporary milieu—the upper-class European and American society that fueled her stories."[19] I contend that Wharton works on a wider "mythology" of her own, rooted in the edgelands at altitude. This is apparent when she presents Mount Athos in *The Cruise at Vanadis* thus:

> we caught sight of the peak of Athos rising faint and blue from the sea ahead of us. The nearer we drew the more beautiful it became, until at last its mighty wall was close before us, dark against the brilliant sky as the sun set in a yellow blaze behind the low hills of the Sithonian promontory.[20]

This extract implies that Wharton is not so much interested in continuing an existing literary tradition or restaging a "mountain cult" of Romanticism that had descended into what Remy de Gourmont impatiently labelled in 1895 "sentimental mishmash."[21] Instead she crafts an alternative mountain mythology, one that probes and builds on the poetic, architectural and scientific descriptions of the terrain synonymous with admired precursors like John Ruskin, whose "wonderful [...] pages" according to Wharton, "woke in me the habit of precise visual observation."[22] Wharton "repeatedly cite[d] Ruskin as a shaping influence" on her "experience of various sites."[23] His expressive accounts of travelling through the Alps in Western Switzerland and Savoy, one of the most celebrated modern tourist destinations, casts a long shadow across the first part of this chapter.[24] Wharton does, of course, register and react to certain narrative codes and conventions—she observes a peak's geological and botanical singularity, for example. Her imaginative engagement with these well-trodden ruins of hard ice, rock and snow is active yet suspicious, her reactions conditioned more by her own enthusiasms than by the vagaries of Alpine fads or transatlantic tourist routes.

Virginia Woolf's short story "The Symbol" (c. 1941) presents an unnamed protagonist who sits on the balcony of an Alpine hotel taking in the views and writing letters home. Woolf remarks: "She had written the mountain was a symbol. But of what?"[25] This is a question that may well have exercised Woolf's father, Leslie Stephen (1832-1904), a leading light of the Alpine Club whose book *The Playground of Europe* (1871), like Edward Whymper's *Scrambles Amongst the Alps* (1871), attracted many intrepid climbers and sensation-seekers to this region. Woolf's question is also one that Wharton weighs, since her goal is to test and enlarge the possibilities of the mountain as a poetic and philosophical construct—even a symbol of how the sacred "sublime" itself had become, in the first decades of the twentieth century, merely "scenic."

The first mountaineering metaphor in Wharton's fiction is found in the 1900 novella *The Touchstone*. The protagonist Glennard "felt the sudden dizziness of the mountaineer on a narrow ledge, and with it the sense that he was lost if he looked more than a step ahead."[26] Mountaineering here is depicted as a dangerous endeavor that exemplifies the difficulties and frustrations of navigating the unforgiving rocky terrain of New York upper class society. Wharton revisits and extends this figuration in the 1907 novel *The Fruit of the Tree*: "It is as though a mountain-climber, braced to the strain of a hard ascent, should suddenly see the way break into roses, and level itself in a path for his feet."[27] This implies that Wharton saw her own literary endeavor as a form of mountain trek, and it is useful to scrutinize the stages of this "ascent" to see where the winding "path" takes us.

Janet Beer states of Wharton that: "In all sorts of ways the impetus for telling the story of her own life follows the same patterns as the momentum behind the writing for her previous works of non-fiction: the desire to explain the aesthetic effect, whether it is the effect of a culture, a landscape."[28] How can we be more exact about this "aesthetic effect" when Wharton describes mountainous "landscape" in her fiction though? Marion Shoard, in her analysis of "edgelands," acknowledges that perceptions of space and place are "changing all the time. Hitherto reviled landscape types have constantly re-emerged as desirable and fascinating as the tides of fashion ebb and flow."[29] She add that "In the eighteenth century the idea that stretches of grassland dotted with trees should be viewed as the new top landscape— parkland—must have been quite revolutionary. Moors and mountains were once considered hideous places."[30] Wharton certainly refines this tradition of foregrounding the summits as sites of geographic and affective complexity. It is most evident perhaps in novellas, *Ethan Frome* and *Summer*. As a purgatory or no-man's land, the *mise-en-scene* is desolate, inhospitable, austere and full of tension. *Summer* boasts arguably the most famous peak in Wharton's oeuvre, the "Mountain"—a "hideous" presence that bespeaks her deeply vexed relationship with rural New England.

However, to focus only on the "Mountain" in *Summer* affords a very limited view of lofty ecozones in Wharton's writing. Janet Beer posits that "[s]ix formative years in Europe were sufficient to induce what the adult Edith Wharton would describe as her lack of affection for either the rural or the urban American landscape."[31] It is not necessarily a "lack of affection" for American mountains or how they become symbols of a relatively young nation's democratic ideals, beliefs and opportunities. It is rather a detached and critical perspective on the home/land resulting from extensive foreign travel coupled with a wariness of transatlantic polemics and shrill nationalist ideologies. Wharton was conscious that "sublime" sentiments and beautiful mountain vistas could be converted into markers of the republic's moral exceptionalism.[32] In *Italian Backgrounds*, the description of "An Alpine Posting Inn" is revealing in this regard. Wharton opens with the direct and spare declaration: "[t]he landscape is simple, spacious and serene."[33] This succinct phrase leads into a more involved chain of subordinate clauses and Latinate flourishes: "The fields suggest the tranquil rumination of generations of cattle, the woods offer cool security to sylvan life, the mountains present blunt weather-beaten surfaces rather than the subtle contours, wrinkled as by meditation, of the Italian Alps."[34] This could very well be an extract from a mountain encounter in *The Children*. It is the last sentence in this passage that resonates: "One feels that it is a scene in which *nothing has ever happened*; the haunting adjective is that which Whitman applies to the American landscape—'the large *unconscious* scenery of my native land'."[35] In this perceptual exercise, Wharton evokes a European topography, all the while citing arguably the most influential American poet (who appears as a crucial character in *The Spark*, one of Wharton's *Old New York* novellas), describing an American natural environment.[36] Regardless of what material terrain Wharton surveys and depicts, she reveals how the American and European perspectives overlap, interact and feed into her own distinct "peak practice." I propose that the New England novellas do not show outright aversion to an American expanse that Whitman commemorates with often patriotic verve, but rather an attempt to harness in original terms the "large unconscious scenery" of her "native" soil. Equally, this passage signals Wharton's admiration for the alpine zones that become a vehicle for expressing and extending her geographical imagination, as I will explain in the next part of this book.

Notes

1 Wharton, *The Letters of Edith Wharton*, 551.
2 Sharon L. Dean writes that: "Wharton liked her mountains in the distance". This chapter intends to "bridge" the distance between Wharton and that mountainous landscape. See Sharon L. Dean, *Constance Fenimore Woolson and Edith Wharton: Perspectives on Landscape and Art*. University of Tennessee Press, 2002, 72.
3 Linda Costanzo Cahir, "Wharton and the American Romantics." *Edith Wharton in Context*, edited by Laura Rattray. Cambridge University Press, 2012, 335–43, 335.
4 As Patrick Vincent argues: "Nineteenth-century commentators on natural landscape often combined the Christian tradition of moralized landscape, which viewed nature as a divine second book open to typological interpretation, with Romantic aesthetic theory, enabling them to draw analogies between the experience of nature and moral perception". See Patrick Vincent, "The Moral of Landscape: John Ruskin and John Muir in the Swiss Alps." *Literature, Ethics, Morality: American Studies Perspectives*, edited by Ridvan Askin and Philipp Schweighauser. Tubingen, 2015, 175–94. The "sublime spectacle of Mont Blanc" which greets Lewis Raycie in Part II of Wharton's novella *False Dawn* is one of the more striking examples of this tendency. *False Dawn* is discussed in a later chapter.
5 Astrid Bracke, "Wastelands, Shrubs and Parks: Ecocriticism and the Challenge of the Urban." *Frame*, vol. 26, no. 2, Nov. 2013, 7–21, 7.
6 Marion Shoard, "Edgelands of Promise." *Landscapes*, vol. 1, no. 2, 2000, 74–93, 74, doi:10.1179/lan.2000.1.2.74.
7 See Sean Ireton and Caroline Schaumann, *Heights of Reflection: Mountains in the German Imagination from the Middle Ages to the Twenty-First Century*. Bowdell & Brewer, 2012, 1–19. See also Cian Duffy, *The Landscapes of the Sublime, 1700-1930: Classic Ground*. Palgrave Macmillan, 2013, 34.
8 Edith Wharton and Vivienne De Watteville, "Preface." *Speak to the Earth: Wanderings and Reflections Among Elephants and Mountains*. Methuen and Co., 1936, 1–2, 1.
9 Edith Wharton, *Edith Wharton Abroad: Selected Travel Writings, 1888-1920*. Edited by Sarah Bird Wright. Robert Hale, 1995, 9.
10 Edith Wharton, *In Morocco*. John Beaufoy Publishing, 2015, 16.
11 Edith Wharton, "The Looking Glass." *Ghost Stories of Edith Wharton*. Vintage, 2009, 223–39, 227.
12 For example, Byron's speaker in *Manfred* (Act 2, Scene 2, l. 62) asserts that "My joy was in the wilderness, to breathe the difficult air of the iced mountain-top." See *Lord Byron: The Major Works*, edited by Jerome J. McGann. Oxford University Press, 2008, 281. P. B. Shelley states that "Danger, which sports upon the brink of precipices, has been my playmate. I have trodden the glaciers of the Alps, and lived under the eye of Mont Blanc." See Shelley, Percy Bysshe. "Preface." *Revolt of Islam; a Poem, in Twelve Cantos*. C. And J. Ollier, 1818. These perceptions of mountains have been studied closely by academics, especially how Romantic poets responded to – and reimagined – discoveries in geology and physical geography. See, for example, Martin Rudwick, *Bursting the Limits of Time: The Reconstruction of Geohistory in the Age of Revolution*. Chicago University Press, 2005; Nigel Leask, *Curiosity and the Aesthetics of Travel Writing, 1700-1800*. Oxford

University Press, 2002; Noah Heringman, *Romantic Rocks, Aesthetic Geology*. Cornell University Press, 2004; Scott Hess. *William Wordsworth and the Ecology of Authorship: The Roots of Environmentalism in Nineteenth Century Culture*. University of Virginia Press, 2012.

13 Shari Benstock, "Landscape of Desire: Edith Wharton and Europe." *Wretched Exotic: Essays on Edith Wharton in Europe*, edited by Katherine Joslin and Alan Price. Peter Lang, 1996, 19–42. XXIV American Literature.

14 Leslie Stephen, "A Substitute for the Alps." *The National Review*, vol. 23, no. 136, June 1894, 460–67.

15 Original text: "Dans leur diversité, les référents *réels* abondent: villes, îles ou archipels, pays, montagnes, fleuves, mers ou lacs, détroits et presqu'îles, deserts, continents et poles, etc. La variété des paradigmes est considérable, au point que la géocritique pourrait leur consacrer l'ensemble de son programme d'application. Mais le réalème n'est pas toujours implanté dans la réalité sensible du monde, car le monde se scinde – du moins dans les univers de la fiction – en la pluralité des mondes possibles du plan de représentation. Transcrit dans le texte littéraire, le référent determine une option de monde." Bertrand Westphal, *Geocriticism: Real and Fictional Spaces*. Translated by Robert T. Tally. Palgrave Macmillan, 2011, 117.

16 Robert T. Tally, "Review of Bertrand Westphal, *La Géocritique: Réel, fiction, espace*." *L'Esprit Créateur: The International Quarterly of French and Francophone Studies*, vol. 49, no. 3, 2009, 134. For James Duncan and Derek Gregory, weighing Westphal's research, "all geographies are imaginative geographies – fabrications in the literal sense of 'something made' – and our access to the world is always made through particular technologies of representation." See James Duncan and Derek Gregory, eds., *Writes of Passage: Reading Travel Writing*. Routledge, 1999, 5–6.

17 Mountains in Wharton's work bring to mind what French philosopher Henri Lefebvre describes as "absolute space": "Absolute space was made up of fragments of nature located at sites which were chosen for their intrinsic qualities (cave, mountaintop, spring, river), but whose very consecration ended up by stripping them of their natural characteristics and uniqueness." Original text: "*L'espace absolu* consiste en fragments de la nature, en lieux élus pour leurs qualités intrinsèques (caverne ou sommet, source ou rivière) mais dont la consecration aboutit à les vider de ces caractères et particularités naturelles." See Henri Lefebvre, *La production de l'espace*. Anthropos, 2000, 59.

18 Wharton. *A Backward Glance*, 33.

19 Myrto Drizou, "Edith Wharton's Odyssey." *The New Edith Wharton Studies*, edited by Jennifer Haytock and Laura Rattray. Cambridge: Cambridge University Press, 2019, 65–79. Twenty-First-Century Critical Revisions, 65.

20 Wharton, *The Cruise of the Vanadis*, 171. This description is all the more significant because Lewis Wright believes that Edith Wharton was the first American woman to write an account of Mount Athos.

21 Remy de Gourmont, quoted in Jean Pierrot, *The Decadent Imagination, 1800-1900*. Translated by D. Cottman. Chicago University Press, 1981, 63.

22 Edith Wharton, quoted in Mary Ann Caws, "Translation of the Self: Ruskin and Wharton." *The Massachusetts Review*, vol. 40, no. 2, 1999, 165–73, 165. On Wharton and Ruskin see Emily J. Orlando, *Edith Wharton and the Visual Arts*. University of Alabama Press, 2007.

23 Mark Scroggins, "Review: *Constructing Cultural Tourism*." *Journal of Tourism History*, vol. 3, no. 3, 2011, 333.

24 In *A Backward Glance*, Wharton recalls her father giving her "'Stones of Venice' and 'Walks in Florence', and gently lent himself to my whim of following step by step Ruskin's arbitrary itineraries," 87. E.M. Forster's early draft for *A Room with a View* mischievously suggests the impact which, in the early years of the twentieth century, Ruskin had on the way genteel sight-seers *consumed* archaeological sites, landmarks and European art: "[Lucy] had Ruskin's *Mornings in Florence* with her, and Santa Croce was her first experience of that invaluable and exasperating book. She began by finding a sepulchral slab, the book informing her that if she did not like it, she was to leave Florence at once." See *A Room with a View*, edited by Oliver Stallybrass. Edward Arnold, 1977, 22.

25 Virginia Woolf, "The Symbol." *A Haunted House: The Complete Shorter Fiction*, edited by Susan Dick. Vintage, 2003, 282.

26 Wharton, "The Touchstone," 17–118, 68.

27 Edith Wharton, *The Fruit of the Tree*. Wildside Press, 2006, 56.

28 Janet Beer, *Edith Wharton*. Liverpool University Press, 2001, 16.

29 Shoard, "Edgelands of Promise," 92.

30 Shoard, "Edgelands of Promise," 92.

31 Beer, *Edith Wharton*, 6.

32 For example, in William Cullen Bryant's sonnet "To Cole, An American Painter, Departing for Europe" (1829), the speaker reminds his friend not to become overly swayed by the Old World's myriad historical associations and "fair scenes," which in the Alps reveals "the trace of men, / Paths, homes, graves, ruins" (ll. 10-12). The speaker urges patriotic readers to cherish instead America's pristine wilderness, whose peaks voice the nation's vigour and freedom from European problems and prejudices. Six years later, Thomas Cole published his "Essay on American Scenery" – a seminal statement of the moral energies of American localities, whose mountains, forests, and lakes represent a unique facet of the American picturesque. See J. Baird Callicott, "A Critique of and an Alternative to the Wilderness Idea." *Environmental Ethics: An Anthology*, edited by Andrew Light and Holmes Roston III. Malden: Blackwell, 2003, 437–43; see also Vincent, "The Moral of Landscape," 175–94.

33 Edith Wharton, *Italian Backgrounds*. Scribner, 1905, 6.

34 Wharton, *Italian Backgrounds*, 6.

35 Wharton, *Italian Backgrounds*, 6.

36 See Edith Wharton, "The Spark." *Old New York*. Simon & Schuster, 1995, 181–234. Wharton's admiration for Whitman was such that she planned at one stage to write a critical essay on his verse. Unfortunately, this plan never came to fruition. See Susan Goodman, "Edith Wharton's 'Sketch of an Essay on Walt Whitman'." *Walt Whitman Quarterly Review*, vol. 10, Summer 1992, 3–9. https://doi.org/10.13008/2153-3695.134

Chapter 7

EDITH WHARTON'S EUROPEAN MOUNTAINS OF LEISURE

Edith Wharton's first experience of European mountains almost killed her. During a stay at a Black Forest resort, Bad Wildbad, in 1870, young Edith came down with typhoid fever and nearly died.[1] It is revealing that during this time in Bad Wildbad she practiced her German by reading the New Testament, and she singles out one chapter that reverberated powerfully with her:

> After six days Jesus took with him Peter, James and John the brother of James, and led them to a high mountain by themselves. There he was transfigured before them. His face shone like the sun, and his clothes became as white as the light. Just then appeared before them Moses and Elijah talking with Jesus. (*Matthew* 17:1–3)[2]

In the Christian tradition, Mount Tabor is the site of the transfiguration of Jesus, a turning point in the gospel narratives, and it relates to Wharton on both a personal and a literary level in *A Backward Glance.* Hermione Lee develops this point by suggesting that "Europe" becomes "the stage" for "a more disturbing event, which Wharton marks as a moment of profound change in her character."[3] Lee's account reminds us that in the Old Testament, mountains—just like the seemingly limitless desert sands—become sites of grueling trial and testing, revelatory vision and heavenly intercession.[4] Wharton is fascinated by the biblical tales of ascending a peak, confronting its atmospheric extremes and discovering a new grammar and syntax of felt sensation. This becomes a crucial facet of her European mountain texts.

The earliest account of a mountain holiday features in a letter to Anna Bahlmann from St. Moritz, in the 1890s, when Edith and Teddy spent a few days in the Alps.[5] It opens with a brisk account of reaching "the top of the mountains in safety."[6] But it soon becomes a vivid word-painting of her surroundings, marked by the ebullience of an amateur geographer keen to

share an awareness of how topographical curiosities emerge through deter-
mined bodily and mental endeavor: "The scenery was fairy-like – hills & valleys clothed with snow more blindingly white than you can conceive of, pine
woods powdered with glittering crystals & feathery fringes of white, waterfalls
turned into deep blue icicles, & suspended thus over the sheer edge of the
rocks."[7] Here Wharton artfully evokes St. Moritz. Her excitement is apparent
through the intricately structured clause that enacts—as well as reflects—the
feeling for scale and distinguishing surface features in this layered landscape:
"at each ascent the snow grew thicker & more dazzling, the pines rarer &
more deeply buried in it."[8] Wharton's lexis blends fear and rapt fascination:
"the next day the ascent of the Julier began. Here the line of vegetation was
left far below & we entered on a region of wild white grandeur which was
absolutely awful."[9] The ascent is a journey to be savored every step of the way:

> At each turn in the road a new & wilder vista of tossed & broken snow
> peaks unfolded itself, with the road winding between them only marked
> by the occasional tall pole in the snow—while the only sign of life was
> afforded now & then by a snow-laden roof & steeple of a half-buried vil-
> lage which barely broke the level of the whiteness[10]

Wharton's letter can be construed as an example of one of two ways of "writing the peaks" that the agnostic Victorian mountaineer, editor and biographer
Leslie Stephen describes in his 1871 essay "The Regrets of a Mountaineer":
"One is to indulge in fine writing about them, to burst out in sentences
which swell to paragraphs, and in paragraphs which spread over pages."[11]
Wharton "encountered" Stephen through his critical study of George Eliot,
which Wharton reviewed for *The Bookman* in May 1902.[12] Stephen's real tar-
get in "The Regrets of a Mountaineer," we might speculate, is John Ruskin.
Stephen's essay accepts, even celebrates, how physical geography "moves"
through the filter of authorial imagination, is reshaped by all sorts of personal
quirks, prejudices, sense-impressions and rhetorical bravura. His complaint
is that Ruskin's prolix and intensely lyrical word pictures in *Modern Painters*
exerted a pernicious influence over aesthetic constructions of the Alps in the
second half of the nineteenth century and even beyond. Stephen's emphasis on
"spread" hints at the contagion of cliché—a "disease" from which Wharton
herself may not have been entirely immune.[13] Wharton's "fine writing" in
the letter above, with its alliterative effects ("pine woods [...] powdered,"
"feathery fringes"), implies a Ruskinian rhetorical flight triggered by the
sensuous immediacy of the snowy peaks.[14] In Stephen's critique, this exhila-
rated "bursting out" across sentences—and in Ruskin's stylistically ornate
and digressive Alpine texts, across "paragraphs" and entire tomes—does not

foster new cultural ways of being and seeing.[15] Rather, for Stephen at least, Ruskin's advice to the traveler-acolyte on how "to visit" the Alpine "shrine in a becoming spirit" merely reheats orthodox narrative tropes and patterns.[16] For example, in the opening chapter of Wharton's 1922 novel *Glimpses of the Moon*, her literary language diffuses the beauty of the setting in which the characters find themselves: "The ripples of the lake had gradually widened and faded into silken smoothness, and high above the mountain the moon was turning from gold to white in a sky powdered with vanishing stars."[17] These terms exemplify what Stephen calls a tendency "to plunge into ecstasies about infinite abysses and overpowering splendors, to compare mountains to arch- angels lying down in eternal winding-sheets of snow, and to convert them into allegories about man's highest destinies and aspirations."[18] For Stephen, such narrative strategies dilute and domesticate the very real hazards, challenges and rewards of "a first ascent of the Matterhorn" or "a precipitous mountain gorge."[19]

Stephen contends that affective and rhetorical excess ("plunge into ecsta- sies") creates a misleading narrative not dissimilar to what we find in Ruskin's 1856 essay "The Moral of Landscape." In this piece Ruskin posits that responsiveness to mountain scenery—a "pure landscape instinct"—evinces the viewer's essential "goodness of heart and justness of moral perception."[20] This is a perspective that Wharton tests in her own writing about European peaks, and as Stephen states: "It is not everyone who can with impunity compare Alps to archangels."[21] If Wharton's short story "The Duchess at Prayer" published in 1900 and originally written in Italian[22] is any indica- tion, then she furnishes such a Ruskinian evocation "with impunity": "Below the terrace, where chrome-colored lichen had sheeted the balustrade as with fine *laminae* of gold, vineyards stooped to the rich valley clasped in hills."[23] However, the boundless and beautiful milieu evoked at the beginning of her story is crucially contrasted with—and slowly gives way to—the smothering and deadly ending of it. In the case of Wharton's other fictional texts, how do these rich word-paintings of elevated—and sometimes spiritually elevat- ing—natural landscapes serve the thematic trajectory itself? And does she push against the grain, or debunk, the Ruskinian approach to high altitudes that Stephen deplores?

Mountaineering occasionally operates in Wharton's fiction as a favored pas- time of New York upper class society. As Maureen E. Montgomery remarks: "nature was seen as a great restorative and living by the sea or camping and hiking in the mountains were among the physical recreations recommended as beneficial to one's health."[24] In *The Age of Innocence*, Newland Archer and May Welland spend their honeymoon in Europe, and visit the Alps: "They had not gone to the Italian Lakes: on reflection, Archer had not been able to picture his wife in that particular setting. Her own inclination (after a month with the Paris dressmakers) was for mountaineering in July and swimming in August."[25] Wharton hints—in a way that reminds us of the phrase "plays of mountain forms" from the previous chapter—how socially refined travelers are prone to aestheticize the summits and passes as a "stage" on which to "perform" elegant taste, class privilege and inherited power. Newland can "picture" May among the peaks, and it is no accident that May is standing in a flowerbed, as if she is a bloom herself: "Once or twice, in the mountains, Archer had pointed southward and said: 'There's Italy'; and May, her feet in a gentian-bed, had smiled cheerfully, and replied: 'It would be lovely to go there next winter, if only you didn't have to be in New York'."[26] This is an example of pastoral cosmopolitanism. Newland and May long for a bucolic refuge but are instead irrevocably drawn into New York City rhythms and routines from which they cannot and will not escape.

As in *The Age of Innocence*, *The Custom of the Country* (1913) shows the protagonist Undine Spragg and her second husband Ralph Marvell honeymooning in Western Europe. The narrator captures an Edenic quality, again reminiscent of the "fine writing" Leslie Stephen disparages in his essay: "Four months of beauty, changeful, inexhaustible, weaving itself about him in shapes of softness and strength; and beside him, hand in hand with him, embodying the spirit of that shifting magic, the radiant creature through whose eyes he saw it."[27] This intense self-awareness gives way to a scrupulous rendering of the natural landscape that surrounds them, the summits of southern Italy:

> This was what the hastened marriage had blessed them with, giving them leisure, before summer came, to penetrate to remote folds of the southern mountains, to linger in the shade of Sicilian orange-groves, and finally, travelling by slow stages to the Adriatic, to reach the central hill-country where even in July they might hope for a breathable air.[28]

It becomes clear that Ralph and Undine's version of the unfolding events is quite disparate. Regarding *The Custom of the Country*, Hermione Lee posits that "[i]n Europe the landscapes are painted both as Undine sees them and as they might look to others."[29] This reading however overlooks Ralph's vision, through which Wharton provides us with an impeccable cartography of Italy. Conversely, Undine is unable to register fully the majesty of this locality since *where* one "summers" is an index only of the cultural kudos that accrues to a dominant caste. Perhaps the crucial term in the extract above is "leisure." Undine is trying to play a "role" among mountains which are packaged as a theatrical backdrop—an upmarket leisure product that should constitute and affirm her status as a well-heeled and carefree consumer. Her version of the peaks reveals her faltering attempts to "arrange" herself in a bucolic "scene." This is comically illustrated in the next sentence: "Undine, nearby, leaned against a gnarled tree with the slightly constrained air of a person unused to sylvan abandonments."[30] Undine's fantasy of "bliss ineffable" in a more refined setting than the frontier wilderness is always beyond her reach, and the narrator emphasizes Undine's discomfort: "Her beautiful back could not adapt itself to the irregularities of the tree-trunk, and she moved a little now and then in an effort to find an easier position."[31] The narrator's mordant depiction of the *nouveau riche* reveals here gaps and tensions between a high altitude honeymoon as a fleeting, showy and inauthentic diversion and holidaying in Ruskin's terms—an anti-capitalist Romantic stress on becoming more deeply attuned to the *genius loci*, cultivating first of all a corporeal, haptic and kinetic engagement with the mountainous ridges. Undine's "vacation pastoral"—what Stewart O'Nan defines as "the illusion of an escape into simplicity and beauty"—becomes increasingly fraught and fevered rather than liberating. Any serenity or spiritual balm is "replaced, quickly enough, by the complexity of human relations and the self. Because desire never takes a vacation."[32] We are reminded of the differences between gazing through an impatient tourist's eyes—Undine evokes the sight-seer who, in Leslie Stephen's critique, "despatches Switzerland as rapidly and thoughtlessly" as she does "Olympia"[33]—and learning to assert one's own standpoint: "But there were hours of solitary striding over bare grassy slopes, face to face with the ironic interrogation of sky and mountains, when his anxieties came back, more insistent and importunate."[34]

Undine is consistently delineated in terms of her physical traits and sartorial choices. In reality this is what she truly cares about: "Slim and tall in her trim mountain garb."[35] The narrator describes how the "high air brightened her cheeks and struck new lights from her hair, and Ralph had never seen her so touched with morning freshness."[36] Here she is rendered as an artificial feature and extension of the mountain itself. Rather than appreciating her surroundings as a touristic outsider or frivolous dilettante, she *is* (momentarily at least) the landscape. This particular scene highlights, first of all, the "stagey" qualities of the mountains in Wharton's European texts. It also invites us to ponder the tangled associations that cluster about these liminal sites: the peaks as both seasonal haven and locus of belonging; synonymous with leisure and pleasure but also a source of fretful self-scrutiny ("anxieties came back"). A honeymoon resort can be construed as the windswept, thrilling, more glamorous double of the *nouveau riche* townhouse. But in sharp contrast to the murky and malign geographies synonymous with Romantic-era Gothic texts, which variously depict the incarceration of "home," Wharton's Alpine milieu can prompt dissatisfaction with its promise of epiphany or mental illumination. So, in the Alps it becomes clear how Ralph and Undine embody two distinct ways of living that cannot be reconciled. The vacation is where they cannot escape themselves or each other. The narrator is not afraid to proclaim the source of this discord: "It was a point of honor with him not to seem to disdain any of Undine's amusements."[37] Undine, lacking what Wharton terms in *False Dawn* the judicious Ruskinian "seeing eye,"[38] is far more preoccupied by opportunities for sociability in the mountains, not the "spiritual satisfaction" that, for example, Georg Simmel scrutinizes in his 1895 essay on "The Alpine Journey."[39] Undine revels in the "noisy interminable picnics, the hot promiscuous balls, the concerts, bridge-parties and theatricals which helped to disguise the difference between the high Alps and Paris or New York."[40] This enumeration of events recalls Mark Twain's evocation of Victorian sightseers as "buzzing hives of restless strangers."[41] It also underlines Wharton's canny grasp of how the mountain "getaway" is institutionalized as a fundamental aspect of American bourgeois power and privilege—an experience that blurs "here" and "there," "home" and "away."[42] Consequently, the "very name of the Alps, so musical in the ears of those" like Ruskin who once savored "their mysterious charm" and awesome solitudes, now conveys, in Leslie Stephen's more jaundiced view, "little more than the hurry and jostling of an average sight-seeing trip."[43]

Undine pays little heed to the marketing of the Alps as a place that "fills us," in Georg Simmel's words, "with an unrivalled intensity of feeling."[44] Instead, the "picnics" are "interminable"—a droll reminder of the etymological link between *travel* and *travail* to show the cheerless, wearying effects of the organized tours that are supposed to furnish refreshment, relaxation, even spiritual fulfilment. The peaks, passes and summits had always been part of Undine's imagination, and a facet of her social achievements in her youth:

> Yielding to the inevitable, they suffered themselves to be impelled to a Virginia "resort," where Undine had her first glimpse of more romantic possibilities—leafy moonlight rides and drives, picnics in mountain glades and an atmosphere of Christmas-chromo sentimentality that tempered her hard edges a little, and gave her glimpses of a more delicate kind of pleasure.[45]

The Alps in *The Custom of the Country* offers a platform on which Undine enacts these adolescent fantasies, and also augurs the beginning of the end of her second marriage.

Not all mountain scenes in Wharton's fiction set in motion the fracturing and dissolution of matrimonial contracts. In *False Dawn*—one of Wharton's four *Old New York* 1924 novellas—the protagonist, Lewis Raycie, has a life-altering encounter in the Alps. During his Grand Tour, Raycie pauses "on a projecting rock and surveyed the sublime spectacle of Mont Blanc."[46] This image immediately evokes Caspar David Friedrich's 1818 painting "Wanderer Above Sea of Fog," positioning Raycie as the quintessential "Romantic" pilgrim-hero, though the weather sharply contrasts with the meteorological effects evoked in Friedrich's canvas: "It was a brilliant August day, and the air, at that height, was already so sharp that he had to put on his fur-lined pelisse."[47] Raycie is seeking refuge in this area, though it will not be a solitary interlude. He is about to meet a most culturally significant figure among these jagged crags and "awful pinnacles," one whose mind "moved in a world of associations and references far more richly peopled" than that of the "simpler youth."[48]

The narrator of *False Dawn* is aware that myriad earlier visual and verbal texts have sought to do justice to Mont Blanc, the "monarch of mountains" on its "throne of rocks."[49] It is no accident that Raycie meets in this locality an affable "stranger" named John Ruskin,[50] who has devoted himself "to the extremely inadequate rendering of some of these delicate *aiguilles*; a bit of drudgery not likely to interest you in the face of so sublime a scene."[51] Here *False Dawn* adroitly catches the tone of Ruskin's own diary entries, especially those composed in Chamonix at the base of Mont Blanc (June 28, 1844): "For an hour before, the *aiguilles* had appeared as dark masses against a sky looking as transparent as clear sea, edged at their summits with fleeces of cloud breaking into glorious spray and foam of white fire."[52] That Ruskin makes such a vivid and decisive appearance in *False Dawn* shows Wharton's keen interest in the elaborate theory of observation and representation in art that he devised. Wharton's narrative evinces a special concern with Ruskin's endeavor to tease out what she calls "a new angle [...] a new train of thought"[53]—schooling audiences in the correct way to envisage and conceptualize the Alps. Ruskin, before first visiting the Alps in 1833, had travelled with his family to the peaks of the Lake District, Scotland and North Wales.[54] Ruskin's notebooks and correspondence suggest that while some botanical and geological curiosities appealed to his "seeing eye,"[55] such palpable facets could not match the European crests and precipices in terms of elemental grandeur, scale and scientific importance. The most extraordinary articulation of this conviction is *Modern Painters* published in five volumes between 1843 and 1860. In the terms of *False Dawn*, *Modern Painters* shows how a seemingly "commonplace item of experience" can be transfigured into "a multi-faceted crystal flashing with unexpected fires."[56] Of these volumes perhaps *Modern Painters Vol. IV* (1856) entitled *Of Mountain Beauty* best illustrates Ruskin's attempt to capture imaginatively both the detail and the sublimity of Alpine peaks. The book ends with a celebratory final chapter "The Mountain Glory" that was viewed as a seminal text among those who explored the Alps, from often skeptical contemporaries like Leslie Stephen to present-day landscape historians such as Robert McFarlane in *Mountains of the Mind* (2003).[57]

Wharton's fictional sketch of the young Ruskin as a visionary "blue-eyed Englishman" in *False Dawn*,[58] points to a close familiarity with his *Modern Painters* methodology—a program elegantly summarized in his "Preface" to the second edition of Volume I. Here Ruskin sets forth the need to assess mountain phenomena as natural features before elaborating any aesthetic and philosophical resonances that might derive from them:

> I shall endeavor to investigate and arrange the facts of nature with sci-entific accuracy. This foundation once securely laid, I shall proceed, in the second portion of this work, to analyze and demonstrate the nature of the emotions of the Beautiful and Sublime; to examine the particular characters of every kind of scenery; and to bring to light, as far as may be in my power, that faultless, ceaseless, inconceivable, inexhaustible loveliness, which God has stamped upon all things, if man will only receive them as He gives them. Finally, I shall endeavor to trace the operation of this on the hearts and minds of men[59]

This passage reveals Ruskin's conception of a movement from empirical and scientific observation through to the aesthetic affect the object provokes—and then to the intellectual, moral and spiritual significance that might be adduced. The process, as Keith Hanley and other Ruskin experts have noted, is sequential and entirely "interdependent."[60] Therefore, one can argue that the intensely lyrical, even florid reactions to material nature conveyed in some Romantic poetry and novels, as well as earlier analysis of the sublime and picturesque by seminal commentators such as Edmund Burke and Joseph Addison, were unsatisfactory for Ruskin in *Modern Painters*—and for Wharton too—not least in their stress on the psychological impact of nature over the external source of the mountain range itself.[61] What Wharton's European mountain texts take from Ruskin is the need to render scrupulously the lofty and august landforms that produce such potent affect.[62]

This is why Ruskin's argument in "The Lamp of Truth" and elsewhere, is echoed by Wharton's version of Ruskin in her novella: "For instance: I desire to give an account of a mountain or of a rock; I begin by telling its shape. But words will not do this distinctly, and I draw its shape, and say, 'This was the shape'."[63] Such a view resonates with Wharton's *False Dawn*, since writing is a Ruskinian "communicated act of imagination, but no lie."[64] The young Ruskin in *False Dawn* tells Lewis that "privileged beings" are not necessarily affluent, stylishly dressed New Yorkers; rather they are ones who can cherish and develop "the seeing eye" as the very basis for this "communicated act."[65] The "lie" here suggests a tendency to make barren, silent rocks speak through extravagant, glib or grandiose word-painting that Leslie Stephen also targeted in his published critiques.[66]

Wharton's Mountain Novel, *The Children*

If there is a definitive "mountain text" in Wharton's oeuvre, then it might be her 1928 novel *The Children*. The action takes place in various settings across Europe, to emphasize the nomadic existence of an upper-class American social set. At the outset, the Wheater children's nanny Scopy wryly remarks: "The wilderness? The real wilderness is the world *we* live in; packing up our tents every few weeks for another move [. . .] And the marriages just like tents—folded up and thrown away when you've done with them."[67] Here the phrasing signals how wealthy urban sophisticates are, on one level, self-interested hunter-gatherers in a different kind of wilderness, oddly "primitive" and unrefined with regard to matrimony as a shallow exercise in seizing then casually discarding "trophy" partners. Martin Boyne, the protagonist is consistently portrayed as an American patrician scaling the metaphorical peaks of the Old World. Key events are set against the Alps, more precisely the Dolomite mountains in Italy, where Boyne seeks Rose Sellars.[68]

The Children is unusually preoccupied by tropes and processes of visual observation and representation; how to separate, for example, mere "picturesque description" from "rapturous communion."[69] Such emphases bring into sharper focus Ruskin's core proposition that "mountains are the beginning and end of all natural scenery; in them, and in the forms of inferior landscape that lead to them, my affections are wholly bound up."[70] The crucial term here is "forms," and whether it is possible to appreciate them fully given the broader environmental and geopolitical crises in the first three decades of the twentieth century. As Wharton's *False Dawn* illustrates through the portrayal of a charismatic young Ruskin, it is "the cardinal importance of eyesight"[71] that matters—prioritizing the keenest scrutiny (line, color, texture) in one's experience of, the "forms" of the "Cristallo group."[72] Ascribing this significance to mountain phenomena makes it all the more revealing that the watchful Boyne must traverse the slopes to meet Rose: "But perhaps it added to the mystery and enchantment *to see her* he had to climb from the dull promiscuity of his hotel into a clear green solitude alive with the tremor of water under meadow-grasses, and guarded by the great wings of the mountains" (my italics).[73] The mountains are personified, the narrator gives them "wings." But they do not "take flight"; instead, they guard Rose's chalet as if it were a nest. Moreover, these Alpine "forms" provide a constant backdrop to

Boyne and Rose's highly charged moments together: they "watched the cliffs across the valley slowly decompose from flame to ashes."[74] The peaks seem to be in eerie mutation—fleeting effects of climate and light that mirror the shifting, nebulous quality of Boyne and Rose's attachment.

This uncertain quality is implied by Rose's ostensibly casual, light-hearted remark: "I'd a good deal rather be a sunny balcony than a crystal peak. But I enjoy looking out on the peak."[75] One effect of "looking out"—this slippery phrase suggests more the mannered enthusiasm of a moneyed tourist-consumer than a serious aesthetic experience?—prompts us to revisit Burke's conception of the sublime, one that Ruskin had deemed peculiarly problematic and ultimately too narrow for his own ambitious interpretive scheme in *Modern Painters I*. *The Children*'s scenes on the slopes "above the big hotels" gestures to Burke's largely secular discussion of the "passion caused by the great and sublime in *nature*, when those causes operate most powerfully" to engender "Astonishment."[76] This overwhelming affect—the term "astonish/ment" features nine times in *The Children*—seems to reverberate through Rose and Boyne's burgeoning relationship. The mountain becomes their own pastoral idyll, and Rose is entranced by the phenomena—contours, climatic conditions, flora, fauna—that envelops them:

> Every day they went off on an excursion. Sometimes they hired a motor, leaving it, far afield, for a long climb; but neither could afford such luxuries often, nor did they much care for them. Usually they started on foot, with stick and rucksack, getting back only as the great cliffs hung their last luster above the valley.[77]

An "excursion" not only suggests a short, bracing leisure activity but also points to William Wordsworth's lengthy experiment in the georgic mode, *The Excursion* (1814).[78] The intertextual resonance here is complex: Wordsworth's poem hints at a Romantic aesthetic bequest that has *manufactured* the mountains in a way that hampers acts of sympathetic engagement with those remote communities that live and undertake grueling, dangerous work on the slopes. So, if the passage above reflects the multiplied consciousness that Rose and Boyne share on "great cliffs," then it is a fragile feeling that also reveals a core weakness of the Burkean sublime, according to Ruskin's aesthetic precepts in *Modern Painters*. That weakness is the dominance of soaring lyrical subjectivity—two people reveling in their own self-created paradise—over sober empirical study of natural objects like passes, peaks and glaciers. The Burkean mind "so entirely filled with its object, that it cannot entertain any other" can lead to solipsistic self-indulgence—a perilous state, as *The Children* and other Wharton texts illustrate.[79] That peril, however, is not yet explicit

given Rose's excited immersion in the "delicate detail" of their palpable surroundings, which the narrator enhances through eye-catching effects of lush
locution, opulent imagery and phonology:

> She loved all the delicate detail revealed only to walkers: the thrust of
> orchis or colchicum through pine-needles, the stir of brooks, the uncurl-
> ing of perfume fronds, the whirr of wings in the path, and that con-
> tinual pulsation of water and wind and grasses which is the heartbeat
> of the forest.[80]

The narrator skillfully stirs the reader's five senses through alliterative flourishes ("whirr of wings") and verbs of organic activity ("thrust," "uncurling").
This vibrancy and dynamism—a piercing intensity of perception mirrored
and enacted in syntactical structure—underlines how Boyne, though "always
alive to great landscape had hitherto been too busy or preoccupied to note
its particulars."[81] It seems that Boyne's reaction to the forest implies not the
Burkean "effect of the sublime in its highest degree" but rather "the inferior,"
more muted "effects" of "admiration, reverence and respect."[82] These "inferior effects" hint at Boyne's sentiments for Rose by the end of the novel. As
with the mountain peaks, he will be admiring her from afar.

Boyne's "respectful," reticent attitude to the summits is justified to some
extent by his professional background as a consultant engineer. But the
"excursions" at least make possible a different habit of vision: "It was years
since he had rambled among mountains without having to look at them
with an engineering eye, and calculate their relation to a projected railway
or aqueduct; and these walks opened his eyes to unheeded beauties."[83] The
liberating potential of his unhurried, meandering "ramble" is implicitly
measured against the immersive, rigorous attention to panoramic vistas that
Ruskin's disciples endorsed—cultivating over time a "gaze" through which
the pilgrim-traveler might appreciate the imbricated layers of resonance
(numinous, archaeological, botanical) in, say, the Dolomites.[84] This "gaze,"
geared towards moral and aesthetic enlightenment, is presumably very different from Boyne's "engineering eye"—especially given Ruskin's fierce and
outspoken opposition to railway construction and the catastrophic ecological harm it caused in areas of outstanding natural beauty.[85] This ominous
note makes all the more poignant the narrator's remark: "It was like being
led through the flowered borders of an illuminated missal of which he had
hitherto noticed only the central pictures."[86] Here is a reminder that what the
narrator evokes is not just on the horizon but also in written text, an intricate
discursive design. *The Children* is the "illuminated missal"[87] and the narrator
a scribe faithfully committing unspoiled natural scenery to the page. The

narrator's religious terminology—echoed elsewhere in "the smell of crushed herbs" rising "like incense"[88]—implies the alternative, spiritual, anti-capitalist values synonymous with Ruskin's learned gaze, especially his effusive accounts of peaks as natural cathedrals, and his early ardent embrace of Natural Theology, construing Alpine summits as, "in Aquinas's term, God's created Second Book," the organic domain "already textualized."[89]

The narrator is especially adept at showing the vastness of this physical terrain and how it contrasts with the solitude and smallness of the two figures within in: "He and Mrs. Sellars were reclining at ease on a high red ledge of rock, with a view plunging down by pineclad precipices, pastures and forests to illimitable distances of blue Dolomite."[90] The lexis and the alliterative effects ("plunging ... pineclad") convey a note of ease and relaxation, contrasting with the tension Boyne felt on the route there. Again, the narrator appeals to all five senses through narrative strategies, with a particular emphasis on the musicality of the "great billowing landscape": "The air sang with light [...] and the hearts of the lovers were glad with sun and wind, and the glow of a long climb followed by such food as only a rucksack can provide."[91] The mountain phenomena provide a sensory concert for Rose and Boyne, but Rose experiences it more intensely.[92]

What is clear here is that while Rose reacts to the sensory stimulus of this austere grandeur, Boyne is still caught in the meshes of his own professional and affective detachment, never becoming completely enthralled.[93] That is underscored when he is left alone to survey "the world of light and freedom before him": "its spreading mountain slopes, its spires of granite reared into a cloud-pillared sky, and the giant blue shadows racing each other across the valleys, he saw nothing but the narrow thread of railway winding down to Venice and the Wheaters."[94] Here the verbal texture, with its focus on topographical specificity, skirts around the extravagantly "purple," "fine writing" critiqued by the Alpinist Leslie Stephen. Instead, the phrasing reminds us of how new technologies of motion (train, automobile)—and plot trajectories ("the Wheaters")—will radically alter, and "cloud," Boyne's future "prospects."

Wharton complicates Rose and Boyne's brittle pastoral idyll by re-introducing Judith Wheater. One of the eponymous children of this novel, Hermione Lee describes her as "an energetic young heroine who loves racing up forest-clad mountains."[95] Boyne is torn between Rose and Judith, inappropriately so. The mountain walk Judith shares with Boyne is just as significant as the ones he conducted with Rose. However, the vocabulary Wharton's narrator uses to conjure the landscape with Judith reveals vital differences: "The air on that height was as fresh as youth, and all about them were the secret scents that dew and twilight waken into life."[96] Even though it is exactly the same material ground as before, Boyne experiences it (the sibilance of "secret scents") as if he is borne aloft to "fresh heights": "It was no longer Judith drawing him on, but the night itself beckoning him."[97] This is implied by how "the wandering man in him, the man used to mountains, to long lonely tramps, to the hush and mystery of nights in the open, felt himself in the toils of the old magic."[98] Here the lexis carries a mischievous echo of John Greenleaf Whittier's "Prelude" to "Among the Hills" in which he famously declared that North America should deliver a pioneering "man to match his mountains."[99] Boyne's masculinity is of a very different order, and the "magic" quality here seems to evoke, yet also transcend, intimations of Burkean sublime. This is because the entrancing quality is set forth as an intensely private, "lonely" experience. It suggests something of Ruskin's own deep suspicion of succumbing to mere sensations, instead of affirming particular observation of tangible mountain structures: Boyne's "highest moments had always been solitary."[100] A passing statement maybe, but in fact it foreshadows how the novel ends, with Boyne's isolation and the mountain but a mere interlude of companionship and family in his peripatetic existence.

During the mountain walk, Boyne quotes four verses from Robert Browning's poem "A Grammarian's Funeral." If Boyne and Judith's mountain ramble has a magical aspect to it, then the verses Boyne cites become an incantation: "*All the peaks soar, but one the rest excels; / Clouds overcome it; No, yonder sparkle is the citadel's / Circling its summit –*"[101] It is not by chance that the text prioritizes this poem, "set in 14th-century Italy, at the time when Renaissance scholars were beginning to revive the ancient learning of Greece and Rome."[102] In it, the "Grammarian, one such scholar, is dead; and his students sing this song as they carry his corpse to the mountaintop where it is to be buried."[103] This can be construed as an allegory for Boyne himself, who after this mountain sojourn will lose the woman he loves as well as the children he has vowed to protect. He is all but dead. I argue that its significance lies with Rose rather than Boyne however, given the narrator's remark that: "He [Boyne] remembered, at a similar moment, Rose Sellars's quoting."[104] The precise moment when Rose cites this poem to Boyne happens "off page"—it is introduced as a new element during Boyne and Judith's mountain trek. Browning's poem also reverberates here as a cryptic commentary on Rose Sellars, a woman who represents the "ideal" qualities of elite, well-heeled American femininity: she is patient, kind and cultured. Just as he cites those verses, Boyne has unwittingly realized he does not love Rose, and in an echo of the grammarian's fate must set his affection for her "to rest" on the Dolomites.

Rose and Boyne's relationship is crumbling, and this is evidenced through the fact that the mountain scenes are no longer intimate. There is one last brief glimpse of Boyne and Rose among the peaks. It suggests the narrator is striving to take a photograph of the moment for posterity: "Boyne had removed his eyes from Mrs. Sellars's face, and was staring out the familiar outline of the great crimson mountains beyond the balcony."[105] The peaks, no longer enchanting, instead seem merely "familiar." It deviates from the pastoral of Terry Gifford's definition: "The reader recognizes that the country in a pastoral text is an Arcadia because the language is idealized. In other words, pastoral is a discourse, a way of using language that constructs a different kind of world" from that of mimetic "realism."[106] For Boyne, the cosmopolitan fret of the populous and prosperous city has infiltrated the mountain sanctuary. He reflects: "A phrase of Stevenson's about 'the lovely and detested scene' (from 'The Ebb-tide', he thought?) strayed through his mind as he gazed."[107] This allusion to one of Stevenson's last works (co-authored with his stepson Lloyd Osbourne), detailing the misadventures of three beachcombers, is suggestive.[108] First of all Stevenson, unlike one of his editors, Leslie Stephen, did not share Burke's "Astonishment" at snow-covered peaks or gorges. Indeed, Stevenson's disappointed travel essays furnish a piquant contrast to the effusive and buoyant style of Ruskin's Alpine acolytes.[109] Moreover, Boyne's recall of the words that describe Papeete, the capital of Tahiti, also apply to Cortina, in Italy. This reference to a sea adventure serves as a pointed reminder that *The Children* began on a boat departing from Algiers. Ultimately, moneyed, elite American tourists in Europe are "beachcombers" of sorts—a faint echo of the nanny's earlier judgment of the patrician class as rootless, rapacious and nomadic tribes: "It was hateful to him to think that he might hereafter come to associate those archangelic summits with [...] Mr. Dobree's knowledge of the inner history of the Westway divorce."[110] This is because Boyne, unlike Rose, has never truly *inhabited* the Burkean sublime. So, he exclaims: "'Aren't you getting rather sick of this place?'." Boyne clarifies what he means:

> "Of the whole show." His sweeping gesture gathered up in one contemptuous handful the vast panorama of mountain, vale and forest. "I always feel that scenery gets mixed up with our personal bothers and all the virtue goes out of it—as if our worries were so many locusts, eating everything bare."[111]

Boyne's telling remark—"scenery gets mixed up with our personal bothers"—returns us to Ruskin's and Wharton's concern with the Burkean sublime, and how in the first volume of *Modern Painters* the subjectivist emphasis ("a strictly sensual pleasure") ultimately encroaches upon, pollutes and overwhelms the greatness of dimension of the singular natural object itself.[112] "To see clearly," Ruskin posits in *Modern Painters III*, "is poetry, prophecy, and religion—all in one."[113] As *False Dawn* reveals, Wharton appreciates the centrality of the process of observation itself rather than brittle emotional conclusions extracted from it. But here, Boyne implies that the "vast panorama of mountain" has been rather *consumed* in a heedless and hectic fashion to the point where "everything" is eaten "bare."

Through evocations of seasonal rhythms, the text signals that the mountain stay is ending. Just as the landscape will "freeze" over, so will this story between Rose and Boyne and Judith. "But summer was waning in the high valleys of the Dolomites; tourists were scattering, the big hotels preparing to close."[114] The lexis of this finale is performative—as if nature's "curtain" is closing and the mountain events were an Act in a pastoral cosmopolitan drama: "Two days afterward, the ship which had brough him to Europe started on her voyage back to Brazil. On her deck stood Boyne, a lonely man."[115] Given the destination, we are left to speculate that Martin Boyne took an engineering job at Fordlândia,[116] Henry Ford's utopian project in the Amazon that was founded the same year as *The Children* was published.

Notes

1 Wharton recounts that: "one morning, climbing a woodland path with my governess and some other children, I was seized by an agony of pain – and after that for many long weeks life was confused and feverish misery. I was desperately ill with typhoid fever". See *A Backward Glance*, 41.

2 Wharton, *The Holy Bible*, 1091.

3 Lee, *Edith Wharton*, 17.

4 For a detailed account of these Old Testament and symbolic resonances see Tynan, *The Desert in Modern Literature*.

5 "Whenever this trip took place, it must have been an amazing experience to climb the Swiss Alps in an open sleigh. The Whartons' young servants, Gross and White, must also have been thrilled by this kind of travel, which they would surely not have experienced had they not been employed by people as adventurous as the Whartons." See Wharton, *My Dear Governess*, 99.

6 Wharton, *My Dear Governess*, 99.

7 Wharton, *My Dear Governess*, 99.

8 Wharton, *My Dear Governess*, 100.

9 Wharton, *My Dear Governess*, 100.

10 Wharton, *My Dear Governess*, 100.

11 Leslie Stephen, "The Regrets of a Mountaineer." *The Playground of Europe*. Longmans, Green and Co., 1871, 263–98, 268. Stephen was an influential member and a President (1865-1868) of The Alpine Club, a dining society which John Ruskin was, at one point, invited to join.

12 Edith Wharton, "George Eliot [Review of Leslie Stephen's *George Eliot*]." *The Bookman*, vol. 15, May 1902, 247–51. Wharton's discerning piece uncovers the sexual double standard which is at the core of an eminent Victorian male writer's account of a female novelist's literary lexis and technical achievements.

13 Stephen records how Ruskin's "*Modern Painters* infected me and other early members of the Alpine Club with an enthusiasm for which I hope, we are still grateful." See Stephen, "John Ruskin" [1900], *The National Review.* In *Studies of a Biographer.* Vol. 3, Duckworth, 1902, 83–118.

14 Wharton's lexis echoes Ruskin when he conducts an "examination of the principal precipices among the Alps," especially the "mountain paths [...] *all fringed* under its shuddering curve with the *ferns that fear* the light" (my emphasis). See Ruskin, John. *Modern Painters, Part V: Of Mountain Beauty.* Volume IV. Smith, Elder and Co., 1904, p. 319.

15 Stephen's journalism and letters frequently register exasperation with what he considered Ruskin's highly eccentric and "excessive sensibility which *bursts* all restraints of logic and common sense" (my emphasis). See Leslie Stephen, "Mr. Ruskin's Recent Writings." *Fraser's Magazine,* vol. 9, no. 54, 1874, 688–701; also, Stephen, "Mr. Ruskin's *Fors Clavigera.*" *Saturday Review,* vol. 31, no. 7, 1871, 13–14. On Stephen's awkward personal and professional relationship with Ruskin see Gregory C. G. Moore and Helen Fordham, "The Victorian Effort to Exclude the Amateur 'Public Intellectual' from Economics: The Case of Stephen Versus Ruskin." *History of Economics Review,* vol. 66, no. 1, 2017, 19–43.

16 Stephen, "A Substitute for the Alps," 460.

17 Wharton, *Glimpses of the Moon,* 11.

18 Stephen, "The Regrets of a Mountaineer," 268.

19 Stephen, "A Substitute for the Alps," 461.

20 Ruskin, *Complete Works,* vol. 5, 375. According to Brian Day, Ruskin's landscape aesthetics here carries echoes of the Kantian aesthetic judgement that refines Rousseau's linking of human affect and moral compass. This judgement, anchored in awareness of the sublime, ministers to one's spiritual nobility. See Day, "The Moral Intuition of Ruskin's 'Storm-Cloud.'" *Studies in English Literature, 1500-1900,* vol. 45, no. 4, 2005, 917–33. *JSTOR,* www.jstor.org/stable/3844621. Accessed May 28, 2021.

21 Stephen, "The Regrets of a Mountaineer," 268.

22 The original Italian manuscript can be found in the Duke University Library Archive: https://archives.lib.duke.edu/catalog/whartonedith

23 Wharton, "The Duchess at Prayer," Vintage, 110–27, 110.

24 Maureen E. Montgomery, "Leisured Lives," *Edith Wharton in Context,* edited by Laura Rattray. Cambridge University Press, 2012, 234–42, 240.

25 Wharton, *The Age of Innocence,* 118–19.

26 Wharton, *The Age of Innocence,* 119.

27 Wharton, *The Custom of the Country,* 259–555.

28 Wharton, *The Custom of the Country,* 331.

29 Lee, *Edith Wharton,* 429.

30 Wharton, *The Custom of the Country,* 331.

31 Wharton, *The Custom of the Country,* 331.

32 Stewart O'Nan, *Wish You Were Here.* Grove Press, 2002, 89.

33 Stephen, "A Substitute for the Alps," 461. On Stephen in relation to the history of tourism see Malcolm Andrews, *The Search for the Picturesque: Landscape Aesthetics and Tourism in Britain, 1760-1800.* Scholar Press, 1990.

34 Wharton, *The Custom of the Country,* 339.

35 Wharton, *The Custom of the Country,* 340.

36 Wharton, *The Custom of the Country,* 340.

37 Wharton, *The Custom of the Country,* 340.

38 Wharton, "False Dawn," 70.

39 Georg Simmel, "The Alpine Journey." *Theory, Culture and Society*, vol. 8, 1991, 95–98. Simmel's slyly phrased article, originally published in 1895, suggests how the Alpine holiday is marketed to the tourist with deep pockets, as a "profound" moral and educational experience. For Simmel, such marketing conceals what is, at best, only a trite, "momentary rapture." Ultimately, the "power of capitalism extends itself to ideas [...] it is capable of annexing such a distinguished concept as education as its own private property."

40 Wharton, *The Custom of the Country*, 340.

41 Mark Twain, *A Tramp Abroad*. American Publishing Co., 1880, 345–46.

42 John Urry's research is revealing in this regard. See his *Consuming Places*. Routledge, 1995, 129–63; *The Tourist Gaze: Leisure and Travel in Contemporary Societies*. Sage, 1990; Margaret Grieco and John Urry, eds., *Mobilities: New Perspectives on Transport and Society*. Routledge, 2012.

43 Stephen, "A Substitute for the Alps," 461.

44 Simmel, "The Alpine Journey," 97.

45 Wharton, *The Custom of the Country*, 287–88.

46 Wharton, "False Dawn," 7–80, 39.

47 Wharton, "False Dawn," 39.

48 Wharton, "False Dawn," 42, 73.

49 Lord Byron, "Savoy: Mont Blanc," *Manfred*, Act 1, Scene 1, 1817.

50 Keith Hanley and John K. Walton have explored in searching detail the influence of eighteenth-century theories of the sublime and Romantic depictions of vertiginous landscapes on Ruskin's initial conception of the Alps. Ruskin especially valued Sir Walter Scott's evocation of the Scottish Highlands in his *Waverley* novels and Byron's portrayal of Alpine sublimity in *Childe Harold's Pilgrimage* (1812-18) and *Manfred* (1817). When young Ruskin glimpsed the Alps for the first time in 1833 whilst travelling around Europe, his response is expressed both in his poem "The Alps from Schaffhausen" composed at the time and recollected in *Praeterita*. See Hanley and Walton, *Constructing Cultural Tourism: John Ruskin and the Tourist Gaze*. Channel View Publications, 2010, 1–24; John Hayman, *John Ruskin and Switzerland*. Wilfred Laurier University Press, 1990, 3–28; Ann C. Colley, "John Ruskin: Climbing and the Vulnerable Eye." *Victorian Literature and Culture*, vol. 37, no. 1, 2009, 43–66. *JSTOR*, www.jstor.org/stable/40347213. Accessed May 28, 2021.

51 Wharton, "False Dawn," 44. Key secondary sources on Ruskin and the Alps include Dinah Birch's *Ruskin on Turner* (1990), George Landow's *The Aesthetic and Critical Theories of John Ruskin* (1971), Paul Walton's *The Drawings of John Ruskin* (1972), and Robert Hewison's *John Ruskin: The Argument of the Eye* (1976), in addition to his publication to coincide with an exhibition at Tate Britain: "Ruskin, Turner and the Pre-Raphaelites" (2000).

52 John Ruskin, *Praeterita and Dilecta*. Edited by E. T. Cook and Alexander Wedderburn. George Allen, 1908, 330.

53 Wharton, "False Dawn," 73.

54 See Hanley and Walton, *Constructing Cultural Tourism: John Ruskin and the Tourist Gaze*, 3–24.

55 Wharton, "False Dawn," 70.

56 Wharton, "False Dawn," 73.

57 Other important texts by Ruskin with Alpine themes include *The Elements of Drawing* (1857), *Lectures on Landscape* (1871) and *Deucalion: Collected Studies of the Lapse of Waves*,

and Life of Stones (1879). These books suggest an interest in the region well into the 1870s according to Ann C. Colley in *Victorians in the Mountains: Sinking the Sublime.* Routledge, 2010.

58 Wharton, "False Dawn," 72.

59 Ruskin, *Modern Painters* I, 48.

60 See Hanley and Walton, *Constructing Cultural Tourism: John Ruskin and the Tourist Gaze*; Dinah Birch, *Ruskin on Turner*, Cassell, 1990, 11–13.

61 Ruskin's response to Burke's thought is found in his chapter "Of the Sublime," which closes part one of *Modern Painters I.* Ending the text in this manner lends greater rhetorical force to Ruskin's critique: "Beauty is not so often felt to be sublime; because in many kinds of purely material beauty there is some truth in Burke's assertion that 'littleness' is one of its elements [...] I take the widest possible ground of investigation, that sublimity is found wherever anything elevates the mind." See Ruskin, *Modern Painters I*, 129–30.

62 As John Batchelor contends, for Ruskin sublimity "expresses the effect of greatness, including great beauty, on the temperament" but the fundamental issue remains the essence of that original greatness in the mountain ranges which trigger sublime affect. See John Batchelor, *John Ruskin: A Life.* Carroll & Graf, 2006, 57–58.

63 John Ruskin, *The Seven Lamps of Architecture.* Dover Publications, 2017, 33.

64 Ruskin, The *Seven Lamps of Architecture*, 33.

65 Wharton, "False Dawn," 70.

66 John Ruskin, *Little Masterpieces.* Doubleday and McClure, 1898.

67 Wharton, *The Children*, 23.

68 The "quest" element in Wharton's text evokes Ruskin's terms: "Before it, all had been ascent; after it, all was decline; both, indeed by winding paths and varied slopes; both interrupted, like the gradual rise and fall of the passes of the Alps, by great mountain outliers." See Ruskin, *Works* 8: 90.

69 Wharton, *The Children*, 151.

70 E. T. Cook and Alexander Wedderburn, eds., "The Mountain Glory." *The Works of John Ruskin*, by John Ruskin. vol. 6, Cambridge: Cambridge University Press, 2010, 418–66. Cambridge Library Collection – Works of John Ruskin, 418.

71 Michael Wheeler, *Ruskin's God.* Cambridge University Press, 1999, 22.

72 Wharton, *The Children*, 22.

73 Wharton, *The Children*, 83.

74 Wharton, *The Children*, 83.

75 Wharton, *The Children*, 83–84.

76 Edmund Burke, *Philosophical Enquiry into the Origin of Our Ideas of the Sublime and Beautiful.* Edited by Adam Phillips. Oxford University Press, 1990, 53. See also Philip Shaw, *The Sublime.* Routledge, 2006. Burke continues: "In this case the mind is so entirely filled with its object, that it cannot entertain any other, nor by consequences reason on that object which employs it," 53.

77 Wharton, *The Children*, 85.

78 On Wharton's admiration for Wordsworth's oeuvre see *My Dear Governess*, 51–52.

79 Burke, *Philosophical Enquiry*, 53.

80 Wharton, *The Children*, 85.

81 Wharton, *The Children*, 85.

82 Burke, *Philosophical Enquiry*, 53.

83 Wharton, *The Children*, 85–86.

84 Ruskin's cultural kudos in the world of "travel-adventures" is felt at the start of *The Children*: "Ruskin on the lake of Geneva," 1–2.

85 Ruskin became increasingly agitated by the combined "blight" of mass tourism and railroad expansion, especially in the Alps: "Chamouni itself and the rest of Switzerland are completely spoiled by railroads, huge hotels, and architects out of employ." See Ruskin, *Complete Works*, vol. 36, 340.

86 Wharton, *The Children*, 86.

87 This phrase evokes Ruskin scholars Hanley and Walton, who describe the publications of Ruskin's travels – such as *Stones of Venice* and *Mornings in Florence* – as "precious volumes, often bound in leather and vellum, with rich tooling and florally decorated inner linings, which resemble missals," 52.

88 Wharton, *The Children*, 97.

89 Hanley and Walton, *Constructing Cultural Tourism: John Ruskin and the Tourist Gaze*, 58. For these scholars, Ruskin's account of European mountains "never entirely loses the trace of a pre-evolutionary sense of deist design coupled with an evangelical reading of Biblical theology," 58–59.

90 Wharton, *The Children*, 97.

91 Wharton, *The Children*, 97.

92 Wharton, *The Children*, 99.

93 It is worth recalling Burke on "Astonishment" as "the effect of the sublime in its highest degree; the inferior effects are admiration, reverence and respect," 53.

94 Wharton, *The Children*, 144.

95 Lee, *Edith Wharton*, 663.

96 Wharton, *The Children*, 186.

97 Wharton, *The Children*, 186.

98 Wharton, *The Children*, 186.

99 John Greenleaf Whittier, "Prelude", "Among the Hills." *The Poetic Works of John Greenleaf Whittier*. Vol. 1, Houghton Mifflin, 1892. 4 vols, 263.

100 Wharton, *The Children*, 186.

101 Wharton, *The Children*, 184.

102 Robert Browning, *The Major Works*. Edited by Adam Roberts. Oxford University Press, 1997, 767.

103 Browning, *Major Works*, 767.

104 Wharton, *The Children*, 184.

105 Wharton, *The Children*, 202.

106 Gifford, *Pastoral*, 45.

107 Wharton, *The Children*, 202.

108 Vanessa Smith, "Piracy and Exchange: Stevenson's Pacific Fiction." *Robert Louis Stevenson*, edited by Harold Bloom. Chelsea House Publishers, 2005, 261–306.

109 Four essays by Stevenson – "Davos in Winter" (1881), "Health and Mountains" (1881), "Alpine Diversions" (1881) and "The Stimulation of the Alps" (1881) evoke his first winter in Davos, Switzerland where he was sent to cure his weak chest. He resided in Davos from early November 1880 to April 1881. He returned for his second sojourn in October 1881. On Stevenson's very flat feelings for the lofty heights (the immediate terrain induced in him a bout of writer's block), see Colley, *Victorians in the Mountains*, 201–16; see also Susan Barton, *Healthy Living in the Alps: The Origins of Winter Tourism in Switzerland 1860-1914*. Manchester University Press, 2008.

110 Wharton, *The Children*, 202–03.

111 Wharton, *The Children*, 203.

112 "All high or noble emotion", Ruskin remarks, "is [...] rendered physically impossible while the mind exults in what is very likely a strictly sensual pleasure". See *Modern Painters I*, 102. It is tempting to conclude that Ruskin is targeting the problems of Burke's conception of sublime affect here.

113 Ruskin, *Modern Painters III*, 333.

114 Wharton, *The Children*, 271.

115 Wharton, *The Children*, 347.

116 For more on Fordlândia, see Greg Grandin, *Fordlandia: The Rise and Fall of Henry Ford's Forgotten Jungle City*. Metropolitan Books, 2009.

Chapter 8

RURAL AMERICANA AND THE "NEW WORLD" MOUNTAINS

Wharton's perception and relation to the mountain phenomena of her "homeland" differs markedly from her aesthetic engagement with Alpine topography. Sharon Dean notes how Wharton "preferred the rises and dips and curves against a backdrop of hills to the overpowering quality of mountains made visible in so many paintings and illustrations of America's western landscapes."[1] This is, however, a rather reductive view. It buttresses the stereotype of Wharton as a haughty cosmopolite who is far too genteel for North American soil, its rustic communities, earthy manners and idioms—an image that situates her as an advocate of James Fenimore Cooper's thesis that "any well-delineated view of a high-class Swiss scene, must at once convince even the most provincial mind among us that nothing of the sort is to be found in America, east of the Rocky Mountains."[2] In fact, Wharton's depictions of summits and ridges in the "New World" are dynamic, nuanced and highly variegated. A brief description of the landscapes of the American West, as in "The Journey," is relevant here: "The train was rushing through a region of bare hillocks huddled against a lifeless sky. It looked like the first day of creation."[3] The stillness of this barren terrain is indicative of how Wharton views the American peak as a locus of unexplored possibility.

Wharton's rural New England narratives evoke and interrogate the second way of "writing peaks" that Leslie Stephen articulates in "The Regrets of a Mountaineer"—what he terms "the sporting view of the mountains."[4] He records how such authors "affect something like cynicism; they mix descriptions of scenery with allusions to fleas or to bitter beer."[5] Wharton's myriad accounts of the "New World" peaks often partake of this "cynical" element, incorporating the ornate yet ominous lexis synonymous with an "Old World" *fin de siècle* stylistic register. Nevertheless, it is not for the reasons Stephen alludes to: "they humbly try to amuse us because they can't strike us with awe."[6] Wharton's European texts furnish various expressions of "awe." The

New England narratives meanwhile reveal a different rhetorical and affective lexicon to portray these lofty landforms.

New England topography haunts Wharton to such an extent that it can be summoned imaginatively in the middle of a bustling Paris, as is the case with *Madame de Treymes*: "A vision of earnest women in Shetland shawls, with spectacles and thin knobs of hair, eating blueberry-pie at unwholesome hours in a shingled dining-room on a bare New England hilltop, rose pallidly between Durham and the verdant brightness of the Champs Elysées."[7] Moreover, the American mountain range can be a place of contemplation and relief, as is the case for Dexter Manford in Wharton's 1927 novel *Twilight Sleep*: "He stretched himself out under a walnut tree on a sunlit slope, lit his pipe and gazed abroad over the fields and woods. All the land was hazy with incipient life."[8] A Whitmanesque resonance can be felt here, but terms like "bare," "hazy" and "incipient" evoke *forms* that require literary treatment beyond the standard tropes and narrative tactics synonymous with the Romantic sublime.

The Derelict Mountain Villages of New England

In *A Backward Glance*, Wharton reflects: "For years I had wanted to draw life as it really was in the derelict mountain villages of New England."[9] From that desire *Ethan Frome* came to fruition and it was published in 1911. Coincidentally this was the year Wharton sold The Mount, her home in the Berkshire mountains and moved permanently to Europe. What started as a French language exercise,[10] entitled "Hiver," went on to become one of her few fictional pieces that take place in an austere New England:

> Before my own time there was up, I had learned to know what that meant. Yet I had come in the degenerate day of trolley, bicycle and rural delivery, when communication was easy between the scattered mountain villages, and the bigger towns in the valleys, such as Bettsbridge and Shadd's Falls, had libraries, theatres and Y. M. C. A. halls to which the youth of the hills could descend for recreation.[11]

The opening chapter of Ethan Frome suggests an account drawn from oral tradition, measuring the spontaneity of speech against the permanency of print.[12] The narrator, by emphasizing the lonely and "scattered mountain villages" and "bigger towns in the valleys," shows how the rugged higher altitudes become geographic saliences of remoteness. The mountains rise above and (even with the means of communication available at the time) are difficult to reach. This is why Alan Henry Rose proposes that "*Ethan Frome* offers the first full expression of the effects of New England in Wharton's fiction."[13] He adds that one of the "components" of these effects is "the void characteristic of the setting."[14] However, is the "setting" completely "void," or rather inaccessible due to harsh terrain and weather: "winter shut down on Starkfield and the village lay under a sheet of snow perpetually renewed from the pale skies, I began to see what life there—or rather its negation—must have been in Ethan Frome's young manhood."[15] Frome seems to embody the forlorn qualities of his "scattered mountain village": he becomes "a part of the mute melancholy landscape, an incarnation of this frozen woe, with all that was warm and sentient in him fast bound below the surface; but there was nothing unfriendly in his silence."[16]

This "mute melancholy landscape"—so far removed from the glossy lawns and "amenity" of Bellomont in *The House of Mirth*—gestures at what critic Leo Marx calls a "wholly new conception of the precariousness of our relations with nature" and how it is "bound to" elicit "new versions of pastoral."[17] What "new version"—if indeed it is new—does Wharton craft here, portraying a "winter morning" where "sunrise burned red in a pure sky [...] and beyond the white and scintillating fields patches of far-off forest hung like smoke"?[18] The temperature is evoked by "clear as crystal," "pure," "white" and "scintillating"—while the "sunrise burned red" it cannot melt the snow.[19] Barbara A. White contends that Wharton "uses snow and cold" to generate "a frightening" ambience at odds with the orthodox consolations of a pastoral mode.[20] This rural New England may seem a lackluster hinterland, offering only "frozen woe" when compared to the more populous towns, but it is not necessarily "frightening." The setting of *Ethan Frome* is an edgeland, remodeling pastoral tropes to represent and reflect upon environmental concerns in a very different way: "It was in the early morning stillness, when his muscles were swinging to their familiar task and his lungs expanding with long draughts of mountain air, that Ethan did his clearest thinking."[21] In his misery, habituated to hardscrabble toil, Ethan seems to experience a moment of peace and clarity. This condition invites comparison with one of the six aspects of the "post-pastoral" that Terry Gifford discusses:

> It has been known for some time that people who live beside a tree or with a cat, or tend a garden or a horse, gain some sense of themselves, or their own circles of growth and decay, and of their emotional ebbs and flows that are unavailable to the inhabitants of the concrete tower blocks.[22]

What "sense" of himself does Ethan gain in such grim physical surroundings, though—a milieu that appears to "seize the characters in its steely grip"?[23] It can be argued that Ethan's mountain moment of vision gives him the idea that is ultimately his undoing: "He knew a case of a man over the mountain—a young fellow of about his own age—who had escaped from just such a life of misery by going West with the girl he cared for."[24] This is not the fate of Ethan, Zeena and Mattie. It is as if Ethan is bound to the "mountain itself," which engenders feelings of indecision and stasis, caught as he is in the meshes of economic necessity. This sense of confinement is what Lawrence Buell ascribes to *Ethan Frome*: "Yet increasingly unfamiliar exurban landscapes could easily transmute themselves from pastoral spaces apart to spaces of entrapment."[25]

There is, however, a crucial exception to this feeling of "entrapment" and suffocation. As Ethan Frome develops feelings for Mattie Silver, he starts to regard the bleak small villages differently. The narrator uses the window to "frame" a picture of the physical environment, defined by subtle gradations of light and darkness: "As he lay there, the window-pane that faced him, growing gradually lighter, inlaid upon the darkness a square of moon-suffused sky."[26] The Frome farmhouse is Zeena's "territory," whereas the desire for Mattie is experienced outdoors, in the New England mountainous terrain. Birdsong reminds Ethan of Mattie's "laughter," and she later "becomes" part of this natural milieu:

> Then, toward sunset, coming down from the mountain where he had been felling timber, he had been caught by some strayed revelers and drawn into the group by the lake, where Mattie, encircled by facetious youths, and bright as a blackberry under her spreading hat, was brewing coffee over a gipsy fire.[27]

The extract is marked by some peculiar tonal and intertextual resonances. The unaffected spontaneity, grace and vigor of Mattie "bright as a blackberry" clashes with the faint trace of mannered artifice in "facetious youths" and "gipsy fire." "[S]trayed revelers" evokes Matthew Arnold's 1849 unrhymed lyric poem whose enigmatic ambivalence about whether to detach oneself from or ecstatically embrace the multifarious forms of elemental nature compels us to reappraise Wharton's lexis—and Ethan's plight more broadly. Arnold's potent descriptive and rhythmic strategies, charting and enacting the Youth's delirious immersion in his palpable locale haunts the edges of the passage above: "Where *red-berried* ashes fringe / The clear-brown shallow pools; / With streaming flanks, and heads / Rear'd proudly, snuffing /The *mountain wind*" (my emphasis). The "frozen" features of Wharton's fictional milieu seem to be "thawed" momentarily by the bracing, raucous pursuits of the nomadic "revelers." This is why it is particularly suggestive when Mattie loses her locket in the grass, and it is Ethan who finds it: "They had sat for a few minutes on the fallen log by the pond, and she had missed her gold locket, and set the young men searching for it; and it was Ethan who had spied it in the moss."[28] Ethan and Mattie's relationship is tied to the mountains—and the life of bare subsistence—that they are unable to leave. This novella is a fragment of their story: "That was all; but all their intercourse had been made up of just such inarticulate flashes, when they seemed to come suddenly upon happiness as if they had surprised a butterfly in the winter woods."[29] Butterflies mostly hibernate during the winter, and they live for a few days during the summer. This imagery foreshadows the other Wharton novella that takes place in this comfortless region, during summer, dealing "with the same type of people involved in a different tragedy of isolation."[30] In a letter to American historian Gaillard Lapsley on December 21, 1916, Wharton tells him about her latest fictional enterprise: "It is known to its author & her familiars as the Hot Ethan, the scene being laid in the neighborhood of Windsor Mountain, & the time being summer which is also the title of the book."[31]

The Case of "The Mountain" in *Summer*

In *A Backward Glance*, Wharton relates that: "I may mention every detail about the colony of drunken mountain outlaws described in 'Summer' was given to me by the rector of the church at Lenox (near where we lived), and that the lonely peak I have called 'the Mountain' was in reality Bear Mountain, an isolated summit not more than twelve miles from our own home."[32] The mysterious "Mountain" in Wharton's 1917 novella *Summer* is repeatedly identified as "the bad place."[33] This landform in *Summer* descends from a literary tradition where these peaks are "craggy, inaccessible and intimidating," as Fred Botting states in his seminal account of the Gothic mode.[34] Charity Royall, the protagonist, is born in poverty on the Mountain, a mark of "lowly" status, a fact that is never forgotten or overlooked: "She had been 'brought down from the Mountain'; from the scarred cliff that lifted its sullen wall above the lesser slopes of Eagle Range, making a perpetual background of gloom to the lonely valley."[35] This "cliff," forbidding rather than fertile, supplies the starkest contrast to the glamorous Alpine resorts in Wharton's oeuvre—chic chalets and hotels cannily packaged for moneyed New Yorkers as commodities which reproduce cozy familiarities of "home."[36] That the uninviting cliff is "scarred" implies both the violence of geological processes over immense stretches of time and more recent, irreversible, man-made disfigurements to the "face" of Mother Nature.

In the same year that *Summer* was published, Wharton embarked on a tour of Morocco. The travelogue, *In Morocco*, was the result. It records how women in harems *"are brought down from mountains* and cedar forests, from the free life of the tents where the nomad women go unveiled" (my emphasis).[37] Charity in *Summer* is not yet an ornamental or "harem" woman, as she was merely a child when she left the Mountain: "She had been told that she was ill of a fever [...] and she could only remember waking one day in a cot at the foot of Mrs. Royall's bed."[38] The Mountain is first introduced in the text as the very antithesis of Mount Olympus in Greek mythology. Only at the end of the novella, when Charity ascends it, are we shown the miserable conditions of these altitudes. Denis Cosgrove and Stephen Daniels remind us that a "landscape is a cultural image, a pictorial way of representing, structuring or symbolizing surroundings."[39] This is especially true of the Mountain: though it "was a good fifteen miles away [...] it rose so abruptly from the lower hills that it seemed almost to cast its shadow over North Dormer."[40]

While the narrator notes the Mountain's geological features, there is also a stress on the symbolic resonances of the site: "If ever, in the purest summer sky, there trailed a thread of vapor over North Dormer, it drifted to the Mountain as a ship drifts to a whirlpool, and was caught among the rocks, torn up and multiplied, to sweep back over the village in rain and darkness."[41] Comparing the Mountain to the locus of a shipwreck invites comparison with Simon C. Estok's definition of "ecophobia" in a 2009 essay as "an irrational and groundless hatred of the natural world, as present and subtle in our daily lives and literature." In this section I will show that the Mountain in *Summer* illustrates ecophobia, where characters cannot help but think and speak of this material "nature" as a "hostile opponent."[42] No matter how much figures try to engage with, domesticate or dominate the Mountain zone, it is an implacable entity which eludes or thwarts their efforts to comprehend it. The Mountain represents a place of malign inscrutability, foreboding, even Gothic terror; variously suggested by Charity, its geographical specificities and its mythology. When Charity remarks that "a cloud over the Mountain always means trouble," we are alerted to how this terrain can have its own *unearthly* aura. It is here that Estok's recent coinage usefully overlaps with the "ecogothic," as Keetley and Wynn Sivils propose in their 2018 essay collection *Ecogothic in Nineteenth-Century American Literature*: "At the broadest level," the ecogothic "inevitably intersects with ecophobia, not only because ecophobic representations of nature will be infused, like the gothic, with fear and dread but also because ecophobia is born out of the failure of humans to control their lives and their world. And control, or lack thereof, is central to the gothic."[43]

Those who live in and around North Dormer voice ecophobic sentiments, since the Mountain exists beyond the "harsh" and hypocritical "code of the village."[44] That is why *Summer* is not an example of an American "regional" text in the strictest sense, as Martha Billips indicates: "The Mountain colony which looms above North Dormer, the place from which Charity comes and to which she later flees" is a "significant alteration to the regional story."[45] This "alteration" is suggested by the Mountain's status as an edgeland at altitude, where the apparent absence of agriculture signals a life of profound hardship and lawless penury. In fact, Charity makes the only reference to agriculture in the text: "the savage misery of the Mountain farmers."[46] Although a contributor to *The New York Times Book Review* oddly described *Summer* in 1917 as "a pleasing romance of village life," there are no thriving agrarian businesses, no carefree shepherds or plentiful harvests in this novella.[47] Wharton's portrayal of Mountain "outlaws" and their "little independent kingdom"—a "bare ground overgrown with docks and nettles"[48]—avoids the soothing pastoral flourishes synonymous with the work of Sarah Orne Jewett or similar local colorists. *Summer* demands a different kind of ecocritical analysis, one that registers Dana Phillips's call, in *The Truth of Ecology* (2003), for the environmental humanities to show "a less devotional attitude" towards "the outdoors" by prioritizing the lonely backwoods and edgelands, as well as the negative, disturbing facets of human-nature relations.[49] Martha Billips's recent interpretation develops this view: Wharton "seems to shift attention from the soil to the individuals who till it, and to find both wanting."[50]

We are informed of the tangled history of the Mountain colony by two different sources. Curiously, the first one is a second-hand account from a New Yorker, Lucius Harney: "Down at Creston they told me that the first colonists are supposed to have been men who worked on the railway that was built forty or fifty years ago between Springfield and Nettleton."[51] The denizens of the Mountain, who came to New England to improve the infrastructure, later reject this modern technology by retreating further into "austere seclusion."[52] That they are designated as "colonists" seems to hint at the very foundation of the United States itself and its people as hunter-gatherers or savage "outlaws," which Harney explains: "Some of them took to drink, or got into trouble with the police, and went off—disappeared into the woods. A year or two later there was a report that they were living up on the Mountain. Then I suppose others joined them—and children were born."[53] The last sentence is especially foreboding, since by the end of the novella Harney and Charity's unborn child almost becomes a "heathen" Mountain dweller.[54] The apparent disorder of this community—reflecting how the Mountain subverts "laws" of genre (literary regionalism, pastoral and georgic traditions)—is highlighted in Harney's next remark: "Now they say there are over a hundred people up there. They seem to be quite outside the jurisdiction of the valleys. No school, no church—and no sheriff ever goes up to see what they're about." In the grim parlance of interwar race science and social hygiene, the Mountain ghetto seems dysgenic.[55] Untethered from the status quo and the spurious fictions of citizenship—"on top of the hill" a "handful of people who don't give a damn for anybody"[56]—these figures are depicted as if they are waste(d). A rudimentary *refuge*—the Mountain—has become a place of *refuse* (human detritus) and stubborn *refusal* (of "civilized" decorum).[57] Frequently portrayed as a mass or herd, the Mountain folk—"poor swamp-people living like vermin in their lair"—represent a racial and class taint to the prim defenders of the village hierarchy.[58] (Charity is, of course, painfully conscious of her own "tainted origin" and "*swarthy*" face).[59] *Summer* addresses this prejudice fostered by the "valley" people who, lacking a modicum of environmental empathy, treat unhusbanded "nature"—and the undesirables associated with it—as an adversary that, in Estok's terms, "hurts, hinders, threatens, or kills."[60]

This ecophobic sentiment is thrown into sharper relief by Lawyer Royall's remarks: "Why, the Mountain's a blot—that what it is, sir, a blot. That scum up there ought to have been run in long ago—and would have, if the people down here hadn't been clean scared of them."[61] The lawyer's earthy vernacular reveals not only a fake moral "high ground" but also deep-seated anxieties about monitoring an edgeland at altitude—what separates the pure/genteel from sullied, drunken and abject bodies ("scum," "*clean* scared"). His crude phrasing does not evince the morbid fear of nature that is anchored in our behavior patterns and survival mechanisms. A rational and basic wariness of certain wild animals, for instance, is, as Estok contends, "written into our genes."[62] Rather, the lawyer's intemperate view of the Mountain folk has been distorted into an instinctual loathing of those classified as *feral*, utterly beyond the "pale" (evoking the "pale walls" of Mrs. Hatchard's "sitting-room"). The lawyer's misgivings are based on the fact that Mountain people are "herded together in a sort of passive promiscuity in which their common misery was the strongest link."[63] Here "link" hints at *missing links*—the bestial other like Charity's pitiful, impoverished mother, whose corpse resembles "a dead dog in a ditch" and the Mountain folk whose movements ape "the heads of nocturnal animals."[64] "[P]romiscuity" suggests incest or at least some violation of the bourgeois family model and taboos that define wholesome living, according to the lawyer. Moreover, the social structures implied by "up there" (a denigrated atavistic enclave) and "down here" (the *clean*-living, law-abiding villagers) invert those in Wharton's European narratives where the elite New York tourists savor the rarefied atmosphere of Alpine peaks while the "lowly" travelers are consigned to cheaper, shabbier lodgings closer to earth.

Lawyer Royall's locutions also demonstrate how a "blot" on rural New England cannot be erased nor can it be aligned with the disciplinary frameworks and respectability synonymous with "down here." "[B]lot" also points to the lamentable condition of Mountain dwellings. These shanties are far

worse than anything depicted in *Ethan Frome*—"hardly more than sheds," we
are told. Charity's mother's house is in "the most ruinous" state: "a stove-pipe
reached its crooked arm out of one window, and the broken panes of the other
were stuffed with rags and paper." Here the "body" of the Mountain shack
seems to mirror that of Charity's dead mother: "her *ragged* disordered clothes"
and "*broken* teeth" (my emphasis). We are also reminded of Charity's endeavor
"to picture to herself what her life would have been like had she grown up on
the Mountain, running wild in *rags*" (my emphasis).[65] Questions of ownership
arise, as Lawyer Royall argues: "The Mountain belongs to this township,
and it's North Dormer's fault if there's a gang of thieves and outlaws living
over there, in sight of us, defying the laws of their country. Why, there ain't
a sheriff or a tax collector or a coroner'd durst go up there."[66] Charity cannot fully grasp the class and cultural connotations of what it means to be
"descended" from the Mountain. Lacking a sense of roots herself she has little time for any mawkishly sentimental sense of home: "the best way to help
the places we live in is to be glad we live there."[67] She does, however, notice a
radical disconnection between the two localities and populations: "She knew
the Mountain had but the most infrequent intercourse with the valleys."[68] For
Charity however, "the valleys" are a backwater, a zone of frustrated aliena-
tion, petty provinciality and depression:

> But anyway we all live in the same place, and when it's a place like
> North Dormer it's enough to make people hate each other just to have
> to walk down the same street every day. But you don't live here, and
> you don't know anything about any of us, so what did you have to
> meddle for?[69]

The residents of North Dormer are *dormant*, their place of residence a shop-
soiled, charmless nullity. The self-appointed guardians of North Dormer
manners exemplify what Immanuel Kant calls "unsocial sociability"[70]. They
have come together because they exist in the same locale, but their urge is to
bicker, bully, break apart and scatter. However, this puts Charity in a complex position, as Donna Campbell contends: "Shuttling between the torpor
of North Dormer, the primitive civilization of earlier centuries represented
by the Mountain, and the cosmopolitan center of Nettleton, Charity steps
beyond the bounds of pastoral."[71] I propose that she is not so much step-
ping "beyond the bounds of the pastoral" but yearning for a specific kind
of pastoral cosmopolitanism. She shows an affinity with a modest patch of
local earth, even while she contemplates what life might be like beyond the
suffocating parochialism, uncaring morality and "furtive malice" of her
neighbors.[72] While an aversion to the Mountain triggers among some North

Dormer figures fantasies of obsessive policing and regulation of organic nature, Charity tries to grasp that she is a part of that "nature"—hinting at communion with, rather than angry rejection of, the soil and trees.

So, the tangible specificities of the material world play a decisive role in *Summer*.[73] Hermione Lee describes Charity as one who "feels and thinks through her blood, she lies on the ground like an animal."[74] Charity lacks the precise terminology to capture the exacting complexities of felt sensation—the natural energies she feels pulsing through her. The narrator fills this gap with an account of her physical setting, replete with botanical detail: "This was all she saw; but she felt, above her and about her, the strong growth of the beeches clothing the ridge, [...] and the crowding shoots of meadowsweet and yellow flags in the pasture beyond."[75] That final part of the sentence evidences how Charity is a particular *form* in the vast arena of the natural world. "All this bubbling of sap and slipping of sheaths and bursting of calyxes was carried to her on mingled currents of fragrance."[76] The narrator displays her own scientific *knowledge*—as measured against Charity's intuitive *understanding*—by employing technical terms such as "sheaths" and "calyxes." The intoxicating buoyancy of these figurations—which hint at a mythic association between Charity and the goddess of blossoms Persephone—seems to furnish a robust response to, or antidote for, the ecophobia synonymous with those North Dormer residents who castigate the Mountain folk and their surroundings ("[t]hey ain't half human up there").[77]

> Every leaf and bud and blade seemed to contribute its exhalation to the pervading sweetness in which the pungency of pine-sap prevailed over the spice of thyme and the subtle perfume of fern, and all were merged in a moist earth-smell that was like the breath of some huge sun-warmed animal.[78]

This extract appeals powerfully not only to sight and smell—a pointed reference to the aromatic herb thyme evokes the sense of taste. The lexis deepens the earlier perception of Charity as one who can process the palpable cosmos through a version of what D.H. Lawrence's 1920s fiction terms "blood-consciousness"—she is divested, however fleetingly, of the burden of socially constructed selfhood.[79] "She was blind and insensible to many things, and dimly knew it; but to all that was light and air, perfume and color, every drop of blood in her responded."[80] Charity translates her physical surroundings (colors, fragrance, fluctuations of light) through the empirical means that her own body provides, which lends the cadences a bewitching and visionary splendor: "She loved the roughness of the dry mountain grass under her palms, [...] the fingering of the wind in her hair and through her cotton blouse."[81] Shortly thereafter, the narrator describes Charity's romantic interest, Lucius Harney, using tropes that revisit and reinforce this association with seasonal cycles and thriving abundance:

> His hair was sunburnt-looking too, or rather the color of bracken after frost; his eyes grey, with the appealing look of the shortsighted, his smile shy yet confident, as if he knew lots of things she had never dreamed of, and yet wouldn't for the world have had her feel his superiority.[82]

The disparity between Harney's so-called "superior" culture of abstract ideas and Charity's instinctual grasp of her palpable organic milieu is made explicit. Harney's hair is "sunburnt-looking" not because it has been burnished by beams of sunlight. Rather this is how Charity reacts to a figure who seems to bring the mental *illumination* and delightful novelty of a world beyond the unrelieved squalor of the Mountain. That Harney's hair is "the color of bracken after frost" reminds us however that these characters belong to very different worlds: Charity is the vibrant eruption of summer while Harney points to the cold hibernation of winter.

The final image of the Mountain is a sunset witnessed by Charity and Harney in the abandoned house where they meet.[83] "Behind the swarthy Mountain the sun had gone down in waveless gold."[84] The phrase "swarthy Mountain" reminds us of Charity's "small swarthy face" in the opening chapter which signals her uneasy sense of being an ethnic outsider among straitlaced, philistine and judgmental palefaces. This description also evokes a Hudson River School painting, such as Thomas Cole's 1846 work "The Mountain Ford." Once night falls, a pulsating natural expanse is replaced by the uncompromising harshness of Mountain soil and the people who scratch out the meanest existence on it.

Charity's draining ascent of the Mountain comes as a moment of closure in the text, the culmination of her search for answers about her own origins. The Mountain becomes an infernal location, and as Campbell reminds us: "For Wharton, the limits of biology and culture dictate the limits of pastoral and in framing this inevitable and uncomfortable conclusion, she reveals the necessary price for women who live in its world out of time."[85] There is a shocking aspect to Charity's grueling quest. She discovers that the one person she was seeking—her mother—was "dying [...] and she would find herself as much alone on the mountain as anywhere else in the world."[86] Unlike the European peaks in Wharton's work, the Mountain at this stage conveys to the protagonist no sense of redemptive release. The landscape of rural New England that Charity knew so well at the start of the novella becomes a "strange land," and she no longer recognizes the place where she has lived the eighteen years of her life:

> She knew them all, mere lost clusters of houses in the folds of desolate ridges: Dormer, where North Dormer went for its apples; Creston River, where there used to be a paper-mill, and its grey walls stood decaying by the stream; and Hamblin, where the first snow always fell. Such were their titles to fame.[87]

The narrator suggests here the undoing of earlier hopes, sentiments and lyrical reflections. The mountain grass that previously carried the stirring scent of thyme is now "faded." The terrain is stripped of any sensuous and enlivening immediacy: "In the hollows a few white birches trembled, or a mountain ash lit its scarlet clusters; but only a scant growth of pines darkened the granite ledges."[88] The mention of birches can be read as an allusion to Robert Frost's poem "Birches," published a year before *Summer*, but without the fond nostalgia Frost implies.[89] The forlorn sense of finality is conveyed by a ragged settlement, a "nest of misery," that seems to exist on a different timeline to that of the villages below.[90]

The Mountain colony in this text points to a landscape of extremes. Overnight, summer transitions directly to "icy cold" winter. As Candace Waid notes: "Wharton draws a world in *dishabille*, a world which offers no warmth or continuity [...] a place beyond the hearth—where cold, hunger and deprivation interfere with any conception of tradition, human relationship, or memory beyond the struggle for animal survival."[91] Waid's stress on "a place beyond the hearth" directs attention to how the Mountain has its own ecosystem, or a layering of memory and action embedded in the earth, that cannot be *translated* using glib literary-critical terminology—is it, we wonder, "a place beyond" conventional genre classifications? Or, to cite Oakes and Price in *The Cultural Geography Reader* (2008), one of those "landscapes that exist beyond humans and their dominant interpretive filters"?[92]

We glimpse that ecosystem when the narrator describes Charity the morning after on the Mountain: "under a wind-beaten thorn, a mound of fresh earth made a dark spot on the fawn-colored stubble."[93] This "mound" is Charity's mother's grave: "As she approached it she heard a bird's note in the still air, and looking up she saw a brown song-sparrow perched in an upper branch of the thorn above the grave."[94] Unlike the bird-song in *Ethan Frome*, which serves as a wakeup call to Ethan that he loves Mattie, this sound does not rouse Charity. She feels completely rudderless, traversing a site without embracing it on an instinctual level ("the cold wind of the night before *sprang out on her*," my emphasis).[95] By having Charity continue her trek along the

Mountain the narrator underscores this feeling of bitter disconnection: "She [...] sat down under a ledge of rock overhung by shivering birches."[96] The narrator revisits the image of birches—but Charity seems the very opposite of those carefree "girls on hands and knees" that Frost describes in his poem of the same name.[97] The "granite wall of the Mountain falling away to infinite distances"[98] makes it all the more threatening, fixing it at a remove from the "village roofs and steeples" below. By ascending the Mountain, suffering the loss of her mother, Charity now registers the ecophobia that Estok summarizes: "Nature becomes the hateful object in need of our control, the loathed and feared thing that can only result in tragedy if left in control."[99] Only by performing a sweeping survey of the terrain beyond is Charity able to see Lawyer Royall arriving. He will "bring her down from the Mountain" for the second time in her life. With this deeply ironic "rescue," Charity's plight prompts comparison with the harem women Wharton saw in Morocco: "Others come from harems in the turreted cities beyond the Atlas, where blue palm-groves beat all night against the stars and date-caravans journey across the desert from Timbuctoo."[100] In the case of *Summer*, the Atlas mountains become the New England range, and Lawyer Royall's act of "charity" is to "claim" a trophy bride who "had never learned any trade that would have given her independence in a strange place."[101]

In this second part of the book, I have shown how Wharton's fictional peaks and summits can be construed as "edgelands at an altitude"—intricate geographical and symbolic entities that raise urgent questions about the homestead and the hinterland, the civilized and the feral, the sublime and the sinister. As Marjorie Hope Nicolson proposes, in her landmark study *Mountain Gloom and Mountain Glory*: "Like men of every age, we see in Nature what we have been taught to look for, we feel what we have been prepared to feel."[102] Wharton's sophisticated habits of *seeing* "in Nature" take us well beyond what "we have been taught to feel" by bourgeois custom and convention. Indeed, there is ample scope here to reappraise Wharton's "mountains of the mind" through the critical prism of the environmental humanities. Shari Benstock posits that "desire and landscape are joined" in Wharton's artistic vision: "she creates landscapes of desire, but desire is disclosed as landscape."[103] Wharton's fiction furnishes much more than this. We register summits as sites of fantasy yes, but also ideation, desolation, identity crisis and blighted hope. Hermione Lee argues that rural New England was "a place that would haunt" Wharton "forever," that "she would rewrite over and over."[104] Taking this notion further, I contend that Wharton's fictional peaks, rather than "landscapes of desire," are in fact landscapes of *re-vision*—part of a geographical palimpsest that will be explained and developed in the next part of this book.

Notes

1 Dean, *Constance Fenimore Woolson and Edith Wharton*, 72–73.
2 James Fenimore Cooper, "American and European Scenery Compared." *The Homebook of the Picturesque, or American Scenery, Art, and Literature*. George Putnam, 1852, 51–70, 60.
3 Edith Wharton, "The Journey." *The New York Stories of Edith Wharton*. New York Review of Books, 2007, 88–99, 92.
4 Stephen, "The Regrets of a Mountaineer," 268.
5 Stephen, "The Regrets of a Mountaineer," 268.
6 Stephen, "The Regrets of a Mountaineer," 268–69.
7 Wharton, "Madame de Treymes," 211–82, 217.
8 Wharton, *Twilight Sleep*, 228.
9 Wharton, *A Backward Glance*, 293.
10 Wharton relates that: "I have a clearer recollection of its beginnings than most of my other tales, through the singular accident that its first pages were written in French!" Wharton, *A Backward Glance*, 295.
11 Edith Wharton, *Ethan Frome*. In *"Ethan Frome"; "Summer"; "Bunner Sisters"*. Alfred A. Knopf, 2008, 1–104. Everyman's Library, 5.
12 On the formal and affective complexity of *Ethan Frome*, especially its deft use of an analeptic, heterodiegetic framing narrative see Lee, *Edith Wharton*.
13 Alan Henry Rose, "'Such Depths of Sad Initiation': Edith Wharton and New England." *The New England Quarterly*, vol. 50, no. 3, 1977, 423–39. *JSTOR*, www.jstor .org/stable/364277. Accessed Oct. 2, 2020, 427.
14 Rose, "'Such Depths of Sad Initiation': Edith Wharton and New England." 427.
15 Wharton, *Ethan Frome*, 5.
16 Wharton, *Ethan Frome*, 9.
17 Leo Marx, "Does Pastoralism Have a Future?" *The Pastoral Landscape*, edited by John Dixon Hunt. Washington National Gallery of Art, 1992, 222.
18 Wharton, *Ethan Frome*, 33.
19 Barbara A. White argues that "Wharton's snowy settings are organic and not just decorative". See White, "Introduction." *Wharton's New England: Seven Stories and Ethan Frome*, edited by Barbara A. White. University Press of New England, 1995, vii–xxviii, xx.
20 White, "Introduction," xx.
21 Wharton, *Ethan Frome*, 33.
22 Gifford, *Pastoral*, 156.
23 Edith Wharton, *The Writing of Fiction*. Scribner's, 1925, 132–33.
24 Wharton, *Ethan Frome*, 74.
25 *Oxford English Dictionary 3* online defines the adjective "exurban" as: "Of or belonging to a district outside a city or town; suburban; *spec.* pertaining to, or characteristic of, an exurb." See Lawrence Buell, *Writing for an Endangered World: Literature, Culture, and Environment in the U.S. and Beyond*. Harvard University Press, 2001, 143.
26 Wharton, *Ethan Frome*, 77.
27 Wharton, *Ethan Frome*, 88.
28 Wharton, *Ethan Frome*, 88.
29 Wharton, *Ethan Frome*, 88.
30 Edith Wharton, "The Writing of *Ethan Frome*." *The Colophon: The Book Collectors' Quarterly*, vol. 2, no. 4, 1932, 261–63.

31 Wharton, *The Letters of Edith Wharton*, 385.
32 Wharton, *A Backward Glance*, 294.
33 Wharton evokes a "mountain colony" setting in the 1926 short story "Bewitched",
    where she describes that: "People said there had once been other houses like it, form-
    ing a little township called Ashmore, a sort of mountain colony created by the caprice
    of an English Royalist officer, one Colonel Ashmore, who had been murdered by the
    Indians, with all his family, long before the Revolution." See "Bewitched." *Ghost
    Stories of Edith Wharton*. Vintage, 2009, 139–59, 142.
34 Fred Botting, "Introduction: Negative Aesthetics." *Gothic*. Routledge, 2014, 1–19, 4.
35 Edith Wharton, *Summer*. In *"Ethan Frome"; "Summer"; "Bunner Sisters"*. Alfred A.
    Knopf, 2008, 109.
36 See Sidonie Smith, *Moving Lives: Twentieth-Century Women's Travel Writing*. University
    of Minnesota Press, 2001; Sara Mills, *Discourses of Difference: An Analysis of Women's
    Travel and Colonialism*. Routledge, 1991; Eric J. Leed, *The Mind of the Traveller: From
    Gilgamesh to Global Tourism*. Basic Books, 1991; Casey Blanton, *Travel Writing: The Self
    and the World*. Routledge, 2002.
37 Wharton, *In Morocco*, 86.
38 Wharton, *Summer*, 117. See also Veronica Makowsky and Lynn Z. Bloom, "Edith
    Wharton's Tentative Embrace of Charity: Class and Character in *Summer*." *American
    Literary Realism*, vol. 32, 2000, 220–33.
39 Denis Cosgrove and Stephen Daniels, "Introduction: Iconography and Landscape."
    *The Iconography of Landscape: Essays on the Symbolic Representation, Design, and Use of Past
    Environments*, edited by Denis Cosgrove. Cambridge University Press, 1988, 1–10, 1.
40 Wharton, *Summer*, 109.
41 Wharton, *Summer*, 109.
42 Simon C. Estok, "Theorizing in a Space of Ambivalent Openness: Ecocriticism and
    Ecophobia." *ISLE: Interdisciplinary Studies in Literature and Environment*, vol. 16, Issue 2,
    Spring 2009, 203–25. https://doi.org/10.1093/isle/isp010, 208.
43 See Dawn Keetley and Matthew Wynn Sivils, *Ecogothic in Nineteenth-Century American
    Literature*. Routledge, 2018, 3–4. The first attempt to theorize and map out this criti-
    cal terrain by fusing Gothic studies and ecocriticism was *Ecogothic*, edited by Andrew
    Smith and William Hughes. Manchester University Press, 2013.
44 Wharton, *Summer*, 143.
45 Martha Billips, "Edith Wharton as Regionalist: A New Context for Reading
    Summer." *Edith Wharton Review*, vol. 34, no. 2, 2018, 146–66. *JSTOR*, www.jstor.org
    /stable/10.5325/editwharrevi.34.2.0146. Accessed Aug. 15, 2020, 160. See also
    Rhonda Skillern, "Becoming a 'Good Girl': Law, Language, and Ritual in Edith
    Wharton's *Summer*." *The Cambridge Companion to Edith Wharton*, edited by Millicent
    Bell. Cambridge University Press, 1995, 117–36.
46 Wharton, *Summer*, 251. Wharton's depiction seems to offer a New England equivalent
    of the hardscrabble Alpine lives glimpsed in some of Ruskin's writing: gloomy cycles
    of "black bread, rude roof, dark night, laborious day, weary arm at sunset". See
    Ruskin, *Complete Works*, vol. 6, p. 388; also Billips, "Edith Wharton as Regionalist: A
    New Context for Reading *Summer*," 160.
47 [Anon.], *New York Times Book Review*, July 8, 1917, 253.
48 Wharton, *Summer*, 56, 249.
49 Dana Phillips, *The Truth of Ecology*. Oxford University Press, 2003, 240. Michael
    Bennett also stresses the need for ecocriticism to make "room for […] small-town,
    rural, and wild spaces that fill the physical and cultural landscape of the United

States, West and East, and its literature". See "From Wide Open Spaces to Metropolitan Places." *Interdisciplinary Studies in Literature and Environment*, vol. 8, no. 1, 2001, 31–52.

50 Billips, "Edith Wharton as Regionalist: A New Context for Reading *Summer*," 160.
51 Wharton, *Summer*, 141.
52 Wharton, *Summer*, 145.
53 Wharton, *Summer*, 141.
54 The Mountain people "herd together like the heathen". See Wharton, *Summer*, 39.
55 For more on these issues see Karen Weingarten, "Between the Town and the Mountain: Abortion and the Politics of Life in Edith Wharton's *Summer*." *Canadian Review of American Studies/Revue canadienne d'études americaines*, vol. 40, no. 3, 2010, 352–72, doi: 10.3138/cras.40.3.351; Jennie A. Kassanoff, *Edith Wharton and the Politics of Race*. Cambridge University Press, 2004.
56 Wharton, *Summer*, 65.
57 Wharton, *Summer*, 141.
58 Wharton, *Summer*, 39.
59 Wharton, *Summer*, 188, 3.
60 Estok, "Theorizing in a Space of Ambivalent Openness: Ecocriticism and Ecophobia," 209.
61 Wharton, *Summer*, 143.
62 Simon Estok, *The Ecophobia Hypothesis*. Routledge, 2018, 20.
63 Wharton, *Summer*, 294.
64 "She looked at her mother's face [...] There was no sign in it of anything human". Wharton, *Summer*, 297, 289.
65 Wharton, *Summer*, 287–89.
66 Wharton, *Summer*, 143.
67 Wharton, *Summer*, 258.
68 Wharton, *Summer*, 242.
69 Wharton, *Summer*, 130.
70 Kant, *Political Writings*, 44.
71 Donna Campbell, "Summers in Arcady: The Deep Time of Evolutionary Romance in James Lane Allen, Hamlin Garland, and Edith Wharton." *American Literary Realism*, vol. 52, no. 2, 2020, 105. *Project MUSE* muse.jhu.edu/article/745267.
72 Wharton, *Summer*, 231.
73 I have previously written about this topic in a comparative article published in 2019: Margarida São Bento Cadima, "The Production of Space in Colson Whitehead's *Sag Harbor* and Edith Wharton's *Summer*." *RSA Journal Rivista Di Studi Americani*, vol. 30, 2019, 163–78.
74 Hermione Lee, "Introduction." Edith Wharton, *"Ethan Frome"; "Summer"; "Bunner Sisters"*. Everyman's Library, 2008, xix. Lee references this passage: "Charity Royall lay on a ridge above a sunlit hollow, her face pressed to the earth and the warm currents of the grass running through her".
75 Wharton, *Summer*, 134.
76 Wharton, *Summer*, 134.
77 Wharton, *Summer*, 89. Lewis highlights that it was "a lifelong obsession with Edith Wharton – of Persephone". See Richard Warrington Baldwin Lewis, *Edith Wharton: A Biography*. Harper & Row, 1975, 495. For more on the Persephone myth in Edith Wharton's fiction, see Sarah Whitehead, "Demeter Forgiven: Wharton's Use of the

Persephone Myth in Her Short Stories." *Edith Wharton Review*, vol. 26, no. 1, 2010, 17–25. *JSTOR*, www.jstor.org/stable/43513029. Accessed Mar. 11, 2021.

78 Wharton, *Summer*, 134.

79 See, for example, Lawrence's 1920 novel *The Lost Girl* which presents another boundary-crossing and intrepid Persephone figure, Alvina Houghton.

80 Wharton, *Summer*, 115.

81 Wharton, *Summer*, 115.

82 Wharton, *Summer*, 116.

83 I consider this abandoned house/ruin in the next part of this book.

84 Wharton, *Summer*, 207.

85 Campbell, "Summers in Arcady: The Deep Time of Evolutionary Romance in James Lane Allen, Hamlin Garland, and Edith Wharton," 106.

86 Wharton, *Summer*, 242.

87 Wharton, *Summer*, 113–14.

88 Wharton, *Summer*, 243.

89 For more on Edith Wharton and Robert Frost, see George Monteiro, "Suicide and the New England Conscience: Notes on Edith Wharton, Robinson, and Frost." *American Literary Realism*, vol. 50, no. 2, 2018, 145–51. *JSTOR*, www.jstor.org/stable /10.5406/amerlitereal.50.2.0145. Accessed Mar. 1, 2021.

90 Wharton, *Summer*, 231.

91 Candace Waid, "The Woman Behind the Door." *Edith Wharton's Letters from the Underworld: Fictions of Women and Writing*. The University of North Carolina Press, 1991, 83.

92 Timothy Oakes and Patricia Price, *The Cultural Geography Reader*. Routledge, 2008, 151.

93 Wharton, *Summer*, 253–54.

94 Wharton, *Summer*, 254.

95 Wharton, *Summer*, 254.

96 Wharton, *Summer*, 254.

97 Robert Frost, *The Poetry of Robert Frost*. Edited by Edward Connery Lathem. Henry Holt and Company, 2002, 121.

98 Wharton, *Summer*, 254.

99 Estok, "Theorizing in a Space of Ambivalent Openness: Ecocriticism and Ecophobia," 210.

100 Wharton, *In Morocco*, 86.

101 "The clergyman began to read, and on her dazed mind there rose the memory of Mr. Miles, standing the night before in the desolate house of the Mountain, and reading out of the same book words that had the same dread sound of finality". See Wharton, *Summer*, 239, 261.

102 Marjorie Hope Nicolson, *Mountain Gloom and Mountain Glory: The Development of the Aesthetics of the Infinite*. Cornell University Press, 1959, 1. Nicolson's continuing influence can be felt in Robert Macfarlane's highly successful *Mountains of the Mind*, in which he asserted that "The notion barely existed […] that wild landscape might hold any sort of appeal", 14.

103 Benstock, "Landscape of Desire: Edith Wharton and Europe," 29.

104 Lee, *Edith Wharton*, 158.

Part III

RUIN/ATION

Chapter 9

ROMANTIC RUINS? EDITH WHARTON'S SEDIMENTED VISION

In the second chapter of *A Backward Glance*, Edith Wharton remembers her childhood spent in Rome and muses: "That old city of Rome of the mid-nineteenth century was still the city of romantic ruins."[1] Here, Wharton's terminology—focusing on local landmarks as visual shorthand for an entire culture—registers the widespread literary, philosophical and artistic obsession with monumental ruins, from the Parthenon, the Pyramids to the Colosseum.[2] Broken and disorderly in varying degrees, yet much visited and venerated, ruins—as Tanya Whitehouse notes—symbolize stubborn endurance as much as ephemerality, and are synonymous with nostalgic rumination as well as rigorous scientific enquiry.[3] Such residuals are "romantic" in the sense that Thomas McFarland expresses: "All such disparative *eloignement* testifies to the pervasiveness of Romantic longing and the incompleteness it implies."[4] This "longing"—to revive the dead splendors of historical memory?—is in an ever-evolving state, according to Frederic Schlegel: "The romantic kind of poetry is still in the state of becoming; that, in fact, is its real essence: that it should forever be becoming and never be perfected."[5]

In this chapter I argue that Wharton treats "romantic ruins" not just as instances of pleasurable dereliction or metaphors for a lost past. By scrutinizing a variety of damaged vestiges of the built environment—from massive, imposing archaeological sites with a testimonial resonance for posterity to more recent, ramshackle structures as well as garden "follies"—I show how Wharton converts the ruin into an intricate repository or conduit for her own force of feeling.[6] This enables her to comment on the layered landscapes through which she travelled and their relationship with the "welter" of this "world"—the frenetic rhythms of advanced industrial modernity. In this regard, Wharton may have had in mind John Ruskin's seminal conception of ruins in *The Seven Lamps of Architecture*:

For, indeed, the greatest glory of a building is not in its stones, nor in its gold. Its glory is in its Age, and in that deep sense of voicefulness, of stern watching, of mysterious sympathy, nay, even of approval or condemnation, which we feel in walls that have long been washed by the passing waves of humanity.[7]

This "sense of voicefulness" is crucial to my chapter and usefully links with Andreas Schönle's recent contention that "[s]omehow we cannot leave ruins alone and let them simply exist in their mute materiality. We *need to make them speak* and militate for our theories" (my emphasis).[8] Ruskin's oeuvre can be viewed as a sustained meditation on *why* we are drawn towards battered architecture or shattered natural formations. What makes them edifying or legitimate sources of aesthetic and cultural concern, even worthy of preservation? Here Ruskin implies that the ruins possess a "voicefulness" that, for Wharton at least, triggers a complex dialogue between relics of the past and her own literary interests. Ruskin's focus on the sentient ruin also imbues the work of Wharton's friend Henry James in *The Italian Hours*: "To delight in the aspects of sentient ruin might appear a heartless pastime, and the pleasure, I confess, shows the note of perversity."[9] "Heartless pastime" intimates a sense that the tourist gaze is vulnerable to the charge of being frivolous, exploitative or indifferent to the genuine human suffering that may not be completely "washed" from the walls of citadels and pillaged gardens. Ultimately, for Wharton, as for James, these remnants boast a metaphysical energy and exercise a binding fascination because they epitomize—even transmit—a multitude of ambiguous messages and eerie, unsettling cadences. Such structures have witnessed—and of course bear the obvious marks of—natural calamity, the rise and fall of empires, socio-economic convulsion, conflicts between creeds and beliefs. Wharton is compelled to reflect not just on the Ruskinian "Age" of the landmark itself but how we, as reader-observers, become weary and weathered, studying the depredations of use that Thomas Hardy summarizes as "Time's transforming chisel."[10]

In this chapter I propose that Wharton's writing project can be seen as a type of imaginative archaeology. She ponders and elaborates the representation of "voiceful" classical as well as Romantic ruins.[11] Her fiction explores how these crumbling phenomena may be utilized to complicate or subvert those aesthetic modes which glamorize, sanitize or commodify the stratified past. This puts Wharton in lively "dialogue" with a recent surge of academic fascination—especially among art historians and cultural geographers—with dilapidation, urban and rural waste/lands, problems of materiality and collective memory.[12] While existing scholarship has scrutinized Wharton's Italian-set fictions, little of it focuses specifically on ruin/ation. I also consider a cluster of her overlooked texts that do not use Italy as *mis-en-scene*. For the critic Christopher Woodward, "To a poet, the decay of a monument represents the dissolution of the individual ego in the flow of Time; to a painter or architect, the fragments of a stupendous antiquity call into question the purpose of their art."[13] This is doubly pertinent, as Wharton's interests extended well beyond literature and poetry to include a vast knowledge of visual art and architecture.

When Georg Simmel posits that a "ruin conveys the impression of peace from yet another perspective,"[14] his theory does not quite capture all the meanings that these structures "voice," given how debris makes manifest cycles of depopulation and redevelopment, imperial and geological upheaval.[15] Ruskin reminds us that the "passing waves of humanity" both reveal and conceal a ruin's connection with state articulations of power, and in Rose Macaulay's phrase the acrid "smell of fire and mortality."[16] These less "peaceful" resonances must be unpacked and understood:

> It is in their lasting witness against men, in their quiet contrast with the transitional character of all things, in the strength of which, through the lapse of seasons and times, and the decline and birth of dynasties, and the changing of the face of the earth, and if the limits of the sea, maintains its sculpted shapeliness for a time insuperable, connects forgotten and following ages with each other, and half constitutes the identity, as it concentrates the sympathy, of nations[17]

Ruskin's emphasis on the "transitional *character* of all things" (my emphasis) indicates how material remnants constitute runic clues ("character" as written script)—remainders and reminders of a centuries-old language of human creativity (or creative destruction).[18] Ruskin's mention of "character" here also situates a ruin as an architectural counterpart of a *non sequitur* (Latin "it does not follow") in a sentence. For Wharton, a ruin can seem illogical, weirdly incongruous and startling in its immediate natural locality. It might, for Ruskin, bear "lasting witness" and seem like a precious, unique artwork, but this was not presumably its initial function or value. Moreover, as Wharton shows in her work, the form it once was, is declining, inexorably, into formlessness. A ruin also appears here as a highly sensitive recording instrument—for Ruskin such sites/sights divulge the fortunes of nation-states, the trajectory of dynastic ambitions and even warn would-be makers of memorials.

What Wharton takes from Ruskin's theory—and it imbues her short story "Roman Fever"—is a vivid sense of the ruin as a portal to a venerable past, by turns glorious and gloomy, a textured European chronicle that as a North American she felt she lacked.[19] Wharton uses the "voiceful" Ruskinian ruin to make it "speak" about her own peculiar cultural preoccupations, specifically the value of history from her own non-European perspective. Her representation of ruins is an attempt perhaps to forge a different kind of American chronicle, identifying hitherto unforeseen continuities and conversations between "Old" and "New Worlds," by borrowing from classical civilizations.[20] Having grown up in Europe, and spent some of her childhood years in Rome, Wharton was acutely aware of the importance—and formal challenges—of recovering and "writing time."

This endeavor to "write time" through the depiction of broken buildings imbues her short story "A Bottle of Perrier": "The house, he already knew, was empty save for the quick cosmopolitan man-servant, who spoke a sort of palimpsest Cockney lined with Mediterranean tongues and desert dialects— English, Italian or Greek, which was he?"[21] Here the servant Gosling's accent is like the scarred physical structure he occupies—difficult to "place." It is apt that Gosling, with his oddly "mixed" phrasing, operates in a North African "jumble" of masonry. Wharton's ruin is a syncretic formation, still standing at the borders of civilizations and ethno-cultural practices (in this story Christian and Muslim). Architecture then, like Gosling's accent, can be construed as a "palimpsest" here, which Thomas De Quincey succinctly defines as: "a membrane or roll cleansed of its manuscript by reiterated successions."[22] Wharton's stress on "palimpsest" reminds us of Ruskin's conception of a ruin, which contrasts with the "transitional *character* of all things" (human script rubbed out and overwritten). We can also view her fiction as a palimpsest of her experiences of global history. Such sense-impressions the reader must decipher and translate through fragmentary or partially-erased symbols.[23] Nowhere is this more evident than in Wharton's best-known novel, *The Age of Innocence*: "In reality they all lived in a kind of hieroglyphic world, where the real thing was never said or done or even thought, but only represented by a set of arbitrary signs."[24] In fact, Katie Trumpener and James M. Nyce note that this is a novel "which uses concepts, perspectives and metaphors from archaeology and what was then a new discipline—anthropology—as a way of structuring the story."[25] What Trumpener and Nyce do not account for is that archaeological optics, motifs and methods—anchored in an obsession with the past as palimpsest—are not exclusive to *The Age of Innocence*: they extend across Wharton's oeuvre, including short stories like "A Bottle of Perrier" in which Almodham, a seemingly tireless excavator, "dashes across the desert in quest of unknown ruins" and the "queer sense of otherwhereness" that these sites apparently voice.[26]

The theorist Sarah Dillon fashions a crucial and previously overlooked distinction between "*a* palimpsest" (the paleographic artifact) and "*the* palimpsest" (the metaphorical construct). A palimpsest, as defined in *Oxford*

English Dictionary 2, is "a parchment or other writing-material written upon twice, the original writing having been erased or rubbed out to make place for the second; a manuscript in which a later writing is written over an effaced earlier writing."[27] Dillon argues that the *Oxford English Dictionary* definition omits "the most peculiar and interesting fact about palimpsests," that is, their retention of the earlier, imperfectly erased writing.[28] Does Wharton see in the material leftovers of the palimpsest, and in the mysterious, unplaceable sound of Gosling's accent, a suggestive link with her own writing project, one that is focused on the problems, gaps, omissions and reach of personal, as well as cultural memory? [29]

To answer this question, it is crucial to appraise the layers of meaning imbuing Wharton's painstaking portrayal of the ruined form as a representational device, and how it triggers a yearning which also "saturates" European Romantic poetics according to Thomas McFarland.[30] Such affective complexity is voiced by Giacomo Leopardi, in his poem "On the proposed Dante monument in Florence." Leopardi's poetry collection *Canti* was a valued part of Wharton's personal library, she chose some of his verses as the epitaph to the first novel she published, *The Valley of Decision*, and she even visited his house in Recanati, Italy in May 1932.[31]

> Gaze at these ruins,
> Words and paintings, marbles, temples;
> Think what ground you tread; and if the light
> Of these examples does not stir you,
> Why linger? rise and go.[32]

The "stirring" Leopardi alludes to here transcends the studious watchfulness that Wharton displays in her travel book *In Morocco*, where she records the remnants of Chella thus: "The tracery of the broken arches is all carved in stone or in glaze turquoise tiling, and the fragments of wall and vaulting have the firm elegance of a classic ruin."[33] What Wharton may have found compelling in Leopardi's standpoint is how his image of "temples" signals a partially effaced architectural lexis ("words") both baffling and enticing, that "voices" the pathos of human striving when measured against the stratified past beneath our feet (the portentous "think what ground you tread"). Wharton intimates this sensibility in *The Cruise of the Vanadis*, her account of the Mediterranean. On April 19, 1888, she stopped in Athens and described the ruins thus: "It is interesting to go to the Acropolis from this building, carrying its color in one's eye, and to invest the sunburnt ruins of the Parthenon and the Erectheum with the tints which must once have belonged to them."[34] Wharton adds that: "perhaps they are more beautiful as they are.

The marble has taken a primrose hue, now fading to ivory, now deepening to russet, and the columns absolutely glow in the sunshine against the blue sky."[35] What is perhaps most arresting about this account is how in striving to make the "marble" and "columns" an object of aesthetic splendor that speaks to us in tender personal tones, Wharton has to "frame" the majestic site in such a way that leaves us oddly distanced—so connection becomes severance, mere genteel rumination from afar, or worse, touristic consumption. How does one step through the framing of picturesque nature so as to carry the "sunburnt" ruin's true "color in one's eye"? This is a question that reverberates through many of Wharton's fictional evocations of time-scarred archaeological relics.

By excavating metaphorically the fractured objects and dilapidated spaces depicted in Wharton's oeuvre, we can secure a better purchase on what Michael Shanks calls "the intangible aspects of archaeology: the evocation of ruin, authenticity achieved through digging deep."[36] She mines "stirring" personal experiences, shards and splinters of affect, with a view to reorganizing them in her fiction, which throws into relief her portrayal of uncovered fragments from *In Morocco*: "every inch of soil in the circumference of the city will be made to yield up whatever secrets it hides."[37]

This chapter is followed by two other chapters. The next one deals with ancient ruins by assessing narratives that portray Italy and North Africa respectively; the last considers ruins of the recent past or those produced within living memory, especially sites threatened by encroaching tides of urban modernity or wild nature and it also addresses garden ruins and "follies."

Notes

1 Wharton, *A Backward Glance*, 29.
2 See Jeanette Bicknell et al., eds., *Philosophical Perspectives on Ruins, Monuments, and Memorials*. Routledge, 2020; Susan Stewart, *The Ruins Lesson: Meaning and Material in Western Culture*. University of Chicago Press, 2020.
3 On the ruin as embodiment of both evanescence and obdurate persistence see Tanya Whitehouse, *How Ruins Acquire Aesthetic Value: Modern Ruins, Ruin Porn, and the Ruin Tradition*. Palgrave Macmillan, 2018; *Ruins in the Literary and Cultural Imagination*, edited by Efterpi Mitsi, Anna Despotopoulou, Stamatina Dimakopoulou, and Emmanouil Aretoulakis. Palgrave Macmillan, 2019; Robert Harbison, *Ruins and Fragments: Tales of Loss and Rediscovery*. Reaktion Books, 2015, 11–43; Julia Hell, *The Conquest of Ruins: The Third Reich and the Fall of Rome*. University of Chicago Press, 2019; Gillian d'Arcy Wood, *The Shock of the Real: Romanticism and Visual Culture, 1760-1860*. Palgrave Macmillan, 2001; Sophie Thomas, *Romanticism and Visual Culture*. Routledge, 2010; Leo Mellor, *Reading the Ruins: Modernism, Bombsites and British Culture*. Cambridge University Press, 2011.

4 Thomas McFarland, "Introduction: Fragmented Modalities and the Criteria of Romanticism." *Romanticism and the Forms of Ruin*. Princeton University Press, 1981, 9. "Diasparaction" is a term McFarland borrows from the Greek which means "torn to pieces". He theorizes that the diasparactive triad consists of: "Incompleteness, fragmentation, and ruin". Of course, ruins are "Romantic" in a more immediate and obvious sense: the Romantic period is remarkable for its obsession with "ruin poems" as a distinct subgenre, going back to the Anglo-Saxon poem "The Ruin". Keats, Shelley, Coleridge and Byron all published texts in fashionably "fragmentary" form. See Michael Bradshaw, "Hedgehog Theory: How to Read a Romantic Fragment Poem." *Literature Compass* vol. 5, no. 1, 2008, 73–89.

5 Friedrich Schlegel, *Friedrich Schlegel's Lucinde and the Fragments*. Translated by Peter Firchow. University of Minnesota Press, 1971, 175.

6 On the "testimonial" potency of archaeological residues see Stewart, *The Ruins Lesson*, 6–30.

7 Ruskin, *The Seven Lamps of Architecture*, 186–87.

8 Andreas Schönle, "Ruins and History: Observations on Russian Approaches to Destruction and Decay." *Slavic Review*, vol. 65, no. 4, 2006, 649–69. *JSTOR*, www .jstor.org/stable/4148448. Accessed Mar. 15, 2020, 652.

9 Henry James, *The Italian Hours*. Harper, 1909, 34.

10 Thomas Hardy, "The Revisitation." *The Complete Poems of Thomas Hardy*. Macmillan, 1982, 346.

11 See Michael S. Roth et al., eds., *Irresistible Decay: Ruins Reclaimed*. Getty Research Institute for the History of Art & the Humanities, 1998; Camilo José Vergara, *American Ruins*. Monacelli Press, 1999; Paul Zucker, "Ruins. An Aesthetic Hybrid." *The Journal of Aesthetics and Art Criticism*, vol. 20, no. 2, 1961, 119–30; Nigel J. Thrift, *Spatial Formations*. Sage, 1996; Dan Dubowitz, *Wastelands*. Dewi Lewis Publishing, 2010; Robert Ginsberg, *The Aesthetics of Ruins*. Rodopi, 2004; Caitlin DeSilvey and Tim Edensor, "Reckoning with Ruins." *Progress in Human Geography*, vol. 37, no. 4, Aug. 2013, 465–85.

12 J. Wilford, "Out of Rubble: Natural Disaster and the Materiality of the House." *Environment and Planning D: Society and Space*, vol. 26, 2008, 647–62; H. Somers-Hall, "The Concept of Ruin: Sartre and the Existential City." *Urbis Research Forum Review*, vol. 1, 2009, 17–19; Mélanie van der Hoorn, "Exorcizing Remains: Architectural Fragments as Intermediaries between History and Individual Experience." *Journal of Material Culture*, vol. 8, no. 2, 2003, 189–213, doi:10.1177/13591835030082004.

13 Christopher Woodward, *In Ruins*. Chatto & Windus, 2001, 2.

14 Georg Simmel, "Two Essays." *The Hudson Review*, vol. 11, no. 3, 1958, 371–85, 383. *JSTOR*, www.jstor.org/stable/3848614.

15 See Ann Laura Stoler, *Imperial Debris: On Ruins and Ruination*. Duke University Press, 2013; Dylan Trigg, "The Place of Trauma: Memory, Hauntings, and the Temporality of Ruins." *Memory Studies*, vol. 2, no. 1, Jan. 2009, 87–101, doi:10.1177/1750698008097397.

16 Rose Macaulay, *The Pleasure of Ruins*. Walker and Company, 1966, 454.

17 Ruskin, *The Seven Lamps of Architecture*, 187.

18 See Glenn Parsons and Allen Carlson, *Functional Beauty*. Clarendon Press, 2008.

19 As Annette Larson Benert, Susan Goodman and others have noted, both Wharton's *French Ways and Their Meaning* (1919) and correspondence with her close friend Sara Norton variously document Wharton's acute sense of being "out of place", among the

"wretched exotics produced in a European glass-house," when returning to a United States with its "wild, dishevelled backwoods look" and absence of a deep, substantial history manifested in architectural and horticultural terms. See Benert, "Edith Wharton at War: Civilized Space in Troubled Times." *Twentieth Century Literature*, vol. 42, no. 3, Autumn 1996, 322–43.

20 For critic Sabrina Ferri, the "ever-present ideal of recovering and reappropriating the past weakened the link to the present and the future, because the movement towards the future was also, always, a movement of recovery, an attempt at maintaining a continuity of meaning and identity with what had come before". Sabrina Ferri, *Ruins Past: Modernity in Italy, 1744-1836*. Oxford University Press, 2015, 4.

21 Edith Wharton, "A Bottle of Perrier." *Ghost Stories of Edith Wharton*. Vintage, 2009, 271–92, 271.

22 Thomas De Quincey, "The Palimpsest of the Human Brain." 1845. *Quotidiana*, edited by Patrick Madden. Dec. 1, 2006. Feb. 1, 2020. http://essays.quotidiana.org/dequincey/palimpsest_of_the_human_brain/.

23 This deficiency has since been redressed in the more nuanced revised entry of *Oxford English Dictionary 3* online, which augments the second edition's definition by stating that the original text in a palimpsest may be "partially erased", while the writing surface, although altered and reused, may still retain "traces of its earlier form".

24 Wharton, *The Age of Innocence*, 29.

25 Katie Trumpener and James M. Nyce, "The Recovered Fragments: Archaeological and Anthropological Perspectives in Edith Wharton's *The Age of Innocence*." *Literary Anthropology: A New Interdisciplinary Approach to People, Signs, and Literature*, edited by Fernando Poyatos. John Benjamins Publishing Company, 1988, 161–69, 161.

26 Wharton, "A Bottle of Perrier," 283.

27 " palimpsest, n. and adj." *OED Online*. Oxford University Press, March 2020, www.oed.com/view/Entry/136319. Accessed Apr. 1, 2020.

28 Sarah Dillon, "Introduction: The Palimpsest." *The Palimpsest: Literature, Criticism, Theory*. Continuum, 2007, 1–9. Continuum Literary Studies Series, 12.

29 Gilberto Perez, "Introduction: Film and Physics." *The Material Ghost: Films and Their Medium*. The Johns Hopkins University Press, 2000, 1–28, 22.

30 McFarland, "Introduction: Fragmented Modalities and the Criteria of Romanticism," 7.

31 Ramsden, *Edith Wharton's Library: A Catalogue*, 77. See also Wharton, *The Letters of Edith Wharton*, 552.

32 Giacomo Leopardi, *Canti*. Mondadori, 1987, 58. Own translation. Original text: "Mira queste ruine/ E le carte e le tele e I marmi e I templi;/ Pensa qual terra premi; e se destarti/ Non può la luce di contanti esempli,/ Che stai? levati e parti."

33 Wharton, *In Morocco*, 14.

34 Wharton, *The Cruise of the Vanadis*, 189.

35 Wharton, *The Cruise of the Vanadis*, 189.

36 Michael Shanks, *The Archaeological Imagination*. Left Coast Press, 2016, 21.

37 Wharton, *In Morocco*, 20. Emerton Sillerton in *The Age of Innocence* is an archaeologist. He uses his work as a way of escaping New York high society, as May Welland remarks: "nothing on earth obliged Emerson Sillerton to be an archaeologist, or indeed a Professor of any sort, or to live in Newport in winter, or do any of the other revolutionary things that he did". See Wharton, *The Age of Innocence*, 134. The capacity of Wharton and her characters to "dig deep" in search of semiotic

patterns also informs *Twilight Sleep*: the "void into which Pauline advanced gave prominence to the figure of a man who stood with his back to her, looking through the window at what was to be a garden when Viking horticulture was revived". In reality, what Pauline Manford actually sees is an eerie scene: "Meanwhile it was fully occupied by neighbouring cats and by swirls of wind-borne rubbish". Wharton, *Twilight Sleep*, 132.

Chapter 10

"OLD" RUINS AS A MELANCHOLIC OBJECT AND A CRITIQUE OF EMPIRE

In *Ruin Lust* (2014), Brian Dillon asks: "ruins are still standing—but what do they stand for?"[1] Moreover, how do we explicate what Rose Macaulay terms "this strange human reaction to decay"?[2] These questions resonate through Wharton's short story "Roman Fever," one of her final works, published in 1934, just three years before her death. In this text, two affluent American widows sit on the terrace of a restaurant to reminisce and admire the "august ruins" of the ancient city in the afternoon light. That these women are positioned as "old lovers of Rome" suggests they are not too far removed from critic Joseph Luzzi's thesis that foreign pilgrims to this region, inspired partly by the Grand Tour imaginary and with deep enough pockets to purchase views of the picturesque, ultimately crafted a concept of "Italy without Italians." Such devotion to the relics of Rome's faded glories conveniently elided the messy, unedifying contradictions of contemporary Italy, and Southern Europe more broadly.[3]

Wharton's text deserves to be seen as more than a sketch inspired by Henry James's *Daisy Miller* (1878), because as Christopher Woodward states: "no writer saw the same Colosseum."[4] "Roman Fever" is not only rich in what Denis Diderot described as the melancholy "poetics of ruins," when analyzing the paintings of Hubert Robert at the Salon de 1767.[5] It also brings into relief, as Rachel Bowlby avers, "the excavations of 'old' parental stories": "whether secret or not, they come out looking different in relation to the contexts in which we encounter them now."[6] "Roman Fever" shows the subtle operations of Wharton's imaginative archaeology, shaped by her shrewd awareness of Grand Tour iconography, as well as obsessions in the eighteenth-century imaginary, such as the widely reported discoveries at Herculaneum and Pompeii, and bestsellers of the era like Constantin Volney's *Les Ruines, or Meditations on Revolutions and Empires* (1792).

In "Roman Fever," "ruin" from the Latin *ruere* ("to collapse, fall") signifies both object (a time-worn statue or an amphitheater) and "process" (how

apparently educated, privileged citizens of the world can spoil their own—
and others'—happiness). In a story that uncovers through its closing phase
a buried history of parental intrigue and illicit assignation, the "ruin" or
safeguarding of a woman's personal honor or reputation also plays an unex-
pectedly potent role. What makes "Roman Fever" especially useful in this
chapter is how the exact meaning of the ancient city and its landmarks seem
in constant evolution. Social and cultural codes, artistic and philosophical
credos, become legible through the myriad narratives that "ruins" carry in
this text. The opening sentence introduces Mrs. Slade and Mrs. Ansley without giving their names yet, and it captures the locale to which they give a
rapt regard:

> From the table at which they had been lunching two American ladies
> of ripe, but well-cared-for middle age moved across the lofty terrace
> of the Roman restaurant and, leaning on its parapet, looked first at
> each other, and then down on the outspread glories of the Palatine
> and the Forum, with the same expression of vague but benevolent
> approval.[7]

The figurations establish a duality that invokes and references the two
Capitoline Dioscuri[8] in Piazza del Campidoglio. The two women frame this
landscape of classical wonder the same way the statues of the two Roman dei-
ties, Castor and Pollux, guard the entrance of the summit of the Capitoline
hill. This is underlined by the fact that Wharton's narrator depicts on multiple occasions these two American ladies gazing at each other, just like two
venerable Roman sculptures.[9] The widows' shared experience—they "had
lived opposite each other—actually as well as figuratively for years" in New
York—is disclosed by their mirrored facial features. The emotionless and
contained expressions of these widows is reflected in the two time-crusted
and enigmatic Roman statues as well. Later in the text, Wharton revisits
and extends this imagery and sense of formal design: "The two women stood
for a minute staring at each other in the last golden light. Then Mrs. Ansley
dropped back into her chair."[10]

The text exploits such tropes so that we might measure the classical monuments—the exalted creations of a venerable civilization—against the two
women and their late husbands who are "museum specimens of old New
York."[11] Wharton is writing in the 1930s about New York high society at the
turn of the twentieth century, making Mrs. Slade and Mrs. Ansley, just like
the landmarks they admire, vestiges of a long-gone culture. More specifically,
these ladies are—to adapt anthropologist Edward Burnett Tylor's coinage in
his 2-volume *Primitive Culture* (1871)—"survivals":

These are processes, customs, opinions, and so forth, which have been carried on by force of habit into a new state of society different from that in which they had their original home, and they thus remain as proofs and examples of an older condition of culture out of which a newer has been evolved.[12]

What makes Tylor's definition pertinent to a reading of "Roman Fever" is the sense of Wharton dramatizing the human body as fossil/ized, wreck/ed or ruin/ed, incongruously residing alongside more modish and democratic interwar tribes, attitudes and "customs," wittily symbolized by the appearance, at the end of the text, of a "stout lady in a dust-coat […] asking in *broken Italian* if anyone had seen the elastic band which held together her *tattered Baedecker*" (my emphasis).[13]

The narrator portrays the Roman ruins at one stage as the "accumulated wreckage of passion and splendor," a phrase that also captures the domestic lives of these two women, given their link with a fallen empire of outmoded manners and mores (Tylor's "older condition of culture"). These semantic resonances are extended in *The Age of Innocence*, when Newland Archer describes Mrs. Van der Luyden "as having been rather gruesomely preserved in the airless atmosphere of a perfectly irreproachable existence, as bodies caught in glaciers keep for years a rosy life-in-death."[14] Here the terms suggest not the oddly sumptuous dilapidation synonymous with the European picturesque, but rather a grisly holdover imbued with the merest semblance of animation.

Even though the middle-aged women imply Tylorian "survivals" in "Roman Fever," Wharton's narrator invests them with a crucial measure of dynamism: her "gesture was now addressed to the stupendous scene at their feet."[15] The widow's "gesture" is unspecified, but the reader is led to imagine that it is akin to Chironomia, the rhetoric of hand movements employed in Ancient Greek and Roman oratory. This is a notable and telling exception, because for the rest of the short story, the women's hands will be occupied by their knitting.[16]

The ladies' meditative absorption in their knitting—a careful and creative use of the hands—is measured against the nearby tourist groups who are "fumbling for tips," "detained by a lingering look at the outspread city" and "gathering up guide-books."[17] This reference to "guide-books" is especially curious, given that some of Wharton's travelogues eventually became guidebooks for Americans traveling to Southern Europe and North Africa. What is most marked here is the irony of the two widows' self-placement as custodians of an elevated aesthetic sensibility—"following," like Wharton herself "step by step Ruskin's arbitrary itineraries"[18]—and the loud vulgarity of the tourist "groups."

As Ruskin suggests at the outset of this chapter, ruined sites are far from residual or unproductive. Indeed, they "speak" eloquently, and do so through this short story in a twofold manner. Just as the widows knit their patterns, so the narrator *weaves* into the textual fabric myriad Greco-Roman allusions that complicate the sense of occasion and buttress the theatrical qualities of the classical vestiges below the terrace. The writing from "Delphin"—the French form of this boy's name points to the Greek town of Delphi, home of the oracle—carries an ominous charge in a story that quarries a substratum of illicit affect by its close. Mrs. Ansley's face is, at one stage, portrayed as a "mask" that seems of a piece with a role in timeless ritual or classical tragedy. As Barbara A. White acknowledges: "In the beginning of the story the city seems a mere decorative backdrop. Only gradually, as the past wells up to overwhelm the two women, does the reader come to feel the presence of the Roman past and realize that Rome is an integral part of the story."[19] However, the ruins also alert us to seemingly innocuous tangible data: "Two *derelict* basket-chairs stood near, and she pushed them into the angle of the parapet, and settled herself in one, her gaze upon the Palatine" (my emphasis).[20] The fact that the widows justify their love of Rome and ask for permission to stay on this terrace implies benign indiscretion. However, they are about to uncover a past transgression that completely changes their lives. The details are packaged as a story within a story:

> A few years later, and not many months apart, both ladies lost their husbands. There was an appropriate exchange of wreaths and condolences, and a brief renewal of intimacy in the half-shadow of their mourning; and now, after another interval, they had run across each other in Rome, at the same hotel, each of them the modest appendage of a salient daughter.[21]

The narrator evokes each of the women as a "modest appendage of a salient daughter," which adds to their sense of displacement in this setting—an addition to the landscape rather than rooted in it through long familiarity. The lines of their personal histories will be drawn differently after this meeting, and the narrator, before recounting what happened, evokes the distorted perspective which these widows apparently share: "So these two ladies visualized each other, each through the wrong end of her little telescope."[22] This instrument is necessary to see the landscape in more detail, and it symbolizes the problems of perspective that are at the very heart of the relationship between the two women. Rather than observation, this passage suggests introspection; instead of gazing at the ancient, public history scattered across the horizon, the women will have to reappraise their own, shared history: "to both, there was a relief in laying down their somewhat futile activities in the presence of the vast Memento Mori which faced them."[23] The critic Roxana Robinson acknowledges that they are grieving for their past: "the women are carried by the march of memory to the rising rhythm of animosity, through a landscape of jealousy and deception, illicit assignations, sexual thrall, and unwed pregnancy."[24] However, Robinson's reading does not acknowledge the potency of the Coliseum in this imaginative framework. The two women recall the past differently and imprecisely. Even though they observe the same palpable locality, the same grand remnants as in their youth, each one has a contrasting version of events that they silently carry within them. This notion emerges through the voicefulness of the Roman ruins:

> "I was just thinking," she said slowly, "what different things Rome stands for to each generation of travelers. To our grandmother, Roman fever; to our mothers, sentimental dangers—how we used to be guarded!—to our daughters, no more dangers than the middle of Main Street. They don't know it—but how much they're missing!"[25]

What is most arresting about this extract is how Rome and its relics (especially the "long green hollow of the Forum" and "the outlying immensity of the Coliseum") convey messages that transcend "sentimental dangers."[26] Rereading the text in light of the revelations at the story's end has the effect of investing glib remarks or casual gestures ("time to kill," "so purposeless a wound," knitting falls as "a panic-stricken heap") with an oddly disturbing, even visceral intensity.[27] This is also true of the pointed use of sur/names throughout—Mrs. Slade/slayed and the daughter Barbara (implying the feminine form of the ancient Greek term for the *barbaros* or savage outsider).[28] This violence is, of course, entirely in keeping with the original purpose of the Roman amphitheater. Such semantic ambiguities also point to the very real perils and devastating consequences of geopolitical strife. Wharton, given her own writing in support of Allied participation in World War I as well as French war efforts against German aggression, was keenly aware of how concepts of ruin had altered irrevocably and tragically over the course of the first three decades of the twentieth century.[29] Her articles collected in *Fighting France*, especially her reaction to the fire-scorched walls of Rheims Cathedral, confront what happens to cherished sites under technologically advanced and sustained "German bombardment."[30] Such a history of traumatic violence—producing meanings and modes of encounter that are far from "delightful"—evokes Nathaniel Hawthorne's sense of the Coliseum's physical scale and structure in *The Marble Faun*:

The Coliseum is far more delightful, as we enjoy it now, than when eighty thousand persons sat squeezed together, row above row, to see their fellow-creatures torn by lions and tigers limb from limb. What a strange thought, that the Coliseum was really built for us, and has not come to its best uses till almost two thousand years after it was finished![31]

Hawthorne's terms are applicable to Wharton's story because, unbeknownst to them, Mrs. Ansley and Mrs. Slade will engage in metaphorical gladiatorial combat—an increasingly bitter verbal sparring—that will culminate with the last sentence of the story, when the genteel fiction of a "delightful" Roman ruin can no longer be sustained.

One of the last images in "Roman Fever," before the painful truth is revealed, is of Mrs. Ansley searching for the Coliseum in her line of sight: "Mrs. Ansley stood looking away from her toward the dusky secret mass" of the ancient structure.[32] This is significant because it evokes Georg Simmel's theorization of a ruin as a form built by humans and decimated by nature: "Nature has transformed the work of art into material for her own expression, as she had previously served material for art."[33] Nature transforms the ruin, and the personal narratives of Mrs. Ansley and Mrs. Slade have been altered by their new status as "secret sharers." Rome is the setting of both betrayal and the inevitable, "indecent" exposure (or excavation) of truths concerning mistaken paternity.

Even though Edith Wharton's short story "A Bottle of Perrier" was praised by English novelist Graham Greene as a "superb horror story,"[34] it remains one of Wharton's least studied fictional works.[35] First published with the title "A Bottle of Evian" in *The Saturday Evening Post* in March 1926, it was then republished with this title in the 1930 volume *Certain People* and again in the 1937 collection of ghost stories.[36] The title is misleading however, for it exists as a negative that will not be: the sparkling water never arrives in the North African desert fortress where the story plays out. This is an unusual location for one of Wharton's fictions, but not altogether unexpected, as she travelled to the region on four different occasions.[37] In this section I gauge the story's precisely evoked geographical milieu, from the dusty interiors of the stronghold to the desert which surrounds (or engulfs) it, focusing especially on the "ancient walls" as constructed barriers between the two spaces, what happens within them and what they stand for. Ultimately the text, by aestheticizing the damaged building, prompts us to consider the political resonances behind such aesthetics. Wharton's "fortress" challenges traditional fields of sight and invites a reading that prioritizes how a physical ruin does not simply *exist* in a condition of sad or mystifying abandonment. Instead, it seems to strike back at empire, defying those warring human tribes that try to claim it as their sole possession and prize.

"A Bottle of Perrier" is an unlikely ghost story. As Carol J. Singley remarks: "Although Wharton included 'A Bottle of Perrier' in a collection she titled *Ghosts*, the only ghost is imagined by Gosling, not actually seen."[38] There is no unearthly or spectral entity then, just the conspicuous absence of the current "tenant," Henry Almodham.[39] Wharton is more exercised by rethinking what the story calls "this castle of romance"—implying the standard Gothic lexicon of ruins, synonymous with dreamlike visions of forbidding citadels and blighted monasteries in Catholic Western Europe.[40] She utilizes the desert ruin to ponder the consequences of admitting the fearful over the threshold into one's psyche or body, which raises persistently vexing questions about personal and imperial dis/possession (via vivid tropes of "opium pipes of jade and amber"). This is why "A Bottle of Perrier" is full of tension. When it finally resolves, rather than being enlightened, we are confronted with a profoundly disturbing moral dilemma.[41] This process of *unsettling* is addressed by Candace Waid from a gender studies perspective: " 'A Bottle of Perrier' is among Wharton's most frightening depictions of entrapment in place by the landscape of the feminine."[42] However the fortress seems to cast a sidelight not so much on "the feminine," but rather the Burkean sublime, which foregrounds "Astonishment" where "all motions are suspended with some degree of horror."[43] When the truth is revealed, that Almodham has been dead at the bottom of the well the entire time, we recall Ruskin's notion of "parasitical sublimity," which he develops in "The Lamp of Memory": "But that character, of which the extreme pursuit is generally admitted to be degrading to art, is *parasitical* sublimity; *i.e.*, a sublimity dependent on the accidents, or on the least essential characters, of the objects to which it belongs."[44] Wharton subtly orchestrates the very "accident" at the center of this short story and the *grand guignol* manner in which it plays out.

The ruin in this text is evoked through the traveler Medford's eyes. Affiliated with "the American School of Archaeology at Athens," he appears both entranced and puzzled at a tangible formation that reveals (and conceals) the marks of colonial conquest, clearance and indigenous dispossession. Does the site gesture at noble (or ruinous) human ambition that was progressively, or suddenly, submerged in the sands of time? For Medford fixing meaning is difficult here given "the mystery of the sands, all golden with promise, all livid with menace, as the sun alternately touched or abandoned them."[45] "*Mystery* of the sands" reminds us that, according to one recent scientific commentator, "no single, conclusive ecological definition of the term 'desert' has been accepted."[46] What Wharton's narrator terms the "omnipresence of the desert" in these opening pages gestures at nebulous, even contradictory associations. Does the desert ruin signify a moment of metaphysical anxiety, as it does in canonical texts ranging from P. B. Shelley's poem "Ozymandias" to Don DeLillo's novel *Point Omega* (2010)? Is the North African desert an impressive natural expanse, a place where we can differentiate "wilderness" (which may wither away over time) from Gary Snyder's concept of "wildness," which exists at both biotic and abiotic levels, and is also a "quality intrinsic to who we are"?[47] We might argue that the *real* ruin in "A Bottle of Perrier" is the desert itself, since it is a partially man-made and unforgiving waste? A complex ecology that sustains a surprising mixture of lifeforms or an exhausted, ravaged earth?[48]

In this possibly cursed expanse can be found the debris of what may once have been an architectural marvel: a "jumble of masonry and stucco, Christian and Moslem." Wreckage from myriad secular and religious traditions has intermingled, making for a stubbornly strange, "in-between" species of space. Medford leans "against the roof parapet of the old building, half Christian fortress, half Arab palace."[49] The Christians, who (presumably) seized what was a strategically valuable site, repurpose a "palace," synonymous with regal comfort, as a "fortress" where austere military discipline is geared towards keeping the former princely "Arab" occupants out. This hint of former imperial strife (and spoils of "gold") is woven into an opulent descriptive flourish: the "afternoon hung over the place like a *great velarium* of cloth-of-gold stretched across the battlements and drooping down in ever slacker folds upon the heavy-headed palms" (my emphasis).[50] A velarium (or "curtain") is a large awning used to protect Roman spectators from the sun in the Coliseum and other Roman amphitheaters.[51]

So "half Christian [...] half Arab" signals how the span and sway of any empire necessitates endeavors to re/claim and assign spiritual, martial and secular meaning to its often-damaged architectural spoils. Are we dealing then with "a legible remnant of the past" or a "scattered cipher," an architectural "text" that is "alternately readable and utterly mysterious"?[52] Medford's initial sense-impressions reveal how this physical site has ongoing, interlinked (Christian-Arab) legacies. The "jumble of masonry" is a historical actuality, an aesthetic object, and a category of thought—does Medford classify it as exotic refuge for "pilgrims of the desert," a makeshift prison or a burial ground? That "the latest tenant of the fortress had chosen a cluster of rooms tucked into an angle of the ancient keep"[53] is telling. The living quarters can be revitalized over time but there are no true "owners" of the ruin in Wharton's text—only "tenants." Rather it is the fortress that eventually "possesses" those who sought sanctuary within its now "dilapidated walls of yellow stone." This image underscores a growing sense of precarity, exposure and insecurity in the text. These walls divide but also seem permeable; they offer Medford a vantage point from which to survey within and without, where East and West meet in an orientalist flourish.[54] While the text "implies the world of North Africa to be a fascinating, exotic, yet threatening place of cultural Otherness,"[55] the fortress walls cannot keep out an estranging alterity for long. These walls are "dilapidated" and the distinction between basic, "airless" living quarters and immeasurable desert will collapse.[56] It is through such nuances that Wharton makes us ponder the blurring of physical partitions between ruin and rubble, between monument and necropolis.

Medford's reaction to his crumbling surroundings is defined increasingly by his engagement with the interior courtyard, at whose center is an "ancient fig tree, enormous, exuberant, writhed over a whitewashed well-head, sucking life from what appeared to be the only source of moisture within the walls."[57] The bizarre and sinister lexis ("writhed," "sucking") undercuts the sacred associations of the fig tree, which is the third tree to be mentioned by name in the Hebrew Bible, after the Tree of Life and Tree of the Knowledge of Good and Evil. Wharton's text also exploits a further irony. In *Deuteronomy*, the Promised Land is an expanse of "wheat and barley, of vines and fig trees and pomegranates [...] where you will eat food without scarcity, in which you will not lack anything" (*Deuteronomy* 8:8–10). This "land" of overflowing ripeness and plenitude furnishes the starkest contrast to the desert outpost in which the key actors of Wharton's text find themselves marooned. The fig tree is a recurrent motif in the story—serving as a macabre *genius loci*, or spirit of place whose purpose is to disrupt the memorable, benign imagery of *Proverbs* 27: 18 which compares tending a fig tree to looking after one's master.[58] In "A Bottle of Perrier," the fig tree is a parasitical entity that, unbeknownst to Medford, feeds off its "master" Almodham, who in death will become an archaeological fragment like those to which he dedicated so much of his professional life. Here we have, not Gustave Flaubert's lyrically evocative trope of "vegetation resting upon old ruins; this embrace of nature."[59] Instead, Wharton's "fig tree" is "*coiled* above the well"[60] (my emphasis)—an oppressive, choking "embrace" that underlines the sense of a predatory, remorseless organic energy establishing the rules of its own green empire, founded upon "secret commerce with the palms"[61] and using a human cadaver as a source of sustenance.

However, Medford is continually drawn to the fig tree, and in this inhospitable setting, it assumes for him a protective, even paternal role. Here, in a further, faint ironic echo of 1 *Kings* 4: 25 in which a man can live safely "under his own vine and fig tree," Wharton's narrator notes: "A seat under the fig tree invited Medford to doze, and when he woke the hard blue dome above him was gemmed with stars and the night breeze gossiped with the palms."[62] It foreshadows Almodham's death when Medford "strolled back and found the court empty of life, but fantastically peopled by palms of beaten silver and a white marble fig tree."[63] The poetic lexis here assumes an eerie resonance. Gosling has to keep Medford away from the well and the fig tree in order to hide his crime. The more he does this, the more he exposes himself, and the more Medford becomes suspicious. Indeed, the earlier conception of the desert fortress as a refuge with some formal aesthetic properties—"[t]o anyone sick of the Western fret and fever the very walls" of this site "exuded peace"[64]— begins to fall apart. Medford "felt himself shut out, unwanted—the place, now that he imagined someone might be living in it unknown to him, became lonely, inhospitable, dangerous."[65] The ruined fortress "voices"—revisiting Ruskin's exact terms—safety and seclusion at first, but this morphs into a growing dread as an empire of stones takes on an uncanny life of its own.

Beyond the fortress walls lies the North African desert, depicted as a "land [...] full of spells."[66] These "spells," synonymous with romantic ruins, now become, at least for the stressed Medford, a Gothic "curse" or hex. This evokes Fred Botting's theory of how "Gothic texts operate ambivalently: the dynamic inter-relation of limit and transgression, prohibition and desire suggest that norms, limits, boundaries and foundations are neither natural nor absolutely fixed or stable despite the fears they engender."[67] Not only are the "boundaries" shifting, but they seem to be removed altogether as the "spell" of the sands engulf these isolated actors. The critic Carol J. Singley argues that with "her desert setting, Wharton is able to achieve both an erotic *and* a gothic effect."[68] However Singley neglects to weigh the earlier biblical resonances of the fig tree and the function of the desert as a barren place of punishment, inimical to human life. An example of this being *Isaiah* 32:16, "Justice will dwell in the desert and righteousness live in the fertile field." This verse is significant given that Gosling has been living out his punishment of twelve years' labor in the fortress without a vacation before he murdered his haughty employer. So a structure that starts as a former "palace," is now more akin to a ghastly wreck on an ocean of sand, which evokes Nietzsche's warning in *Thus Spoke Zarathustra* (1883-5): "The desert grows: woe to him who harbors deserts!"[69] Gosling is not only trapped in an actual wasteland, a place (to him) of physical enervation and despair where there can be no true belonging or home, only the "light monotonous smoothness of eternity."[70] As a criminal he carries a "stony waste," a desert within, an existential void implied by his association with "evil secrets clinging bat-like to the nest of masonry."[71] One of the contributing factors that leads Gosling to murder Almodham is the lack of "measures of time in a place like this."[72] For the transgressor Gosling there can be no redemptive vision of "the dawn break[ing] in all its holiness" or a "fountain of purity welling up into the heavens."[73] Indeed, he seems to apprehend what Martin Heidegger theorizes in "Evening Conversation" as " 'Devastation' [...] that everything—the world, the human, and the earth— will be transformed into a desert."[74]

The "wheeling of the constellations over those ruined walls marked only the revolutions of the earth; the spasmodic motions of man meant nothing."[75]

The closing phase of Wharton's text asks us to imagine what "revolutions" (or crusades based on material gain) have caused those "walls" to burn, shake and decay over centuries. More importantly, Gosling's situation signals how a desert and its rubble challenges "life's ability to make a place for itself." It puts "our conceptions" of space—the relation between earth and heavens— "belonging" and precise location into doubt.[76] The fortress walls serve as a kind of "moon dial" so that nomads and navigators can discern the passage of time—all the more crucial given the acute challenges of establishing permanent marks or settlements on these shifting North African dunes. This is relevant in parsing Gosling's spiritual anguish and homicidal impulse. He has been cloistered within the fortress for many years, which makes him a prisoner of sorts, and it is unclear how well he can determine coordinates in conformity with the rising and setting stars ("wheeling of constellations") and recurrent rhythms of wind or (extreme) weather events. He is also an aggrieved factotum or subaltern caught in the meshes of class and colonial hierarchies. As Rich explains, by murdering Almodham, Gosling may "symbolize the resistant colonial object, breaking through hegemonically inscribed boundaries to rebel against oppression."[77] But Gosling also appears "infected" in these closing pages with the intense affect that Edward Said formulates: "a form of paranoia, knowledge of another kind, say, from ordinary historical knowledge."[78] Gosling's "knowledge" implies how the North African sands not only deplete the possibilities of language itself but becomes the geographical correlate of *vacancy*. Gosling is compelled to glimpse what critic Aidan Tynan terms that "point beyond the buoyancy of the experience of nature that animated Romantic sublimity towards the sheer inescapability of space as a brute and abstract reality."[79] The codes by which he grasps temporality and eternity have been utterly scrambled. Even Medford acknowledges that there "were no time measures in a place like this."[80] Such "paranoia" is at a far remove from the aloof, distanced appreciation of classical ruins that the wealthy widows strive for in Wharton's "Roman Fever."

Crucially, Wharton's conception of the desert in this closing phase implies that we are dealing with a very different type of sublime affect from that synonymous with snow-covered summits or archaic locations like the Acropolis or Coliseum. As Cian Duffy's *The Landscapes of the Sublime, 1700-1830* explains, deserts do not feature conspicuously as sites of "the natural sublime" in Romantic-era cultural production. Wharton's text dramatizes a twilight zone much closer to the ominous and "chastened sublimity" of Egdon Heath in Thomas Hardy's *The Return of the Native* (1878).[81] In this aesthetic and philosophical construct of sublime affect, any Burkean relish or frisson at the boundless is smothered by recognition of very real physical peril, frightening nullity and arid, featureless "uniformity."[82]

Commentators have judged the end of Wharton's short story as lacking in affective impact. While "Wharton's message is subtle" in "A Bottle of Perrier," according to Jenni Dyman, the text is missing "a dramatic moment of epiphany beyond the 'who-dun-it' confession."[83] This can be explained by the fact that Wharton is not primarily exercised by consequences, or even intricate human motivations. In a manner reminiscent of Georg Simmel in his 1911 essay "The Ruin," Wharton's text conveys the profound ecological implications of ancient remnants, which provide a "stage" for an eternal conflict between two cosmic tendencies—tangible nature and the mortal appetite for territorial acquisition. Simmel's concept of the ruin pushes against the grain of, and subverts, a glib anthropocentric faith in the mastery of humankind over the organic environment. In Simmel's essay, as in Wharton's story (via the vivid trope of the fig tree), nature has the power to wrest, reclaim and transmute the built structure—as well as the human remains buried within it—"into material for her own expression."[84] The fortress emerges not just as an autonomous entity, but the *central protagonist* in Wharton's story, overshadowing what the narrator calls "the spasmodic motions of man." The fortress attests its own survival from oblivion, unlike those hubristic wanderers who dared to cross the crumbling threshold.

Notes

1 Brian Dillon, *Ruin Lust: Artists' Fascination with Ruins, from Turner to the Present Day*. Tate Publishing, 2014, 5. See also C. Morgan, "Book review, *Ruins of Modernity*." *Visual Studies*, vol. 26, no. 1, 2011, 84.
2 Macaulay, *The Pleasure of Ruins*, xv.
3 See Joseph Luzzi, *Romantic Europe and the Ghost of Italy*. Yale University Press, 2008, 53–76.
4 Woodward, *In Ruins*, 23. James's story concerns a contemporary American young woman whose behaviour in Rome, including a late-night visit with a man to the Colosseum, ultimately leads to her contracting malaria ("Roman fever") and dying.
5 "The effect of these compositions, good or bad, is to leave us in a sweet melancholy. We gaze upon the debris of a triumphal arch, a portico, a pyramid, a temple, a palace; and we come back on ourselves; we anticipate the ravages of time; and our imagination scatters the very buildings we inhabit on earth. At the moment solitude and silence reign around us. We remain alone of a whole nation that is no more. And here is the first line of the poetics of the ruins". Own translation. Original text: "L'effet de ces compositions, bonnes ou mauvaises, c'est de vous laisser dans une douce mélancolie. Nous attachons nos regards sur les debris d'un arc de triomophe, d'une portique, d'une pyramide, d'un temple, d'un palais; et nous revenons sur nous-mêmes; nous anticipons sur les ravages du temps; et notre imagination disperse sur la terre les édifices mêmes que nous habitons. A l'instant la solitude et le silence régnent autour de nous. Nous restons seuls de toute une nation qui n'est plus. Et voilà la première ligne de la poétique des ruines." Denis Diderot, *Ruines et Paysages: Salons De 1767*. Edited by Else Marie Bukdahl et al. Hermann, 1995, 335.

6 Rachel Bowlby, "'I Had Barbara': Women's Ties and Edith Wharton's 'Roman Fever'." *A Child of One's Own: Parental Stories.* Oxford University Press, 2013, 218–22.

7 Edith Wharton, "Roman Fever." *The New York Stories of Edith Wharton.* New York Review of Books, 2007, 438–52, 438.

8 "The Colossal statues of Castor and Pollux with their Horses standing at the top of the *cordonata* were found in fragments in 1561 on the site of the Temple of Castor and Pollux beside the Circus Flaminius. Originally monoliths of Greek (Pentelic) marble, 5.5 and 5.8 m. high respectively, they were probably not the cult statues of the temple proper, but stood in front of it, on the wings of the front steps. Since the heads are restored (one completely, the other in nose, chin and hair) it is impossible to be sure, but they might have portrayed Augustus' grandsons Gaius (who died aged 24 in AD 4) and Lucius (who died aged 19 in AD 2)." See Amanda Claridge, *Rome.* Oxford Archaeological Guides. Oxford University Press, 1998, 234.

9 Wharton, "Roman Fever," 438.

10 Wharton, "Roman Fever," 448.

11 Wharton, "Roman Fever," 440.

12 Edward Burnett Tylor, *Primitive Culture.* John Murray, 1871, I: 15.

13 Wharton, "Roman Fever," 446.

14 Wharton, *The Age of Innocence*, 89.

15 Wharton, "Roman Fever," 439.

16 Wharton, "Roman Fever," 445.

17 Wharton, "Roman Fever," 439.

18 Wharton, *A Backward Glance*, 87.

19 Barbara A. White, "Wharton's Telling of the Short Story: Theory and Practice." *Edith Wharton: A Study of the Short Fiction.* Twayne Publishers, 1991, 3–26. Twayne's Studies in Short Fiction, 11.

20 Wharton, "Roman Fever," 439–40.

21 Wharton, "Roman Fever," 441.

22 Wharton, "Roman Fever," 443. This is not the only reference to the distorted view through a telescope in Wharton's fiction. In *The Age of Innocence*, Newland Archer considers that: "Viewed thus, as through the wrong end of a telescope, it looked disconcertingly small and distant; but then from Samarkand it would." Wharton, *The Age of Innocence*, 49.

23 Wharton, "Roman Fever," 443.

24 Roxana Robinson, "Introduction." *The New York Stories of Edith Wharton.* New York Review of Books, 2007, xxvi.

25 Wharton, "Roman Fever," 444.

26 Wharton, "Roman Fever," 444.

27 By the end of the story, that is, the very last sentence, Mrs. Slade reveals to Mrs. Ansley that Barbara is Mr. Ansley's biological daughter.

28 On the coded language of belligerence in Wharton's short stories see Bowlby, "'I Had Barbara': Women's Ties and Edith Wharton's 'Roman Fever'," 218–22; Dale M. Bauer, *Edith Wharton's Brave New Politics.* University of Wisconsin Press, 1994.

29 See Shafquat Towheed, "Reading the Great War: An Examination of Edith Wharton's Reading and Responses, 1914–1918." *Reading and the First World War: New Directions in Book History*, edited by Shafquat Towheed, and E. G. C. King. Palgrave Macmillan, 2015, 78–80; Julie Olin-Ammentorp, "Wharton and World War I." *Edith*

Wharton in Context, edited by Laura Rattray. Cambridge: Cambridge University Press, 2012, 293–301. Literature in Context.

30 "And there, before us, rose the Cathedral – *a* cathedral, rather, for it was not the one we had always known. […] the wonder of the impression is increased by the sense of its evanescence; the knowledge that this is the beauty of disease and death, that every one of the transfigured statues must crumble under the autumn rains, that every one of the pink or golden stones is already eaten away to the core". See Edith Wharton, *Fighting France from Dunkerque to Belfort*. Charles Scribner's Sons, 1915, 185–86.

31 Nathaniel Hawthorne, *The Marble Faun*. In *Novels: Fanshawe, The Scarlet Letter, The House of the Seven Gables, The Blithedale Romance, The Marble Faun*. Library of America, 1983, 849–1242, 982.

32 Wharton, "Roman Fever," 450.

33 Georg Simmel, "The Ruin." Translated by David Kettler. *The Hudson Review*, vol. 11, no. 3, 1958, 381.

34 Graham Greene, "'Short Stories'." *Edith Wharton: The Contemporary Reviews*, edited by James W. Tuttleton et al. Cambridge University Press, 1992, 537–42. Greene goes on to argue that the mere premise of this short story is horrifying: "to drink water from a well in which a friend's body is rotting, aware only of an odd smell, an unpleasant taste, is an idea which certainly graduates in horror".

35 See Jenni Dyman, "'A Bottle of Perrier' and 'Mr. Jones'." *Lurking Feminism: The Ghost Stories of Edith Wharton*. Peter Lang, 1996, 115–38.

36 See Charlotte Rich, "Fictions of Colonial Anxiety: Edith Wharton's 'The Seed of the Faith' and 'A Bottle of Perrier'." *Journal of the Short Story in English* [Online], vol. 43, Autumn 2004, Online since Aug. 5, 2008, connection on Apr. 30, 2019, 1–12, 1.

37 Charlotte Rich explains that: "She visited the region four times, calling at the ports of Algiers and Tunis during an 1888 Mediterranean cruise; traveling to Algeria and Tunisia in 1914; touring Morocco in 1917 at the invitation of its French Resident-General at the time, Marshal Louis-Hubert Lyautey; and visiting the port of Alexandria, Egypt during a 1926 cruise of the Mediterranean." Rich, "Fictions of Colonial Anxiety: Edith Wharton's 'The Seed of the Faith' and 'A Bottle of Perrier',", 1.

38 Carol J. Singley, "Gothic Borrowings and Innovations in Edith Wharton's 'A Bottle of Perrier'." *Edith Wharton: New Critical Essays*, edited by Alfred Bendixen and Annette Zilversmit. Garland Publishing, 1992, 271–90.

39 As Jennifer Haytock remarks: "Almodham himself is absent and mythical; we hear stories about him but never meet him." See Haytock, "'Unmediated Bonding Between Men': The Accumulation of Men in the Short Stories'." *Edith Wharton and the Conversations of Literary Modernism*. Palgrave Macmillan, 2008, 75–100, 81.

40 Wharton, "A Bottle of Perrier," 271. David Stuart Davies stresses that the story "demonstrates that one does not need gothic touches, old houses with dark corners or moonlit graveyards to produce fears in the reader". See Edith Wharton and David Stuart Davies, "Introduction." *Ghost Stories of Edith Wharton*. Vintage, 2009, vii–xii. Jorge Freire reminds us that if Wharton's "ghost stories scare us - and they do – it's because of their moral character". Own translation. Original text: "...si sus cuentos de fantasmas asustan – y lo hacen –, es por su carácter moral." Jorge Freire, *Edith Wharton: Una mujer rebelde en la edad de la inocencia*. Alrevés, 2015, 152.

41 Candace Waid posits that "Wharton's tales give voice to these suppressed lives by providing them with listeners, readers of their life stories, but in the end the voices from

the past can tell only the story of their representation and unutterable loneliness". See "Pomegranate Seeds: Letters from the Underworld (The Touchstone and Ghosts)." See Candace Waid, *Edith Wharton's Letters from the Underworld: Fictions of Women and Writing*. University of North Carolina Press, 1991, 173–203, 191–92.

42 Waid, "Pomegranate Seeds: Letters from the Underworld (The Touchstone and Ghosts)," 178.

43 Burke, *Philosophical Enquiry*, 47.

44 Ruskin, *The Seven Lamps of Architecture*, 189.

45 Wharton, "A Bottle of Perrier," 271.

46 Olafur Arnalds, "Desertification: An Appeal for a Broader Perspective." *Rangeland Desertification*. Springer, 2011, 5–15, 10.

47 Snyder argues that "wildness" is located in "the wind, the desert sands", and also represents a quality of selfhood. See *The Practice of the Wild*. Counterpoint, 1990, 16, 194.

48 See Tynan, *The Desert in Modern Literature and Philosophy*, 3.

49 Wharton, "A Bottle of Perrier," 271.

50 Wharton, "A Bottle of Perrier," 276.

51 "velarium, n." *OED Online*. Oxford University Press, March 2020, www.oed.com/view/Entry/221954. Accessed Apr. 14, 2020.

52 Brian Dillon, "Fragments from a History of Ruin." *Cabinet*, vol. 20, 2006. http://www.cabinetmagazine.org/issues/20/dillon.php. Accessed Apr. 13, 2021.

53 Wharton, "A Bottle of Perrier," 273.

54 For Edward Said, the Orient "is not only adjacent to Europe; it is also the place of Europe's greatest and richest and oldest colonies, the source of its civilizations and languages, its cultural contestant, and one of its deepest and most recurring images of the Other." See Edward Said, *Orientalism*. Penguin, 2003, 1.

55 Rich, "Fictions of Colonial Anxiety: Edith Wharton's 'The Seed of the Faith' and 'A Bottle of Perrier'," 8.

56 The walls of the fortress also serve to illustrate the distinction between the tangible and the imagined. This is apparent in Medford's disappointment at the scale of the edifice: "The house turned out to be smaller than he had imagined, or at least the habitable part of it; for above this towered mighty dilapidated walls of yellow stone, and in their crevices clung plaster chambers, one above the other, cedar-beamed, crimson-shuttered but crumbling." Wharton, "A Bottle of Perrier," 273.

57 Wharton, "A Bottle of Perrier," 271.

58 On the philosophical and ecological implications of this "spirit of place" see Edward Casey, *The Fate of Place: A Philosophical History*. University of California Press, 1997; Edward Casey, *Getting Back into Place: Toward a Renewed Understanding of the Place World*. Indiana University Press, 1993.

59 Gustave Flaubert, "Letter to a Friend, 1846." *Selected Letters*. Penguin Classics, 1987, 46.

60 Wharton, "A Bottle of Perrier," 273. Waid posits that the "rigid pose of Almodham in life has passed through rigor mortis to the state of a liquified dissolution, ironically still feeding the greedy fig. In cloying abundance, the life-sucking fig, Wharton has found a figure for the resilience of the master and an image of patriarchy; the thick, ancient trunk of a tree". See Candace Waid, "Pomegranate Seeds: Letters from the Underworld (The Touchstone and Ghosts)," 183.

61 Wharton, "A Bottle of Perrier," 289.

62 Wharton, "A Bottle of Perrier," 273.

63 Wharton, "A Bottle of Perrier," 282.
64 Wharton, "A Bottle of Perrier," 272.
65 Wharton, "A Bottle of Perrier," 288.
66 Wharton, "A Bottle of Perrier," 280.
67 Botting, "Introduction: Negative Aesthetics," 9.
68 Singley, "Gothic Borrowings and Innovations in Edith Wharton's 'A Bottle of Perrier'," 276.
69 Friedrich Nietzsche, *Thus Spoke Zarathustra: A Book for Everyone and None*. Translated by Graham Parkes. Oxford World's Classics, 2008, 248.
70 Wharton, "A Bottle of Perrier," 284.
71 Wharton, "A Bottle of Perrier," 285.
72 Wharton, "A Bottle of Perrier," 276.
73 Wharton, "A Bottle of Perrier," 285.
74 Martin Heidegger, "Evening Conversation." *Country Path Conversations*. Translated by Bret W. Davis. Indiana University Press, 2016, 137–38.
75 Wharton, "A Bottle of Perrier," 276.
76 See Tynan, *The Desert in Modern Literature and Philosophy*, 3.
77 Rich, "Fictions of Colonial Anxiety: Edith Wharton's 'The Seed of the Faith' and 'A Bottle of Perrier'," 8.
78 Said, *Orientalism*, 72.
79 See Tynan, *The Desert in Modern Literature*, 1–3.
80 Wharton, "A Bottle of Perrier," 276.
81 See Duffy, *The Landscapes of the Sublime, 1700-1930*, 4–15; Tynan, *The Desert in Modern Literature*.
82 Wharton's imagery prompts comparison with chronicles by European desert explorers of the Romantic period. These texts are dominated by the notion of geographical precarity and existential emptiness: "The eye wandered in vain to seek relief by a diversity of objects. No huge rocks confusedly scattered on the plain, or piled into mountains, no hills clothed with verdure, no traces of cultivation, not a tree nor a tall shrub, appeared to break the uniformity of the surface, nor bird nor beast to enliven the dreary waste". See John Barrow, *Travels into the Interior of Southern Africa, Vol. 1.* 2nd ed., Cadell and Davies, 1806, 37. The intrepid Scot Mungo Park's *Travels to the Interior of Africa* (1799) registers analogous dread at the interminable "lone and level sands", terra incognita that gives little in the way of sublime excitement: "the disconsolate wanderer, wherever he turns, sees nothing around him but a [...] gloomy and barren void, where the eye finds no particular object to rest upon". See Parks, *Travels in the Interior Districts of Africa; Performed in the Years 1795, 1796, and 1797.* London, 1799, 157.
83 Dyman, "'A Bottle of Perrier' and 'Mr. Jones'," 123.
84 See Simmel, "The Ruin," 379–85.

Chapter 11

STONY WASTE—THE "NEW RUIN" IN THE MODERN METROPOLIS AND GARDEN RUINS

The detailed attentiveness to layered landscapes and their melancholy debris is by no means a facet of Wharton's later literary production. She makes direct reference to antique and modern "stones" in her very first published short story "Mrs. Manstey's View," which brings into sharper focus Christopher Woodward's notion that "[e]very new empire has claimed to be the heir of Rome, but if such a colossus as Rome can crumble—its ruins ask—why not London or New York?"[1] The New York-set "Mrs. Manstey's View" is Wharton's earliest text to be analyzed in this book. While a monumental ruin suggests to many the grandeur of a classical heritage (as in "Roman Fever"), "Mrs. Manstey's View" is important for its focus on a mundane urban site that is falling into desuetude, incrementally abandoned due to dizzying civic and economic flows. For Rose Macaulay, these "new ruins," linked with neighborhood backyards and other non-traditional or unofficial green spaces, do not command our full attention because they "have not yet acquired the weathered patina of age, the true rust of barons' wars, not yet put on their ivy."[2] This is, however, precisely what captures Wharton's literary imagination. In a manner that exposes the shortcomings of some recent ecocriticism, which tends to devalue urban nature writing as "short takes and small grains at micro-level,"[3] Wharton's story extracts a rare emotional power from the fragmented map of Mrs. Manstey's shabby locality.

Charlee M. Sterling points out that to "understand" the intricacies of Wharton's art "we must consider the literary circumstances in which she was writing."[4] Sterling adds that: "Wharton first published a short story ("Mrs. Manstey's View") in 1890, just as the American literary scene was in great flux."[5] This story was published in July 1891 (not in 1890 as Sterling states) in *Scribner's Magazine*, at a moment when not just the "literary scene," but more crucially New York City itself was undergoing an astonishing overhaul and reinvention. Wharton's story can be parsed as a "dwelling" on the rapid cycles of demolition, population reduction, relocation and urbanization that constitutes an emergent global metropolis. The watchwords of capitalist enterprise (progress and profit) exist alongside Mrs. Manstey's fears of erasure of her personal touchstones of horticultural beauty.

In *Imagining New York City*, Christoph Lindner documents the "convulsions of urbanization that culminated in New York's vertical architecture," which "first took hold of the city in the second half of the nineteenth century, before reaching their highest intensity between 1890 and 1940."[6] Wharton published "Mrs. Manstey's View" two years after the start of this intense period of urbanization. As Lindner notes, during this era of escalating "development, encompassing the consolidation of the five boroughs in 1898, New York's physical appearance and character were radically transformed by the widespread construction of skyscrapers."[7]

It is against this backdrop of historical "convulsions" that Mrs. Manstey's desire to safeguard her view of neighborhood backyards acquires its tragicomic force.[8] This effect is enhanced by how, in the second sentence, the narrator draws a sly parallel between the naturalistic rubble synonymous with the seedier streets of a nascent industrial empire and ancient Rome.[9] Mrs. Manstey "occupied the back room on the third floor of a New York boardinghouse, in a street where the ash-barrels lingered late on the sidewalk and the gaps in the pavement would have staggered a Quintus Curtius."[10] The simile directs us—apparently—to the first-century Roman historian Quintus Curtius Rufus whose ten-book life of Alexander the Great is characterized by glaring narrative "gaps." Such lacunae and omissions also define the much better-known chronicles of Livy or Tacitus.[11] However, rather than dismissing this figuration as mere pedantry, it seems likely—and this is a droll, unintended irony in a story centrally concerned with the operations of personal memory and shoring up fragments against one's ruin—that Wharton (or her editor) has confused the relatively obscure historian Quintus Curtius with the Roman hero Marcus Quintius.[12] The "gaps" in the sidewalk form a peculiar signature of Mrs. Manstey's flyblown locality: "She had grown used" to the "disorder and broken barrels. The empty bottles and paths unswept no longer annoyed her; hers was the happy faculty of dwelling on the pleasanter side of the prospect before her."[13] As this quotation implies, underlying the notion of splintering ("broken barrels") is a selective process of remembrance. Mrs. Manstey's "happy faculty," outlined at the start of the story, depends on which fragments—of sense-impression—are to be conserved and embellished. This "faculty" also focuses attention on the semantic resonances of "dwelling."[14] It points, first of all, to Mrs. Manstey's humdrum domestic milieu. The bedraggled area outside her window is a sobering contrast to the "august ruins" admired by affluent visitors from the elegant, spotless terrace of "Roman

Fever." However, "dwelling" also foregrounds a complex habit of mind, a somber thinking backwards that links a chronicler of the Roman Empire like Livy or Quintus Curtius to the stoical Mrs. Manstey. Her unmanicured surroundings prompt lyrical reflection on her own past—and how it blends into a modern moment of diminishing possibilities. Mrs. Manstey, we learn, appreciates the "distant" perspectives and textures synonymous with impressionist painting: "at twilight, [...] the distant brown-stone spire seemed melting in the fluid yellow of the west." At these moments, she "lose[s] herself in vague memories of a trip to Europe, made years ago, and now reduced in her mind's eye to a pale phantasmagoria of indistinct steeples and dreamy skies."[15] Mrs. Manstey's longing for the ruins of Europe prompts comparison with Ruskin's distinctive conception of "voiceful" stones:

> that golden stain of time, that we are to look for the real light, a color, and preciousness of architecture; and it is not until a building has assumed this character, till it has been entrusted with the fame, and hallowed by the deeds of men, till its walls have been witnesses of suffering and its pillars rise out of the shadows of death, that its existence, more lasting as it is than that of the natural objects of the world around it, can be gifted with even so much as these possess, of language and of life.[16]

Ruskin indicates that architectural form becomes a recording instrument, bearing the residuum or patina ("golden stain") of human strivings, struggles and frustrations across time. Ruskin suggests how it is through such patina that material ruins can rise above the "shadows of death." Amenable to perpetual re-interpretation and accretion of new narratives, such physical relics attain an eerie gravitas. It is this power of association that may explain the ageing Mrs. Manstey's fierce attachment to the "stones" of her threatened neighborhood, the way she "stories" her built environment from the very opening lines: the "view from Mrs. Manstey's window was not a striking one, but to her at least it was full of interest and beauty." Her version of Ruskin's *seeing eye* manages to uncover hints of organic nature in a place marked by "chronic untidiness" and the "fluttering" of "miscellaneous garments."[17] Perhaps, the narrator implies, this is less about Ruskinian "seeing" and more about projecting a fantasy of pastoral retreat onto a meagre patch of vegetation—a patch owned by somebody else. So, instead of Ruskin's "golden stain of time" we have Mrs. Manstey who knows "every stain on the wall-paper" of her home.[18] However, capitalist enterprise becomes the ruin of Mrs. Manstey's peace of mind. The extension of a neighboring boarding-house will block her view and compel her to move from an apartment she has occupied for seventeen years. This sense of severance, even traumatic dislocation, is mirrored in violent lexis: "She might move, of course; so might she be *flayed alive*; but she was not likely to survive either *operation*."[19] If this (surgical?) "operation" is conducted then Mrs. Manstey's view ("the hyacinths were budding, the magnolia flowers looked more than ever like rosettes carved in alabaster") will be the last she ever enjoys.[20] The phrase "magnolia flowers" resembling "rosettes carved in alabaster" (mingling the mineral and the organic) foreshadows the trope of the "magnolia" unfolding "a few more sculptural flowers."[21]

In Wharton's story "Confession" the shifting cultural terrain of the modern metropolis seems to signal fresh starts, the erosion of old snobberies and loosening of architectural form into ceaseless movement—"[throbbing] with the stir of innumerable beginnings." By contrast, there is an unsettling hint of endings and mortality in "Mrs. Manstey's View." This is reinforced by a faint echo of Emily Dickinson's powerful poem of death and the afterlife, "Safe in their Alabaster Chambers." Just like the natural world is inexorably choked by "stony wastes"—an unedifying crust of sidewalks, litter and roads—so Mrs. Manstey herself seems to be an endangered species in this socioeconomic jumble.[22] While some neighboring yards are green and inviting, her view also shows there is "*no shade* in spring save that afforded by the intermittent leafage of the clothes-lines" (my emphasis).[23] Indeed, this humble and financially beleaguered protagonist, antipodal to Wharton herself, as Roxana Robinson remarks, may soon become a "shade" or specter in a neighborhood undergoing seismic change.[24] Robert Harbison observes that such patterns of dissolution are inescapable, and lead to the "archetypal place of ruin," the grave.[25] Mrs. Manstey's paltry garden plot will become a burial plot . Demolition, as a historical and capitalist act in a bustling global city, cannot be reversed: "nor ev'n can Fancy's eye / Restore what Time hath labour'd to deface."[26]

What lends Mrs. Manstey's plight an especial resonance is how the "stony waste" is measured against a yearning for other species of spaces: "For many years she had cherished a desire to live in the country, to have a hen-house and a garden."[27] Mrs. Manstey never actually secures this bucolic haven—it only resonates on a spiritual level, as Robinson explains: Wharton "lays claim to both her physical territory—the city of New York—and her metaphysical one—*les choses d'esprit*."[28] When Mrs. Manstey tries to grow plants of her own, the result is failure. "There was no sunny window in our house, and so all my plants died."[29] For Robinson, this "New York seems soulless—but a secret landscape thrives within the slovenly urban one."[30]

The "secret landscape" is Mrs. Manstey's own "artistic" creation—a mental map that exists apart from the unkempt material locality. She has "cultivated"—or trained herself to savor over long years of limited mobility and poor health - an intensely private, joyful and subjective view of nature that flourishes in spite, or perhaps because of, the dingy backyards and detritus:

> In the very next enclosure did not a magnolia open its hard white flowers against the watery blue of April? And was there not, a little way down the line, a fence foamed over every May by lilac waves of wisteria? Farther still, a horse-chestnut lifted its candelabra of buff and pink blossoms above broad fans of foliage; while in the opposite yard June was sweet with the breath of a neglected syringe, which persisted in growing in spite of the countless obstacles opposed to its welfare.[31]

"Enclosure" in this extract reminds us of Karl Marx's coinage "land-grabbing" in 1867, which evokes the "enclosure" of English commons—a brazen, aggressive and highly organized theft of collective property. These nuances cast a shadow over the positive stress on "magnolia" which is a vital leitmotif throughout Wharton's story. Such fauna will be smothered as the city continues its gargantuan growth.[32] When construction of the annex begins, the magnolia is symbolically crushed: "One of the men, a coarse fellow with a bloated face, picked a magnolia blossom and, after smelling it, threw it to the grounds; the next man, carrying a load of bricks, trod on the flower in passing."[33]

"Mrs. Manstey's View" is the first of many short stories that highlight Wharton's readiness to address how New York domestic routines, habits and perspectives (the thwarted old woman's "tenderness" for "plants and animals") are permanently ruptured—figured here as the ruin and rearrangement of urban space and culture. Mrs. Manstey is forced to confront this fact towards the end of the text: "Soon the wisteria would bloom, then the horse-chestnut; but not for her. Between her eyes and them a barrier of brick and mortar would swiftly rise; presently even the spire would disappear, and all her radiant world would be blotted out."[34]

Some of the most "voiceful" ruins in Wharton's fiction do not speak of the glories of Greco-Roman or medieval culture. For example, in texts that portray the "edgelands" described in my previous chapters about mountains, we find occasional descriptions of severely altered, rundown or dilapidated structures, though Wharton's narrators never use the word "ruin/s" to specify them. The 1917 novella *Summer* evokes an abandoned dwelling as well as an overgrown garden and orchard: "The little old house—its wooden walls sun-bleached to a ghostly gray—stood in an orchard above the road."[35] The aestheticization of the tattered, the dingy and the deserted here—through a patterning of alliterative effects ("wooden walls" etc.)—recalls Ruskin's maxim "Better the rudest work that tells a story or records a fact, than the richest without meaning."[36] Although we never discover the full "story" of this "rudest" house, it goes on to have a notable significance in Charity's life. The "ghostly gray" signifies another one of Wharton's humbler ruins where the spectral and the imperfectly remembered seems to saturate the rickety timbers: "The garden palings had fallen, but the broken gate dangled between its posts, and the path to the house was marked by rose-bushes run wild and hanging their small pale blossoms above the crowding grasses."[37] Gardens in Wharton's fiction frequently exist between the dichotomies of supplying sanctuary to visitors and excluding interlopers. However, the "gate" is in such disrepair that there is little keeping this uncultivated private patch from blurring into the wider natural expanse. An "old house" is sliding inexorably into *terrain vague*, even formlessness by *becoming* vegetation ("crowding grasses"). For spatial theorist Luc Lévesque such environments epitomize a weird, interstitial or "indeterminate space without precise boundaries," outside "the circuit of the productive structures" of townships, "the counter image of the city, both in the sense of a critique and a clue for a possible way to go beyond."[38] Perhaps the "old house" of *Summer* goes "beyond" not only the conventional resonances of scenic landscape beauty and the pastoral idyll, but also what Wharton calls "garden-magic" in the horticentric essays collected in *Italian Villas* (1902).[39] The somber word-painting of *Summer* exposes a crucial irony: although gardens are quite literally *rooted*, they are also fragile and ephemeral—"palings" can collapse, and sink into, the native soil. If a garden operates as a liminal zone between private and public, close-knit clan and wider community, intimate place, and wider space, then something is out of joint in *Summer*. Indeed, "run wild" implies it is no longer the clear-cut, man-made plot that it once was. In a culture that affirmed the redoubtable yeoman farmer, private land ownership and the cultural cachet of well-trimmed grass and elegantly arranged ornamental beds how does this forsaken, rather than luxuriant, plot function? Has the once charming site gone to *rack and ruin*—a despondent and jumbled realm, untended, forgotten and with moss and weeds growing over its "wooden walls," revealing only wan traces of what might have been a garden? Or does Wharton's narrator signal, in the style of Henry David Thoreau or local colorist Sarah Orne Jewett, a curious counter-aesthetic here, a different type of elemental energy, found in the unlikeliest of spots—the wretched or ramshackle—yet freed from traditional concepts of horticultural landscaping? In Jewett's *Country By-Ways* (1881) for instance, the narrator confronts a patch with "a straggling orchard of old apple trees." However, the timeworn site sustains nonhuman lifeforms and affords aesthetic, haptic and numinous experiences at variance with the familiar codes of the natural sublime. In this neglected spot is "where" Jewett's speaker is "happiest," "where I find that which is next of kin to me," in "trees [...] or seas, or beside a flower."[40]

At the very least Wharton, an inventive garden historian and theorist in her own right, pushes us to reconsider "ecocriticism's accounts of placeness and place-attachment" as well as the wider question of how American culture should engage with the natural milieu without becoming enmeshed in—and tarnished by—a socially approved drive for possession (and domination).[41] There appears to be no evidence of human occupation, let alone possession of the rundown plot in *Summer*: "Slender pilasters and an intricate fan-light framed the opening where the door had hung; and the door itself lay rotting in the grass, with an old apple-tree fallen across it."[42] The "door itself lay rotting in the grass," evokes a decomposing corpse. Unlike the lush fig in "A Bottle of Perrier," the stunted apple tree cannot hold and will not bear fruits. Charity Royall is forced to return to this tired site at the end of the novel, after she has been rejected (or ruined) by Lucius Harney. The terms used to describe this return echo those of the first visit: "It seemed a cruel chance that compelled her to retrace every step of the way to the deserted house; and when she came in sight of the orchard, and the silver-gray roof slanting crookedly through the laden branches, her strength failed her and she sat down by the road-side."[43] Wharton's narrator makes us feel that this "deserted house" is haunted by the unquiet ghosts of earlier literary texts, especially William Wordsworth's elegiac treatment of pastoral tropes in "The Ruined Cottage" (c.1797), which evokes the incremental disintegration of a human dwelling, and nature's re-wilding of a once ordered family plot. In Wharton's text, the encroaching vegetation seems to mirror Charity's bodily posture—the sight of the shrubbery is depressing rather than healing. Observing the "fallen" elements of this garden, a defeated and disillusioned Charity must sit down to gather her spirits: "She sat there a long time, trying to gather the courage to start again, and walk past the broken gate and the untrimmed rose-bushes strung with scarlet hips."[44] Charity has to "walk past the broken gate," not *through it*—to move beyond the memory of Lucius Harney. Through the raindrops, Charity "thought of the warm evenings when she and Harney had sat embraced in the shadowy room, and the noise of summer showers on the roof had rustled through their kisses."[45] The mention of "showers" in this "tangled garden"—"tangled" because the spontaneous growth of vegetation scrambles the border between the ruin of human hopes, habitation and external nature?—serves a purpose of washing these memories away. "Tangled" also pinpoints our experience of this entire episode. Is the verdure in the garden material evidence of human apathy and wanton disregard, or a clear sign of a natural restorative pattern? Is the "old house" tainted or cleansed by the emergence of "crowding grasses"? While the reader weighs the ambiguities triggered by this "tangle" of human and natural agencies, Charity's "plot" seems fixed in the closing pages. Her existence in the natural realm is doomed, she must become a pallid, domesticated version of herself, by marrying Lawyer Royall and renouncing her instinctive grace that was once connected with this forsaken dwelling and scrubby grass.

There is only one mention of ruins in Edith Wharton's 1912 novella *The Reef*. However, it becomes, as in *Summer*, a multifaceted presence in a narrative similarly preoccupied by the boundaries of personal ownership and the interplay of human soul and native soil, longing and belonging, feeling and losing kinship with organic nature. Anna and Darrow enjoy an outing in the French countryside:

> Once, at the turn of a wall, they stopped the motor before a ruined gateway and, stumbling along a road full of ruts, stood before a little old deserted house, fantastically carved and chimneyed, which lay in a moat under the shade of ancient trees.[46]

The many gardens in Wharton's oeuvre should be "plots" where nature and artifice, wildness and rationality, leisure and labor, are judiciously balanced. These "plots" allegorize—as in *Summer* above—fraught struggles between instinctual yearning and sober rationality, or between sexuality and genteel reserve, untamed expanse and high society mores. However, something more intriguing seems to happen in this extract from *The Reef*. The narrator's sly reference to "fantastically carved" hints at the whimsical distortions, illusions and extravagance synonymous with once-trendy eighteenth-century "sham ruins" in parkland—so-called "follies."[47] In one of Wharton's earlier short stories, "The Duchess at Prayer," set in sixteenth-century Italy, she also evokes a "mock ruin of a temple": "Down the alleys maimed statues stretched their arms like rows of whining beggars; faun-eared herms grinned in the thickets, and above the laurustinus walls rose the mock ruin of a temple, falling into real ruin in the bright disintegrating air."[48] In *The Reef* the hint of landscape kitsch is measured against natural sights, smells and sounds: "Over everything lay a faint sunshine that seemed dissolved in the still air, and the smell of wet roots and decaying leaves was merged in the pungent scent of burning underbrush."[49] There is a cinematic quality to this account, providing initially a wide angle shot before zooming in to linger over minutiae: "They paced the paths between the trees, found a moldy Temple of Love on an islet among reeds and plantains, and, sitting on a bench in the stable-yard, watched the pigeons circling against the sunset over their cot of patterned brick."[50]

Rose Macaulay addresses how artificial ruined temples "proved an immensely charming occupation for estate-owners, and ruins came into their own as objects in a landscape, picturesque and exciting in themselves and artistic in their relation to the design of the whole."[51] What is "exciting" for Macaulay here—the impish mixing of antique and modish, genuine and sham, Gothic and classical, Judeo-Christian and pagan forms—raises more troubling questions in Wharton's text. Her fictional version of a "folly" in *The Reef* mimics the decorative quirks, cultural syncretism and irregularities of other European formal gardens to imply that Anna and Darrow's romantic relationship is itself a "folly"—an elaborate self-deception, exaggerated, stylized, yet brittle. This is implied by the peculiarly problematic thinking behind the construction of artificial ruins and monuments like triumphal arches. Architects pride themselves—we hope—on using the best materials to craft useful, structurally sound and complete buildings that will endure. However, a deliberately truncated folly, diligently aged with vegetation and bits of stone strewn about its base must advertise architectural blunders or inadequacy (things fall apart). Moreover, the building maker is compelled to don the disguise of an archaeologist—*uncovering* rather than *designing*.[52] Later in Wharton's novel, there is another pointed reference to the folly phenomenon and, by extension, Anna and Darrow's inauthentic attachment—itself a kind of projection or *fabrique*: the "sky had cleared after luncheon, and to prolong their excursion they returned by way of the ivy-mantled ruin which was to have been the scene" of the "picnic."[53] This sentence evokes a beautiful painting of an amorous rendezvous ("Temple of Love"), not a meaningful, deeply felt human interaction. The "scene" is stagey, the picnic never happens, and it is implied (or at least foreshadowed) that a satisfying future for Anna and Darrow is a chimera.

This chapter has addressed what Sabrina Ferri terms "the composite symbolism" of ruins, and how such phenomena "speak to our imagination and to our intellect by conjoining in dialectical tension a series of oppositional categories: not only the past and the future, but also culture and nature."[54] Svetlana Boym develops these ideas to argue that the "early twenty-first century exhibits a strange ruinophilia, a material embodiment of the prospective nostalgia that goes beyond postmodern quotation marks."[55] Wharton's fiction probes this "ruinophilia" and offers a remarkable range of standpoints on processes of history and the laws of pastoral, the living and the dead, the immanent and the transcendent, the manicured and the unruly.

Notes

1 Woodward, *In Ruins*, 5.
2 Macaulay, *The Pleasure of Ruins*, 453.
3 Lawrence Buell, *The Future of Environmental Writing*. Blackwell, 1998, 88.

4 Charlee M. Sterling, "Introduction." *Irony in the Short Stories of Edith Wharton*. Mellen Press, 2005, 1–28, 3.
5 Sterling, "Introduction," 3.
6 Christoph Lindner, *Imagining New York City: Literature, Urbanism, and the Visual Arts, 1890-1940*. Oxford University Press, 2015, 26. See also Russell A. Berman, "Democratic Destruction: Ruins and Emancipation in the American Tradition." *Ruins of Modernity*, edited by Hell and Schönle. Duke University Press, 2010; Shannon Lee Dawdy, "Clockpunk Anthropology and the Ruins of Modernity." *Current Anthropology*, vol. 51, no. 6, 2010, 761–93. *JSTOR*, www.jstor.org/stable/10.1086/657626. Accessed Apr. 2, 2020.
7 Lindner, *Imagining New York*, 26–27.
8 This period of transition is evidenced in the depiction of Mrs. Manstey's "real friends" who "were the denizens of the yards, the hyacinths, the magnolia, the green parrot, the maid who fed the cats, the doctor who studied late behind his mustard-coloured curtains; and the confidant of her tenderer musings was the church spire in the sunset". The highest man-made building the ailing protagonist can see is the spire of Trinity Church on Broadway. Lindner explains that: "As late as 1883, the neo-Gothic spire of Trinity Church on Broadway and Wall Street in Lower Manhattan remained the tallest completed structure in the city [...] The spire is 284 feet tall", *Imagining New York*, 26–27.
9 See Tim Edensor, "Walking Through Ruins." *Ways of Walking: Ethnography and Practice on Foot*, edited by Tim Ingold and Jo Lee Vergunst. Ashgate, 2008, 123–42; Tim Edensor, "Waste Matter - The Debris of Industrial Ruins and the Disordering of the Material World." *Journal of Material Culture*, vol. 10, no. 3, Nov. 2005, 311–32, doi:10.1177/1359183505057346.
10 Edith Wharton, "Mrs. Manstey's View." *The New York Stories of Edith Wharton*. New York Review of Books, 2007, 3.
11 On Wharton's (sometimes imperfect) classical erudition and how it is deployed in her shorter fiction see Michael Hendry, "Two Greek Syllables in Wharton's 'The Pelican'." *Notes and Queries*, vol. 255, no. 2, 2010, 224–25.
12 According to Livy, a yawning gulf opened up in the Forum in 362 BC, which soothsayers interpreted as a call for sacrifice. The courageous young soldier Marcus Curtius plunged into the gulf on horseback.
13 Wharton, "Mrs. Manstey's View," 4. As Russell A. Berman argues, "Nature and time generate ruins only where human activity is involved [...] Ruin is a result of culture, not of nature". See Berman, "Democratic Destruction," 105–06.
14 Critic Donna Campbell interprets the story as an example of Wharton "dwelling" on, and exposing, the limitations of the female-dominated "local colour" literary genre. Mrs. Manstey's narrow life experiences and dogged refusal to acknowledge the brave new world of technological advance are construed by Campbell as elements of a "local colour garden plot" that Wharton wishes to move beyond by embracing an outward-looking, formally bold and more naturalistic textual practice. See Donna M. Campbell, "Edith Wharton and the 'Authoresses': The Critique of Local Color in Wharton's Early Fiction." *Studies in American Fiction*, vol. 22, no. 2, 1994, 169–83.
15 Wharton, "Mrs. Manstey's View," 3.
16 Ruskin, *The Seven Lamps of Architecture*, 187.
17 Wharton, "Mrs. Manstey's View," 3.
18 Wharton, "Mrs. Manstey's View," 8.

19 Wharton, "Mrs. Manstey's View," 8.

20 Wharton, "Mrs. Manstey's View," 7.

21 Wharton, "Mrs. Manstey's View," 14.

22 See Scott Emmert, "Drawing-Room Naturalism in Edith Wharton's Early Short Stories." *Journal of the Short Story in English*, vol. 39, Autumn 2002,, 57–71. June 28, 2011. http://jsse.revues.org/index271.html#text; Jennifer L. Fleissner, "The Biological Clock: Edith Wharton, Naturalism, and the Temporality of Womanhood." *American Literature*, vol. 78, no. 3, 2006, 519–48; Hochman, "The Good, the Bad, and the Literary"; Gary Totten, "Imagining the American West in Wharton's Short Fiction." *Journal of the Short Story in English*, vol. 58, 2012, 143–58.

23 Wharton, "Mrs. Manstey's View," 3.

24 "Boldly, she chooses a protagonist and setting that are remote from her own experience." See Robinson, "Introduction," vii–xxviii, xi.

25 Robert Harbison, *Ruins and Fragments: Tales of Loss and Rediscovery*. Reaktion, 2016, 187.

26 Lord Byron, *Childe Harold's Pilgrimage* 2, 85–88. See Byron, Lord. *Lord Byron: The Major Works*. Edited by Jerome J. McGann, Oxford University Press, 2008, p. 253.

27 Wharton, "Mrs. Manstey's View," 3–4.

28 Robinson, "Introduction," xi.

29 Wharton, "Mrs. Manstey's View," 9.

30 Robinson, "Introduction," xi.

31 Wharton, "Mrs. Manstey's View," 4.

32 In *Delirious New York: A Retroactive Manifesto for Manhattan*, Rem Koolhaas attests to this monstrous urban transformation taking place in New York City: "Especially between 1890 and 1940 a new culture (the Machine Age?) selected Manhattan as laboratory: a mythical island where the invention and testing of a metropolitan lifestyle and its attendant architecture could be pursued as a collective experiment in which the entire city became a factory of man-made experience, where the real and the natural ceased to exist". Rem Koolhaas, *Delirious New York: A Retroactive Manifesto for Manhattan*. Monacelli Press, 1994, 9–10.

33 Wharton, "Mrs. Manstey's View," 11.

34 Wharton, "Mrs. Manstey's View," 7–8.

35 Wharton, *Summer*, 197.

36 Ruskin, *The Seven Lamps of Architecture*, 183.

37 Wharton, *Summer*, 197.

38 Luc Lévesque, *The 'Terrain Vague' as Material - Some Observations*. House Boat, 2002, 9.

39 "The traveller returning from Italy, with his eyes and imagination full of the ineffable Italian garden-magic, knows vaguely that the enchantment exists; that he has been under its spell, and that it is more potent, more enduring, more intoxicating to every sense than the most elaborate and glowing effects of modern horticulture; but he may not have found the key to the mystery. Is it because the sky is bluer, because the vegetation is more luxuriant?" See Wharton, *Italian Villas and Their Gardens*, 6.

40 Sarah Orne Jewett, *Country By-Ways*. Houghton, Mifflin and Company, 1881, 98.

41 Lawrence Buell, *The Future of Environmental Criticism*. Blackwell, 2005, 88.

42 Wharton, *Summer*, 197.

43 Wharton, *Summer*, 239–40.

44 Wharton, *Summer*, 240.

45 Wharton, *Summer*, 240.

46 Edith Wharton, *The Reef*. Alfred A. Knopf, 1996, 101.

47 The Temple of Ancient Virtue (1773) at Stowe House in Buckinghamshire, the Grotto
    of Venus (1738) at Rousham House in Oxfordshire and the fake medieval castle (1747)
    at Hagley Hall in Worcestershire are among the most notable examples in the British
    tradition of landscape gardening.
48 Wharton, "The Duchess at Prayer," 110–27, 111.
49 Wharton, *The Reef,* 101.
50 Wharton, *The Reef,* 101–02.
51 Macaulay, *The Pleasure of Ruins*, 24.
52 See Exhibition Catalogue, *Visions of Ruin: Architectural Fantasies and Designs for Garden
    Follies.* Soane Museum, 1999; Inger Sigrun Brodey, *Ruined by Design: Shaping Novels
    and Gardens in the Culture of Sensibility.* Routledge, 2012. Brodey is particularly good on
    these critical and architectural issues, though her discussion is restricted largely to
    pre-1800 British and European texts.
53 Wharton, *The Reef,* 166.
54 Sabrina Ferri, *Ruins Past: Modernity in Italy, 1744-1836.* Oxford University Press, 2015,
    228.
55 Svetlanda Boym, *The Off-Modern.* Bloomsbury Academic, 2017, 43.

CONCLUSION

Where indeed—she wondered again—did one's own personality end, and that of others, of people, landscapes, chairs or spectacle-cases, begin?[1]

In *Twilight Sleep*, the protagonist Nona Manford considers the extent to which "people" interact with, and are transformed by, the cultural "landscapes" they visit or occupy. One of the goals of this book has been to demonstrate that while the pastoral seems to portray troubling fractures between the social self and native soil, Wharton is more struck by how these ostensibly divergent cultural categories superimpose and interpenetrate to form an ecocritical palimpsest.[2] This is a finding that resonates with Greg Garrard's recent claim that the methods, motifs and practices of American "pastoral can be radical." Like Terry Gifford and Lawrence Buell before him, Garrard recognizes that for ecocriticism, pastoral tropes—yearning for a socially stable rustic elsewhere with its pristine lakes and isolated farmsteads, the poetic motifs of "retreat-and-return," plus the ethical unease triggered by unregulated industries—are not simply elements of fanciful literary texts but decisively shape the way contemporary readers grasp and interpret their material surroundings. This notion is elaborated by contributions to the essay collection *Ecocritical Theory: New European Approaches* (2011), which develops Buell's attitude to pastoral by promoting a robust re-orientation of the mode triggered by current environmental anxieties.[3] For Garrard, this makes it all the more crucial to interpret pastoral—and so-called "nature writing" more broadly—not as "a finished model or ideology" but as a literary mode that largely eschews nostalgic posturing in favor of alerting us to the presence of multiple, sometimes conflicting, cultural codes and values. The imagery of apparently carefree and simple rural populations throws into relief the urbane, highly cultured poetic entity that crafts such imagery. Pastoral is therefore, in Garrard's view, an insistent "questioning" regarding the formation of an ethical individual and a good society, "be/longing" and the "root of human being on this earth."[4] It is this type of "questioning" that lends the extract above from

Wharton's *Twilight Sleep* a peculiar intensity. Indeed, one of the central aims of this book has been to treat pastoral as a kind of palimpsest—a "parchment" upon which successive generations of artist-pilgrims have etched their impressions, constantly revising its imagery, formal procedures and lyrical effects.

This notion of the palimpsest also reinforces how my research seeks to extend the range of Wharton studies. First of all, my close reading of selected texts adds another "layer" of sophistication to the ever-evolving field of ecocriticism, whose core ideas and critical standpoints have assumed both an urgency and galvanizing potency given the seismic upheaval to our material localities around the globe—some of the most damaging tornadoes in US history; flooding in the American Midwest; devastating earthquakes in Haiti, China and Japan; stronger and more extensive wildfires in the American Southwest. For ecocritical pundits over the past fifteen years—as for Wharton in the early, war-ravaged decades of the twentieth century—the nightmare of a *ruined earth* has become a powerfully disturbing actuality. In the light of this, I have sought to refine—more than any other recent work of published academic scholarship—a distinctive "green" analysis of Wharton's narrative strategies. While rival commentators have targeted the ecological imagination of other North American women writers of the period, such as Willa Cather, my own book is one of the first full-length projects to place comparable stress on Wharton's abiding engagement with the profound effects of the intersection of bourgeois social mores, burgeoning wealth and the organic palpable milieu.[5] Wharton's oeuvre has much to say about the origins and historical nature of environmental degradation, resource conservation, urban sustainability as well as the often pernicious flows of global capitalism. Her subtle depiction of bucolic hinterlands and urban edgelands also highlights her complex views on individual and institutional political responsibility in the modern moment, as well as the civic dilemmas facing North American and European populations in the interwar period.

What I suggest here then is that a "greening" of Wharton's texts inevitably involves a shift of scholarly focus, re-positioning this North American author as a deeply engaged, animated and intellectually curious citizen of the world. Of course, incisive research has been published throughout the 1980s and 1990s on Wharton's vital place in America's literary tradition, the myriad ways she influenced (and reacted to) other writers. Scholars have alerted us to how *Ethan Frome* and *Summer* have, for example, shaped Sinclair Lewis's satirical debunking of American small-town manners; how Wharton offers us a searching critical perspective on the theories of the novel synonymous with Henry James or so-called "naturalists" like Frank Norris, Jack London and Theodore Dreiser; or how her cosmopolitan enthusiasms resonate through the novels and short stories of Ernest Hemingway and F. Scott Fitzgerald. My own fascination with Wharton's aesthetic practice has less to do with her central part in America's novelistic tradition—her indebtedness to a rich array of nineteenth-century domestic and sentimental authors has, after all, been amply and elegantly chronicled before—and more to do with her evident relish for European writing and thought.

My challenge to future Wharton scholars is this: if we undertake a more thoroughgoing ecocritical assessment of her imaginative enterprise then we need to gauge some of those conceptual motifs and tactics associated with the New Modernist Studies, especially the emphasis on how early twentieth-century authors read, write and journey *across* national frontiers and languages, recalibrating cultural identities along the way. So, a reconsideration of how Wharton weighed the impact of the advance of world trade and industrial capitalism on the tangible environment might involve, rather than a predictable scholarly comparison with, say, a Willa Cather or Sarah Orne Jewett, but rather a Stendhal, Flaubert, George Sand, Goethe, John Ruskin, George Eliot or Oscar Wilde. As a formally ambitious author-traveler, Wharton was suspicious of introspective nativism and sought instead to translate the signatures of the soil in parklands, private gardens and mountains across continents. We must develop, surely, a similarly boundary-defying, multifaceted and expansive critical procedure? This perspective needs to be bold enough to recast standard narratives of the 'International Theme' (as found in secondary texts like Jessica Levine's *Delicate Pursuit: Discretion in Henry James and Edith Wharton*) by debating fresh transatlantic and cross-Channel conversations, affinities, interactions, intellectual and cultural networking clusters that helped mold what we call nowadays the Wharton "brand."

My methodology recognizes the crucial role taken by ecocritical and environmental scholarship in the humanities and invites Wharton's readers to gauge the global nature of economic upheavals as well as highly specific local histories in, for example, Morocco, Italy and elsewhere in Europe. In short, we need to innovate when assessing Wharton's textual repertoire, especially her layered evocations of European or North African species of spaces in an age of acute geopolitical convulsion—how these geographical zones reshape the relation between gendered subjectivity, freedom and justice. My insistence on using the environmental humanities as a lens through which to construe Wharton's fictional strategies is about much more than a preoccupation with her pastoral flourishes. The goal here is to be more conceptually rigorous and original about a central problem of Wharton's oeuvre. Lily Bart, we may recall, proclaims in *The House of Mirth* that it is 'a miserable thing [...] to be a woman'. In the light of this gloomy declaration, how do Wharton's other female characters apprehend, manipulate and seize a space of their own in an age of complacent male landowners? This is the question that reverberates through my chapters, and it is one that future Wharton scholars should be savvier about, by leaning heavily into the findings synonymous with an ecocritical agenda. The advantages of this scholarly "gearshift" are, I think, significant. My book sets forth how the "greening" of Wharton's private and public writings contributes to exciting strands in cultural geography and recent post-colonial theory: for example, biological and political constructions of citizenship, mobility, race and nation; hospitality and hostility towards the "Other"; fraught experiences of exile and competing conceptions of home/land; trans/national selfhood; the figure of the nomad, the outcast or the wanderer.

Wanderers in Wharton's oeuvre frequently encounter sites that dominate my final chapter. Here my research responds to and complicates a remarkable trend over the past decade in the humanities and social sciences, one that has resulted in new periodicals like *Worldwide Waste: Journal of Interdisciplinary Studies*. Literary scholars, researchers in object-oriented ontology, philosophers, sociologists, political scientists, ecologists, environmental activists and landscape historians have started to collaborate and pay closer attention to ruins, rubble, vestiges and obsolete objects in the cultural imagination.[6] Books like Will Viney's *Waste: A Philosophy of Things* (2014), Robert Harbison's *Ruins and Fragments: Tales of Loss and Rediscovery* (2015), Susan Signe Morrison's *The Literature of Waste: Material Ecopoetics and Ethical Matter* (2015), and Rachele Dini's *Consumerism, Waste, and Re-use in Twentieth-Century Fiction* (2016) variously show, like my own project, that we can exploit findings in newly minted sub-disciplines like "Discard Studies" to expand the ecocritical repertoire and also rethink Wharton's myriad fictional depictions of tangible and written detritus, the tumbledown, the corrupted, and the (soon-to-be) evacuated.[7] We might want to reflect further on how Wharton's evocation of palpable wealth and splendor in parkland or garden directs our attention to the inevitable production—and concealment—of dirt, leftovers, unwholesome residues. Indeed, Wharton's trenchant insights—which make us reflect on our current environmental plight - also remind us of Zygmunt Bauman's words: "Waste may be described as simultaneously a most harrowing problem and a most closely guarded secret of our times."[8] Social power and kudos in Wharton's fictional world often resides with those who have special knowledge of the covert, the clandestine and the freshly buried. Prioritizing Wharton's critical interrogation of the socio-economic frameworks in which waste is created and managed—what lies beneath the apparently decorous surface of a country estate?—means we can parse her work in relation to Terry Gifford's call for a more "mature environmental aesthetics," one that acknowledges how "some literature has gone beyond the closed circuit of pastoral and antipastoral to achieve a vision" of a stratified natural milieu "that includes the human."[9]

That "vision," which I have found in the primary texts featured here, warrants detailed scrutiny from the next generation of Wharton experts.

What aspects of Edith Wharton's fictional world do we recover by reconsidering her through a green lens? Where does Wharton's abiding fascination with the countryside, nature and green spaces fit into her fiction? This book addresses these questions, since it is an area of academic research that has been largely neglected or misconstrued. Wharton's fiction can be viewed through the lens of pastoral cosmopolitanism, which is the unlikely and unpredictable pairing of two concepts that seem to be opposites when, in fact, they are not. In Wharton's fiction cosmopolitan characters use pastoral tropes, ideas or beliefs to reimagine their own social identities, ambitions and needs. Cosmopolitanism here is not a place, a large metropolis for example, but rather an attitude. It is the tension between the particular and the universal. The return to various natural localities (such as gardens, edgelands or ruins and follies) reflects how characters seek to forge new relationships with various geographies and the lifeforms that can be found there. The chapters in this book address the different pastoral cosmopolitan tropes Edith Wharton makes use of her in extensive literary production.

In Part I we saw—through, for instance, Lily Bart's responses to the Bellomont estate—a sentimental pastoral synonymous with well-heeled east coast American landowners. Moneyed weekend visitors to Bellomont savor a "romantic" and idyllic view of nonhuman terrain, by turning a blind eye to the rational management and exploited human labor that plants crops, clears woodland and kills wild creatures to make a "countryside" fit for urban consumption. *The House of Mirth* implies that if Lily was more attentive to this hidden history of the lush American Garden, or at least the tensions between rustic myths and brute capitalist facts, then she might have navigated better what Virginia Woolf termed, in her admiring 1905 published review of Wharton's novel, a patrician and blinkered New York "community [...] bound together not only by the possession of wealth, but also by a certain gift [...] 'a force of negation which eliminated everything beyond their own range of perception'."[10] Wharton's multi-layered depiction of private American parks hint at how, in the words of critic Roderick Nash, the American pastoral offers a "middle landscape" between the divergent extremes of unfenced wilderness and civilized culture, but this fusion is deeply "unstable and contradictory at best."[11] In a short story like "Kerfol," we see Wharton making the history of violence partially buried by the parterres, sculptural features and glossy lawns of Bellomont more legible, even explicit, when her narrator decides to explore a European garden and its disturbing feudal residues.

In Chapter 4 I also appraised Wharton's fictional portrayal of America's first large national park, a site whose original designers—Frederick Law

Olmsted and Calvert Vaux—aimed to fuse English picturesque landscaping techniques with popular Jeffersonian ideals of a restorative rustic purity and calm. Wharton is clearly fascinated by the fictional possibilities of Central Park, a locus which promised peace and seclusion from the incessant din, dirt and what Henry James labelled the "impudent" novelty of the skyscrapers that surrounded it.[12] What distinguishes Wharton's typically painstaking evocations of the green zone is her sense of the sheer audacity of this form of urban land development, whose irregular plan and expression of ornamental features were meant to accommodate a diverse array of recreational, aesthetic (and romantic) impulses. Her wonder was shared by numerous cultural pundits after Central Park had been built. In 1868 Junius Henry Brown remarked: "It is not a little remarkable, in a City where every square inch of ground is prized as gold, that so much real estate in the most valuable part of the island should have been appropriated to the public use."[13] Like Brown, Wharton relishes and responds to the notion of a vast *public* park which offered curious New Yorkers an intensely *private* and supposedly numinous experience of a nature artfully designed to look fresh, even "unspoiled." As in the previous chapter, Wharton's characters must learn to *translate* the abstruse script of this green oasis, which brings to mind Clarence Cook's resonant *Description of the New York Central Park* (1869): "it was decided to take the barren tract—the sheet of white paper, and write the future Park poem upon that."[14] In Wharton's fiction, we must decide who has the requisite life experiences or close reading skills to interpret and appreciate the involved cultural meanings of this "Park poem."

In Part II, attention shifted from the garden lowlands to much higher altitudes—European and North American mountains. Wharton's vivid portrayal of the different phenomena located among the European peaks frequently recalibrated the emotions of awe and lyrical communion so often identified with first- and second-generation Romantic aesthetics. Undine Spragg in *The Custom of the Country* wonders whether this Romantic rapture might be purchased as part of a vacation tour. However, as Wharton shows on a number of occasions, the touristic perception of the peaks reduces a mountain to a sleek, enticing "brand," a locus of urban consumption little better than the manicured lawns of Bellomont in the previous chapter. When Wharton's narrative eye moved from "Old" to "New World," the sumptuous vacation hotel is replaced by cheerlessly bleak mountain communities in novellas like *Ethan Frome* and *Summer*, where *prospects* (in every sense of the word) are drastically reduced. Wharton's Gothic accounts of the impecunious and near-feral "Mountain" folk in *Summer*, offers some of the most potent and unsettling word-painting in her entire oeuvre. This is because Wharton's

American pastoral insists upon the links between the "high" and "low," the "chaste/pure" and the "polluted/unclean," the "fertile" and the "barren" as part of her unflinching survey of an evolving democracy.[15] Those at the bottom of the social scale—barely surviving on the "Mountain"—embody a disruptive alterity. On a grim hillside the fictions of an American extrovert virility—the brave pioneer or the tireless farmer—are utterly quashed. The pastoral in *Summer* does not simply allude to but portrays in telling detail a remote site whose occupants epitomize the excessive, the transgressive and the unspeakable, eliciting in Charity an appalled fascination, then existential torment and finally a measure of acceptance. In *Summer*, the "Mountain" men and women are rejected, exiled or "edgeland people"—in Marion Shoard's phraseology. They have been scorned by the custodians of "civilized" decorum as too tricky to classify, carriers of danger and disease, beyond the codes of virtuous and productive citizenship. The "Mountain" folk are segregated from where "orderly business" is conducted down below in the towns.[16]

My third and final part turned from the ravaged and ruined "Mountain" zone in *Summer* to those fastidious descriptions of forlorn, wrecked and crumbling material sites that are scattered across Wharton's oeuvre.[17] Ruin/ation can refer to blighted human hopes, reputations and fortunes. However, my chief preoccupation in Part III was with the eerie, abandoned, yet *voiceful* structures (the Coliseum in "Roman Fever") or plots (the tumbledown cottage in *Summer*) that compel Wharton's protagonists to brood over their own uncertain place in the "welter" of this "world." One of the most poignant articulations of this brooding is found in the early story "Mrs. Manstey's View" which presents a metropolis locked into a seemingly endless (and chaotic) cycle of demolition and redevelopment. Wharton's story invites us to reflect on this contribution to the 1856 *Harper's Monthly*: "New York is notoriously the largest and least loved of any of our great cities. Why should it be loved as a city? It is never the same city for a dozen years together. A man born in New York forty years ago finds nothing, absolutely nothing, of the New York he knew."[18] William Cullen Bryant also worried about this issue, warning readers of *The Evening Post*: "Commerce is devouring inch by inch the coast of the island, and if we would rescue any part of it for health and recreation it must be done now."[19] The pathos of Wharton's story—which says much about the experiences of residential displacement and precarity then and now—is that neither Mrs. Manstey, nor her cherished plot, can be "rescued" from the depredations of time and the maneuvering of speculative land dealers.[20] She treats her ragged home as hallowed ground, which is deconsecrated by the end of the text. All that was solid in her diurnal existence, melts into dusty air.

In terms of sketching out future directions for Wharton scholarship, one crucial area relates to the subject of my final chapter. Over the last decade, geographers, literary scholars, sociologists, environmental activists and landscape historians have started to pay much closer attention to ruins, rubble, vestiges and obsolete objects in the cultural imagination.[21] Books like Robert Harbison's *Ruins and Fragments: Tales of Loss and Rediscovery* (2015) show that there's ample scope to use research in newly minted sub-disciplines like "Discard Studies" to rethink Wharton's myriad fictional depictions of the residual, the waste/d, the tumbledown or the (soon-to-be) evacuated. By scrutinizing Wharton's insights into these species of spaces we can parse her work in relation to Terry Gifford's call for "a mature environmental aesthetics" that acknowledges how "some literature has gone beyond the closed circuit of pastoral and antipastoral to achieve a vision of an integrated natural world that includes the human."[22] That "vision" is something Wharton's texts try to articulate, even while they register seismic socio-economic and geopolitical convulsions.

Finally, I return to Wharton's remarks in *A Backward Glance* concerning the "world is a welter." In this text she adds, "though all the cranks and theorists cannot master the old floundering monster, or force it for long into any of their neat plans of readjustment, here and there a saint or a genius suddenly sends a little ray through the fog, and helps humanity to stumble on, and perhaps up."[23] In this book I have researched the "neat plans" of formal private and public gardens, explored "up" Wharton's fictional mountains before "stumbling on" the debris and ruins that capture her literary imagination. My aim has been to address a knowledge gap in Wharton and the environmental humanities, especially recent debates in ecocriticism. My chapters comprise a "little ray through the fog" in these research fields, and by no means a definitive one. The investigation is ongoing.

Notes

1 Wharton, *Twilight Sleep*, 201.
2 Buell believes that the environmental turn of ecocriticism cannot be understood in terms of 'waves', but rather as a palimpsest of complex debates and ideas. My book proposed that Wharton's fiction be understood through this prism. Buell, *The Future of Environmental Criticism*, 17.
3 Axel Goodbody and Kate Rigby, eds., *Ecocritical Theory: New European Approaches*. University of Virginia Press, 2011, 3. Astrid Bracke, "Redrawing the Boundaries of Ecocritical Practice." *Interdisciplinary Studies in Literature and Environment*, vol. 17, no. 4, 2010, 765–68. *JSTOR*, www.jstor.org/stable/44087670. Accessed May 26, 2021.
4 Garrard, "Radical Pastoral?" 449–65.

5 For more on ecocriticism in Willa Cather see Susan J. Rosowski, ed.. *Willa Cather's Ecological Imagination*. University of Nebraska Press, 2003.

6 Here I pay tribute to Francesco Orlando's massive – and hugely ambitious – work *Obsolete Objects in the Literary Imagination: Ruins, Relics, Rarities, Rubbish, Uninhabited Places, and Hidden Treasures*. Yale University Press, 2008.

7 Morrison's book offers an especially thoughtful and fluent survey of the key commentators who have shaped what is now known as "Discard Studies".

8 Zygmunt Bauman, *Wasted Lives: Modernity and Its Outcasts*. Polity Press, 2004, 26–27.

9 Gifford, *Pastoral*, 147–49. Martin Simonson et al. eds., *A Contested West: New Readings of Place in Western American Literature*. Portal Editions, 2013, 43–60. Martin Ryle, "The Past, the Future and the Golden Age: Some Contemporary Versions of Pastoral." *The Pleasures and Politics of Consuming Differently*, edited by Kate Soper, Martin Ryle and Lyn Thomas. Palgrave Macmillan, 2011.

10 Andrew McNeillie, *The Essays of Virginia Woolf*. Vol. 1. 1904-1912. Harcourt, 1986, 68. See also Katherine Joslin, "'Embattled Tendencies': Wharton, Woolf and the Nature of Modernism." *Special Relationships: Anglo-American Affinities and Antagonisms 1854-1936*, edited by Janet Beer and Bridget Bennett. Manchester University Press, 2002, 202–23; Anne McMaster, "Beginning with the Same Ending: Virginia Woolf and Edith Wharton." *Virginia Woolf: Texts and Contexts: Selected Papers from the Fifth Annual Conference on Virginia Woolf*, edited by Beth Rigel Daugherty and Eileen Barrett. Pace University Press, 1996, 216–22.

11 Nash, *Wilderness and the American Mind*, 392.

12 Henry James, *The American Scene*. Chapman and Hall, 1907, 76.

13 Junius Henry Brown, *The Great Metropolis*. American Publishing Co., 1868, 121.

14 Clarence Cook, *A Description of the New York Central Park*. [1869]. B. Blom, 1972, 39–40.

15 As David Trotter suggests, "mess theory" is indissolubly connected to American "democracy, which would be hard to imagine without litter, or without the historically specific form of disgust aroused by (and in) the spectacle of widespread social mobility". See David Trotter, *Cooking with Mud: The Idea of Mess in Nineteenth-Century Art and Fiction*. Oxford University Press, 2000, 3–16.

16 See Jos Smith, *The New Nature Writing: Rethinking the Literature of Place*. Bloomsbury, 2017. It scrutinizes in scrupulous detail Marion Shoard's conceptual landscape. On the theory of the rejected, discarded, or demonized human body see Zygmunt Bauman, *Postmodern Ethics*. Blackwell, 1993.

17 Wharton scholars have, in the past, restricted their analysis of ruin/ation to war novels such as *The Marne* (1918) and *A Son at the Front* (1922). The protagonist of *The Marne* notes how war "emptied towns of their inhabitants as it emptied veins of their blood; it killed houses and lands as well as men". Wharton captures well the appearance of "these wan ruins, these gutted houses and sterile fields". Edith Wharton, *The Marne*, Scribner's, 1918, 24-25. See also Benert, "Edith Wharton at War: Civilized Space in Troubled Times," 322–43.

18 Quoted in Edwin G. Burrows and Mike Wallace, *Gotham: A History of New York City to 1898*. Oxford University Press, 1998, xxii. See also Edward K. Spann, *The New Metropolis: New York City, 1840-1857*. Columbia University Press, 1981: Hilary Ballon, ed., *The Greatest Grid: The Master Plan of Manhattan, 1811- 2011*. Columbia University Press, 2012.

19 William Cullen Bryant, "A New Public Park." *The Evening Post*, July 3, 1844.

20 See Randall Mason, *The Once and Future New York: Historic Preservation and the Modern City*. University of Minnesota Press, 2009; David Scobey, *Empire City: The Making and Meaning of the New York City Landscape*. Temple University Press, 2002; Max Page, *The Creative Destruction of Manhattan, 1900-1940*. University of Chicago Press, 1999.

21 Here I pay tribute to Francesco Orlando's massive – and hugely ambitious – work *Obsolete Objects in the Literary Imagination: Ruins, Relics, Rarities, Rubbish, Uninhabited Places, and Hidden Treasures*.

22 Gifford, *Pastoral*, 147. See also Simonson et al., *A Contested West*, 43–60. Ryle, "The Past, the Future and the Golden Age."

23 Wharton, *A Backward Glance*, 379.

APPENDIX 1

SPRING IN A FRENCH RIVIERA GARDEN.

The French Riviera, like all the north side of the Mediterranean, is so subject to abrupt changes of temperature that it is hard to say when spring begins in a garden which overflows with roses and carnations in January, yet in which tender growths may be frost-nipped or wind-withered a few weeks later. But on my dry hillside terraces, if the season follows a normal course, the last almond blossoms wave a goodbye to winter toward the middle of February; just as the reddening of the peach-buds begins to announce the new season. By that time, too, Prunus Blieriani is a great rosy cloud, Kennedya trifoliata is hanging out its violet fringes, buds are thick on Deutzias, Exorchorda Grandi-flora, Prunus Moseriana, Paeonia arborea, the hybrid Pyrus Japonicas, and the early-blooming lilacs; and in the hot sheltered rock-garden Aloe Cilaria is covering itself with scarlet spikes and Aloe Salm-Dyckiana and its hybrids are throwing up their fiery rockets.

This transition from winter to spring is perhaps the most exciting moment to garden-lovers in these regions. The roses are over, and have been cut back for April blooming; Narcissus Paper-White and Iris Tingitana have shed their last petals, Bougainvillea Sanderiana has rolled up its magenta tapestries, and the flowerful Bignonia Capensis is only a sheet of brightly varnished foliage. But as one mounts from terrace to terrace what a rush of hurrying flower-feet is in the air! The tireless Laurustinus leads the way, already thrusting its snowy corymbs among last year's blue-black berries; the Photinias are crowning their stately growth with burnished terminal shoots and broad flat flower-clusters; the single-flowered Kerria Japonica is breaking into golden bloom, and the single yellow Banksia that climbs through it is already showing a few flowers.

Here clumps of Eremurus are thrusting up between the faded flowers of the Diplopappus; in another corner, tucked away in warm clefts along the path, the species crocuses Tomasinianus and Sieberi are folding up their last blooms; but the purple cups of Imperati and the great vain-glorious chalices of Enchantress still burn in the sun- shine, and the vivid golden stars of Crocus Susianus nestle low in their striped leaves. Near by the tulip Kaufmanniana spreads its first water-lily petals, the tiny Humilis has already put up a frail flower of pinkish mauve, Sylvestris is hung with dangling buds, and the plump flowers of Tulipa Greigii are forcing apart its thick snake-speckled leaves. Farther on, in another sunny nook, the species Irises are weaving their enchantment; here Sind-pers has already unfurled its ethereally lovely flowers, there the exquisite lilac-blue of Reticulata Cantab lies like a fragment of sky on the brown earth. The yellow remontant Pumila, "Souvenir du Lieutenant Siret", which bloomed all through the summer and autumn, is again thick with bursting blossoms, the outspread blue and purple stars of Histroides Major still linger, and Bucharica and Sind-reichii are unfolding their fluted sheaves, and the Hispanicas thrusting up their frail grassy filaments.

In a half-shady hollow, the great bed of arums already shows a few unfurling trumpets through its lordly leaves, and bordering a long grass walk in full sun sturdy bushes of Raphiolepis Delacourii are covering themselves with rosy waxen flowers. In a warm angle of the house-front the old Wistaria is just venturing into flower, Gera- nium Capitatum is multiplying its scarlet aigrettes beneath the sunny windows, Rosa Anemone Laevigata is blossoming on gates and trellises, and that indefatigable coverer of walls, the climbing rose Noella Nabonnand, is refurbishing her gaunt branches for another crop of

3.

bloom. Countless unopened flower-spikes declare the coming splendours of Echium Fastuosum, Anemone Fulgens flames through the silvery branches of Grevillea Rosmarinifolia, and a sheet of faint blue Ionopsidion is thickly starred with Tritaleias of the same elusive colour.

Everywhere the play of new tints is already a prelude to the great glory that ushers in April, when the Echiums lift their thousand torches of gentian-blue among the blue blossoms of Ceanothus Veitchii, when Xanthocera Sorbifolia droops its white fringes above the salmon and mauve chalices of the Reine Elisabeth tree-paeony, and the later Prunuses Hisakura, Pendula, Sinensis, and the first lovely single-flowered Japanese apples, blend their rose and crimson blossoms. Meanwhile, hyacinths and garden Narcissi are springing up everywhere, and preceded by Tulipa Clusiana, all the garden tulips will soon be unfolding their cups, followed by the delicately tinted Dutch Irises sometimes catalogued as "Hollandia", which so serviceably fill the gap between Tingitana and the hybrid Germanicas. The later Mimosas, such as and Trinervis
Petiolaris, Cyanophylla, Boule d'Or, are already in flower or bud, and the noblest of Bignonias, Venusta, is preparing to weave its vast hangings of crimson bells.

But the tale of April in a Riviera garden is too long to tell: as well try to crowd a symphony into a "Half-hour of music". When the peaches and cherries are in bloom, and all the late tulips, narcissi, ranonculus, anemones and irises come rushing up, mingling with roses, lilacs and paeonies to swell the mighty chorus, one can only fall back on the closing lines of Schiller's Hymn to Joy, to which Beethoven gave the wings of immortality.

APPENDIX 2

DECEMBER IN A FRENCH RIVIERA GARDEN

In writing of southern gardens the gardener is so often
tempted to dilate on the enchanting spectacle they present in the
early spring (when all gardens naturally lend themselves better to the
art of the photographer and of the descriptive writer) that I have
thought it might be interesting to ~~readers of "The Garden Lovers"~~ *garden lovers* to
hear something of the less abundant season as it shows itself on my
Riviera terraces at the close of the year.

In speaking of my garden as being on the French Riviera
I may give a false impression, for the climate of the Var is at once
warmer and more unsettled than that of the actual "Côte d'Azur". My
garden is only a few miles from Toulon, and Toulon only two hours
distant from Marseilles and the dreaded Rhône valley, down which the
north winds pour with fury from the snowy Alps and the frozen heights
of the central plateau. But Hyères is fifty miles farther south than
any other town on the south coast of France, and if one's garden lies,
as mine does, among sheltered ledges protected from the north, one
can triumph over the gardeners of Menton and Cannes by a fortnight's
priority in the bloom of early-flowering plants.

As a drawback to these advantages, the soil of my rocky
terraces is poor and shallow, so that I am deprived of many plants
which flourish in the deep rich earth of the plain; but the garden has
yet to be found in which advantages are not balanced by drawbacks, and
this light warm soil makes happy many moisture-dreading plants.

If the regular rains come, as they should, in November,
and the weather afterward is fine, December and January at Hyères,
are like a belated summer; but though the landscape is supremely

2.

beautiful the flower garden is necessarily far less varied than
later on.

Among irises only "Styloma" and the interesting "remontant"
Hybrid Pumilas, which bloom again so abundantly in the spring, can
be counted on, unless Iri's Tingitana has already begun its long
season of flowering; a result easily secured if one or two beds are
kept watered in summer, with a view to precocious bloom. Of the
narcissi, again, only two or three varieties bloom abundantly in
December, and these not among the most interesting; although the
"Paper White", if planted in drifts in uncultivated nooks, is always
a joy to the eye.

To make up for the lack of bulbs and irises, the violets
are flowering profusely, and the roses (especially teas, and the
old-fashioned "remontant" rose) are in their beauty; indeed some of
the more vigorous shrubby varieties, such as "Pax", "Clytemnestra",
"Cramoisi Supérieur", "Gloire du Rosomane" and "Mme Abel Carrière",
though they seem in full bloom, are still putting forth new buds.

Among the climbing plants in flower there are the
brilliant yellow Senecio Scandens, which lasts for weeks, the two
varieties (orange and scarlet) of Bignonia Capensis, the delicate
purple-and-pink Lopezia Grandiflora, Solanum Jasminoides, the rocket
like scarlet flowers of Aloe C?laria, and great sheets of Bougainvillea *Sanderiana*, so resplendent in its bold magenta bloom
if it is given a green background, and if all other colours but the
pale mauves of Buddleyas and *I*rises, and the soft grays of *S*enecios
and wormwood, are kept away from it.

But perhaps the most interesting element in my December
garden is that contributed by the flowering shrubs, many of them
recent introductions from China or Central America. Among them the

3.

most sensational of December bloomers is the great "Daisy Tree",
Montanoa Grandiflora, which towers up some fifteen feet, forming a
canopy of broad delicately-cut leaves and white flowers which are
like a hybrid between the Shasta Daisy and Clematis Armandi. Its only
rival is the fantastic Dahlia Arborea, shooting up still higher on
its long bamboo-like stalks, and bursting suddenly at the summit into
a great spreading shower of single mauve flowers. Both of these shrubs
carry their fragile flower clusters so high that they need to be
sheltered not only from the cold but from the wind; but in my garden
they have resisted a degree or two of frost.

    Among shrubs in full bloom before Christmas there are also
the winter-flowering Buddleyas (the orange Madagascariensis, the
white Asiatica and the lilac Officinalis), as well as Jasminum
Grandiflorum, Grevillea Rosmarinifolium, the earliest Mimosas (*Mot-
teana, Dealbata,*) and Eleagnus Edulis, which sheds its vanilla-fragrance
Floribunda, so widely on the warm air. The graceful Frelinia Cestroides, with its
slender bamboo-like foliage, is already showing a few feathery sprays
of sulphur-coloured blossom, and the vigorous Escallonia Ingrami is
heavy with bright pink flower-clusters. Other shrubs, such as Nandina
Domestica, Duranta Plumieri, the Pyracanthas Yunnanense and Gibbsii,
and Arbutus Unedo, contribute clusters of orange, flame-red or
crimson berries to the gay December colour-scheme, to which the soft
rose-coloured fruit-clusters of the Schinus and the rosy-mauve of the
new Eucalyptus shoots add their harmonizing tones.

    In warm corners of the rock-garden the brilliant purple
Statice Perezii is already coming into bloom, and Lithospermum Rosmarinifolium beginning to spread its dense masses of gentian-blue
flowers, in exquisite Hispidus, which neighbours it; while wherever
Contrast to the turquoise-coloured heather

4.

a careless hand has scattered Lantana Sellowiana, whether in sun or shade, in rocky clefts or good garden soil, there, equably and continuously for more than half the year, it weaves its lowly tapestry of pinkish-lilac bloom.

Elsewhere the delicate daisy-like Vittadinia is preparing to fringe the paths, Gazania Montana is opening its orange suns, Lavandula Dentata and Diplopappus Fruticulosus are spreading their sheets of mauve between clumps of bright violet Veronica, and the loveliest mauve of all, that of the Iris Stylosa, is adding another note to the purple corner of the garden.

This list comprises all the flowers and shrubs which are in full bloom in December in my garden, but every Riviera garden-lover will reckon in among the pleasurable emotions of the month that of watching for the earliest species crocuses (Tomasinianus and Sieberi among the first), and of going daily to see how far the Saxatilis tulips have pushed up their noses, or how soon the swollen buds of Iris Sind-Pers will release their subtly painted petals. December is of all months perhaps the most exciting in this respect; the soil trembles with promise; every nook shows a green stalk or a bursting bud that was not there yesterday; and in the Christmas dawn some precocious almond-bough is sure to hang out its snowy garlands against the sunrise.

BIBLIOGRAPHY

Primary Sources

Wharton, Edith. "After Holbein." *The New York Stories of Edith Wharton*. New York Review of Books, 2007, pp. 356–80.

Wharton, Edith. *The Age of Innocence*. Edited by Candace Waid, W. W. Norton & Company, Inc, 2003.

Wharton, Edith. *A Backward Glance*. Simon & Schuster, 1998.

Wharton, Edith. "Bewitched." *Ghost Stories of Edith Wharton*. Vintage, 2009, pp. 139–59.

Wharton, Edith. "A Bottle of Perrier." *Ghost Stories of Edith Wharton*. Vintage, 2009, pp. 271–92.

Wharton, Edith. *Bunner Sisters. 'Ethan Frome'; 'Summer'; 'Bunner Sisters'*. Alfred A. Knopf, 2008, pp. 271–366. Everyman's Library.

Wharton, Edith. *The Children*. Virago, 2010.

Wharton, Edith. "Coming Home." *The Collected Short Stories*, vol. 2, edited by R. W. B. Lewis, Scribner's, 1968, pp. 230–56.

Wharton, Edith. *The Cruise of the Vanadis*. Rizzoli International, 2004.

Wharton, Edith. *The Custom of the Country. Three Novels of New York*. Penguin, 2012, pp. 259–555. Penguin Classics Deluxe Edition.

Wharton, Edith. "The Duchess at Prayer." *Ghost Stories of Edith Wharton*. Vintage, 2009, pp. 110–27.

Wharton, Edith. *Edith Wharton: The Uncollected Critical Writings*. Edited by Frederick Wegener, Princeton University Press, 1996.

Wharton, Edith. *Edith Wharton Abroad: Selected Travel Writings, 1888–1920*. Edited by Sarah Bird Wright, Robert Hale, 1995.

Wharton, Edith. *Edith Wharton's New England: Seven Stories and 'Ethan Frome'*. Edited by Barbara Anne White, University Press of New England, 1995.

Wharton, Edith. *Ethan Frome. 'Ethan Frome'; 'Summer'; 'Bunner Sisters'*. Alfred A. Knopf, 2008, pp. 1–104. Everyman's Library.

Wharton, Edith. "False Dawn." *Old New York*. Simon & Schuster, 1995, pp. 7–80.

Wharton, Edith. *Fighting France from Dunkerque to Belfort*. Charles Scribner's Sons, 1915.

Wharton, Edith. *French Ways and Their Meaning*. D. Appleton and Company, 1919.

Wharton, Edith. *The Fruit of the Tree*. Wildside Press, 2006.

Wharton, Edith. "George Eliot [Review of Leslie Stephen's *George Eliot*]." *The Bookman*, vol. 15, May 1902, pp. 247–51.

Wharton, Edith. *Glimpses of the Moon*. Pushkin Press, 2018.

Wharton, Edith. *The House of Mirth*. Edited by Elizabeth Ammons, W. W. Norton & Company, Inc, 1990.

Wharton, Edith. *In Morocco.* John Beaufoy Publishing, 2015.

Wharton, Edith. *Italian Backgrounds.* Scribner, 1905.

Wharton, Edith. *Italian Villas and Their Gardens.* The Century, 1905.

Wharton, Edith. "The Journey." *The New York Stories of Edith Wharton.* New York Review of Books, 2007, pp. 88–99.

Wharton, Edith. "Kerfol." *Ghost Stories of Edith Wharton*, by Edith Wharton. Vintage, 2009, pp. 68–87.

Wharton, Edith. *The Letters of Edith Wharton.* Edited by Richard Warrington Baldwin Lewis and Nancy Lewis, Collier Books, 1988.

Wharton, Edith. "The Looking Glass." *Ghost Stories of Edith Wharton.* Vintage, 2009, pp. 223–39.

Wharton, Edith. "Madame de Treymes." *Madame de Treymes and Three Novellas.* Scribner & Schuster, 1995, pp. 211–82.

Wharton, Edith. *The Marne.* Scribner's, 1918.

Wharton, Edith. *A Motor-Flight through France.* Scribner's, 1908.

Wharton, Edith. "Mrs. Manstey's View." *The New York Stories of Edith Wharton.* New York Review of Books, 2007, pp. 3–14.

Wharton, Edith. *My Dear Governess: The Letters of Edith Wharton to Anna Bahlmann.* Edited by Irene Goldman-Price, Yale University Press, 2012.

Wharton, Edith. *The Reef.* Alfred A. Knopf, 1996. Everyman's Library.

Wharton, Edith. "Roman Fever." *The New York Stories of Edith Wharton.* New York Review of Books, 2007, pp. 438–52.

Wharton, Edith. "Sanctuary." *Madame de Treymes and Three Novellas.* Scribner & Schuster, 1995, pp. 119–210.

Wharton, Edith. *A Son at the Front.* Scribner's, 1923.

Wharton, Edith. "The Spark." *Old New York.* Simon & Schuster, 1995, pp. 181–234.

Wharton, Edith. *Summer. "Ethan Frome"; "Summer"; "Bunner Sisters".* Alfred A. Knopf, 2008, pp. 105–270. Everyman's Library.

Wharton, Edith. "The Touchstone." *Madame de Treymes and Three Novellas.* Scribner & Schuster, 1995, pp. 17–118.

Wharton, Edith. *Twilight Sleep.* Simon & Schuster, 2010.

Wharton, Edith. *The Valley of Decision* [1902]. Project Gutenberg. Aug. 1, 2009. Oct. 16, 2019.

Wharton, Edith. "The Vice of Reading." *The North American Review*, vol. 177, no. 563, 1903, pp. 513–21. *JSTOR*, www.jstor.org/stable/25119460. Accessed May 27, 2021.

Wharton, Edith. "The Writing of *Ethan Frome.*" *The Colophon: The Book Collectors' Quarterly*, vol. 2, no. 4, 1932, pp. 261–63.

Wharton, Edith. *The Writing of Fiction.* Touchtone Book, 1997.

Wharton, Edith and Ogden Codman, Jr. *The Decoration of Houses* [1902]. Introduction and notes by John Barrington Bayley and William A. Coles. Norton, 1978.

Wharton, Edith and Vivienne De Watteville. "Preface." *Speak to the Earth: Wanderings and Reflections Among Elephants and Mountains.* Methuen and Co., 1936, pp. 1–2.

Secondary Sources

Alaimo, Stacy. *Bodily Natures: Science, Environment, and the Material Self.* Indiana University Press, 2001.

Alpers, Paul. *What is Pastoral?* University of Chicago Press, 1996.

Alpers, Paul. "What Is Pastoral?" *Critical Inquiry*, vol. 8, no. 3, 1982, pp. 437–60. *JSTOR*, www.jstor.org/stable/1343259. Accessed May 24, 2021.

Anderson, Donald and Judith Saunders. "Edith Wharton and the Hudson Valley." *The Hudson River Valley Review*, vol. 23, no. 1, 2006, pp. 1–6.

Andreassen, Elin et al. *Persistent Memories: Pyramiden, a Soviet Mining Town in the High Arctic.* Tapir Academic Press, 2010.

Andrews, Malcolm. *Landscape and Modern Art.* Oxford University Press, 1999.

Andrews, Malcolm. *The Search for the Picturesque: Landscape Aesthetics and Tourism in Britain, 1760–1800.* Scholar Press, 1990.

Apel, Dora. *Beautiful Terrible Ruins: Detroit and the Anxiety of Decline.* Rutgers University Press, 2015.

Arnalds, Olafur. "Desertification: An Appeal for a Broader Perspective." *Rangeland Desertification*, by Olafur Arnalds and Steve Archer, Springer, 2011, pp. 5–15.

Aske, Martin. *Keats and Hellenism: An Essay.* Cambridge University Press, 1985.

Bainbridge, Simon. *Mountaineering and British Romanticism: The Literary Cultures of Climbing 1770–1836.* Oxford University Press, 2020.

Balestra, Gianfranca. "Italian Foregrounds and Backgrounds: The Valley of Decision." *Edith Wharton Review*, vol. 9, no. 1, 1992, pp. 12–27. *JSTOR*, www.jstor.org/stable /43512793. Accessed Dec. 11, 2020.

Ballon, Hilary, editor. *The Greatest Grid: The Master Plan of Manhattan, 1811–2011.* Columbia University Press, 2012.

Barnes, Julian. "Introduction." *The Reef*, by Edith Wharton, Everyman's Library, 1996, pp. ix–xviii.

Barillas, William. *The Midwestern Pastoral: Place and Landscape in Literature of the American Heartland.* Ohio University Press, 2006.

Barrell, John and John Bull, editors. *The Penguin Book of Pastoral Verse.* Penguin, 1974.

Barrow, John. *Travels into the Interior of Southern Africa.* Vol. 1, 2nd edn, Cadell and Davies, 1806.

Barton, Susan. *Healthy Living in the Alps: The Origins of Winter Tourism in Switzerland 1860– 1914.* Manchester University Press, 2008.

Batchelor, John. *John Ruskin: A Life.* Carroll & Graf, 2006.

Bate, Jonathan. *The Song of the Earth.* Picador, 2000.

Bauer, Dale M. "'Roman Fever': A Rune of History." *Edith Wharton's Brave New Politics.* University of Wisconsin Press, 1995, pp. 145–64.

Bauman, Zygmunt. *Postmodern Ethics.* Blackwell, 1993.

Bauman, Zygmunt. *Wasted Lives: Modernity and Its Outcasts.* Polity Press, 2004.

Beam, Dorri. *Style, Gender, and Fantasy in Nineteenth-Century American Women's Writing.* Cambridge University Press, 2010.

Beer, Janet. *Edith Wharton.* Liverpool University Press, 2001.

Beer, Janet. *Edith Wharton: Traveler in the Land of Letters.* Palgrave Macmillan, 1990.

Beer, Janet. *Kate Chopin, Edith Wharton and Charlotte Perkins Gilman: Studies in Short Fiction.* Palgrave Macmillan, 1997.

Beer, Janet and Bridget Bennett, editors. *Special Relationships: Anglo-American Antagonisms and Affinities, 1854–1936.* Manchester University Press, 2002.

Beer, Janet and Avril Horner. *Edith Wharton: Sex, Satire and the Older Woman.* Palgrave Macmillan, 2011.

Beer, Janet and Avril Horner. "'The Great Panorama': Edith Wharton as Historical Novelist." *The Modern Language Review*, vol. 110, no. 1, 2015, pp. 69–84. *JSTOR*,www. jstor.org/stable/10.5699/modelangrevi.110.1.0069. Accessed Jan. 20, 2020.

Beer, Janet and Avril Horner. "'This Isn't Exactly a Ghost Story': Edith Wharton and Parodic Gothic." *Journal of American Studies*, vol. 37, no. 2, 2003, pp. 269–85. *JSTOR*, www.jstor.org/stable/27557331. Accessed Apr. 1, 2021.

Bellringer, Alan W. "Edith Wharton's Use of France." *The Yearbook of English Studies*, vol. 15, 1985, pp. 109–24. *JSTOR*, www.jstor.org/stable/3508551. Accessed Mar. 10, 2021.

Bender, Barbara. "Introduction: Landscape - Meaning and Action." *Landscape, Politics and Perspectives*, edited by Barbara Bender, Berg Publishers, 1993.

Benert, Annette. "The Romance of Nature." *The Architectural Imagination of Edith Wharton: Gender, Class, and Power in the Progressive Era*. Fairleigh Dickinson University Press, 2007, pp. 140–65.

Benert, Annette Larson. "Edith Wharton at War: Civilized Space in Troubled Times." *Twentieth Century Literature*, vol. 42, no. 3, Autumn 1996, pp. 322–43.

Benstock, Shari. "Landscape of Desire: Edith Wharton and Europe." *Wretched Exotic: Essays on Edith Wharton in Europe*, edited by Katherine Joslin and Alan Price, Peter Lang, 1996, pp. 19–42. XXIV American Literature.

Berger, Alan. *Drosscape: Wasting Land in Urban America*. Princeton Architectural Press, 2007.

Berger, Alan. *Reclaiming the American West*. Princeton Architectural Press, 2002.

Berman, Russell A. "Democratic Destruction: Ruins and Emancipation in the American Tradition." *Ruins of Modernity*, edited by Julia Hell and Andreas Schönle, Duke University Press, 2010.

Bhabha, Homi K. "Unsatisfied: Notes on Vernacular Cosmopolitanism." *Text and Nation*, edited by Laura Garcia-Morena and Peter C. Pfeifer, Camden House, 1996, pp. 191–207.

Bicknell, Jeanette et al., editors. *Philosophical Perspectives on Ruins, Monuments, and Memorials*. Routledge, 2020.

Billips, Martha. "Edith Wharton as Regionalist: A New Context for Reading *Summer*." *Edith Wharton Review*, vol. 34, no. 2, 2018, pp. 146–66. *JSTOR*, www.jstor.org/stable /10.5325/editwharrevi.34.2.0146. Accessed Aug. 15, 2020.

Birch, Dinah. *Ruskin on Turner*, "Cassell," 1990.

Blackmar, Elizabeth. "Modernist Ruins." *American Quarterly*, vol. 53, no. 2, 2001, pp. 324–39. *Project MUSE*, doi:10.1353/aq.2001.0013.

Blanton, Casey. *Travel Writing: The Self and the World*. Routledge, 2002.

Blazek, William. "Wharton and France." *Edith Wharton in Context*, edited by Laura Rattray, Cambridge University Press, 2012, pp. 275–84.

Bloom, Harold, editor. *Edith Wharton's The Age of Innocence*. Chelsea House Publishers, 2005.

Bloom, Harold. *The Western Canon: The Books and School of the Ages*. Riverhead, 1994.

Borden, Iain et al. *The Unknown City: Contesting Architecture and Social Space*. MIT Press, 1998.

Botting, Fred. "Introduction: Gothic Excess and Transgressions." *Gothic*. Routledge, 1996, pp. 1–13. The New Critical Idiom.

Botting, Fred. "Introduction: Negative Aesthetics." *Gothic*. Routledge, 2014, pp. 1–19.

Bowlby, Rachel. "'I Had Barbara': Women's Ties and Edith Wharton's 'Roman Fever'." *A Child of One's Own: Parental Stories*. Oxford University Press, 2013, pp. 218–22.

Boym, Svetlana. *The Off-Modern*. Bloomsbury Academic, 2017.

Bracke, Astrid. "Redrawing the Boundaries of Ecocritical Practice." *Interdisciplinary Studies in Literature and Environment*, vol. 17, no. 4, 2010, pp. 765–8. *JSTOR*, www.jstor .org/stable/44087670. Accessed May 26, 2021.

Bracke, Astrid. "Wastelands, Shrubs and Parks: Ecocriticism and the Challenge of the Urban." *Frame*, vol. 26, no. 2, Nov. 2013, pp. 7–21.

Bradburne, James M. *Italian Garden Magic*. Fondazione Palazzo Strozzi, 2012.

Bradley, Elizabeth L. "Dutch New York from Irving to Wharton." *The Cambridge Companion to the Literature of New York*, edited by Cyrus R. K. Patell and Bryan Waterman, Cambridge University Press, 2010, pp. 27–41. Cambridge Companions to Literature.

Bradshaw, Michael. "Hedgehog Theory: How to Read a Romantic Fragment Poem." *Literature Compass*, vol. 5, no. 1, 2008, pp. 73–89.

Bratton, Daniel. "Edith Wharton and Louis Bromfield: A Jeffersonian and a Victorian." *Edith Wharton Review*, vol. 10, no. 2, 1993, pp. 8–11. *JSTOR*, www.jstor.org/stable/43512825. Accessed Apr. 3, 2021.

Brodey, Inger Sigrun. *Ruined by Design: Shaping Novels and Gardens in the Culture of Sensibility*. Routledge, 2012.

Brown, Barbara and Douglas D. Perkins. *Place Attachment*. Plenum Press, 1992.

Brown, Bill. *A Sense of Things: The Object Matter of American Literature*. University of Chicago Press, 2004.

Brown, Jane. *The Pursuit of Paradise: A Social History of Gardens and Gardening*. HarperCollins, 2000.

Brown, Junius Henri Brown. *The Great Metropolis*. American Publishing Company, 1868.

Browning, Robert. *Robert Browning*. Edited by Adam Roberts, Oxford University Press, 1997.

Buchan, John. "The Glamour of High Altitudes." *The Spectator*, Jan. 9, 1904, pp. 45–6.

Buell, Lawrence. *The Environmental Imagination: Thoreau, Nature Writing and the Formation of American Culture*. Harvard University Press, 1995.

Buell, Lawrence. *The Future of Environmental Criticism*. Blackwell, 2005.

Buell, Lawrence. *Writing for an Endangered World: Literature, Culture, and Environment in the U.S. and Beyond*. Belknap Press of Harvard University Press, 2001.

Burke, Edmund. *Philosophical Enquiry Into the Origin of Our Ideas of the Sublime and Beautiful*. Edited by Adam Phillips, Oxford University Press, 1990.

Burrows, Edwin G. and Mike Wallace. *Gotham: A History of New York City to 1898*. Oxford University Press, 1998.

Byron, Lord. *Lord Byron: The Major Works*. Edited by Jerome J. McGann, Oxford University Press, 2008, p. 253.

Cahir, Linda Costanzo. "Wharton and the American Romantics." *Edith Wharton in Context*, edited by Laura Rattray, Cambridge University Press, 2012, pp. 335–43.

Callicott, J. Baird. "A Critique of and an Alternative to the Wilderness Idea." *Environmental Ethics: An Anthology*, edited by Andrew Light and Holmes Roston III, Blackwell, 2003.

Campbell, Craig. "Residual Landscapes and the Everyday: An Interview with Edward Burtynsky." *Space and Culture*, vol. 11, no. 1, Feb. 2008, pp. 39–50, doi:10.1177/1206331207310703.

Campbell, Donna M. "Edith Wharton and the 'Authoresses': The Critique of Local Color in Wharton's Early Fiction." *Studies in American Fiction*, vol. 22, no. 2, 1994, pp. 169–83.

Campbell, Donna M. "Summers in Arcady: The Deep Time of Evolutionary Romance in James Lane Allen, Hamlin Garland, and Edith Wharton." *American Literary Realism*, vol. 52, no. 2, 2020, pp. 95–113. *Project MUSE* muse.jhu.edu/article/745267.

Campbell, Gordon. *A Short History of Gardens*, Oxford University Press, 2016.

Campkin, Ben. "Degradation and Regeneration: Theories of Dirt and the Contemporary City." *Dirt: New Geographies of Cleanliness and Contamination*, edited by Rosie Cox and Ben Campkin, I. B. Tauris & Company Limited, 2008, pp. 68–79.

Cannavo, Peter F. "American Contradictions and Pastoral Visions: An Appraisal of Leo Marx, 'The Machine in the Garden.'" *Organization & Environment*, vol. 14, no. 1, 2001, pp. 74–92. *JSTOR*, www.jstor.org/stable/26161714. Accessed May 27, 2021.

Caraccioli, Louis-Antoine de. *Paris, le modèle des nations étrangères, ou L'Europe françoise.* Veuve Duchesne, 1777.

Carver, Steve. "Rewilding in England and Wales: A Review of Recent Developments, Issues, and Concerns." *Science and stewardship to protect and sustain wilderness values: Eighth World Wilderness Congress symposium; September 30–October 6, 2005; Anchorage, AK.* Proceedings RMRS-P-49, comps. Alan Watson, Janet Sproull, and Liese Dean. Fort Collins: U.S. Department of Agriculture, Forest Service, Rocky Mountain Research Station, 2007, 267–72.

Casey, Edward. *The Fate of Place: A Philosophical History.* University of California Press, 1997.

Casey, Edward. *Getting Back into Place: Toward a Renewed Understanding of the Place World.* Indiana University Press, 1993.

Caws, Mary Ann. "Translation of the Self: Ruskin and Wharton." *The Massachusetts Review*, vol. 40, no. 2, 1999, pp. 165–73. *JSTOR*, www.jstor.org/stable/25091519. Accessed Mar. 1, 2021.

Chambers, Dianne L. "Gender and Performance in the Glimpses of the Moon." *Feminist Readings of Edith Wharton: From Silence to Speech.* Palgrave Macmillan, 2009, pp. 125–50.

Chance, Helena. "Interior and Garden Design." *Edith Wharton in Context*, edited by Laura Rattray, Cambridge University Press, Cambridge, 2012, pp. 199–208. Literature in Context.

Chatterton, Paul. "'Squatting Is Still Legal, Necessary and Free': A Brief Intervention in the Corporate City." *Antipode*, vol. 34, no. 1, Jan. 2002, pp. 1–7, doi:10.1111/1467-8330.00223.

Claridge, Amanda. *Rome.* Oxford University Press, 1998. Oxford Archaeological Guides.

Cloke, Paul and Owain Jones. "'Unclaimed Territory': Childhood and Disordered Space(s)." *Social & Culture Geography*, vol. 6, no. 3, 2005, pp. 311–33, doi:1080/14649360500111154.

Cohen, Jeffrey Jerome. *Stone: An Ecology of the Inhuman.* University of Minnesota Press, 2015.

Colley, Ann C. "John Ruskin: Climbing and the Vulnerable Eye." *Victorian Literature and Culture*, vol. 37, no. 1, 2009, pp. 43–66. *JSTOR*, www.jstor.org/stable/40347213. Accessed May 28, 2021.

Colley, Ann C. *Victorians in the Mountains.* Routledge, 2010.

Conan, Michael, editor. *Perspectives on Garden Histories.* Dumbarton Oaks, 1991.

Conlogue, William. *Working the Garden: American Writers and the Industrialization of Agriculture.* University of North Carolina Press, 2001.

Cook, Clarence. *A Description of the New York Central Park.* [1869]. B. Blom, 1972.

Cook, Edward Tyas and Alexander Wedderburn, editors. "The Mountain Glory." *The Works of John Ruskin*, by John Ruskin, vol. 6, Cambridge University Press, 2010, pp. 418–66. Cambridge Library Collection – Works of John Ruskin.

Cook, Ian et al. *Cultural Turns / Geographical Turns: Perspectives on Cultural Geography.* Routledge, 2016.

Cooper, David E. *The Philosophy of Gardens.* Oxford University Press, 2006.

Cornell Dolan, Kathryn. *Beyond the Fruited Plain: Food and Agriculture in U. S. Literature, 1850–1905.* University of Nebraska Press, 2014.

Cosgrove, Denis and Stephen Daniels. "Introduction: Iconography and Landscape." *The Iconography of Landscape: Essays on the Symbolic Representation, Design, and Use of Past Environments*, edited by Denis Cosgrove, Cambridge University Press, 1988, pp. 1–10.

Cowie, Jefferson R. and Joseph Heathcott, editors. *Beyond the Ruins: The Meanings of Deindustrialization*. Cornell University Press, 2003.

Crang, Mike. "The Death of Great Ships: Photography, Politics, and Waste in the Global Imaginary." *Environment and Planning A: Economy and Space*, vol. 42, no. 5, May 2010, pp. 1084–102, doi:10.1068/a42414.

Crèvecoeur, J. Hector St. John. *Letters from an American Farmer and Sketches of Eighteenth Century America* [1782]. Penguin Classics, 1981.

Cullen Bryant, William. "A New Public Park." *The Evening Post*, Jul. 3, 1844.

Cunliffe, Marcus. "The Expatriates (Henry James, Edith Wharton, Henry Adams, Gertrude Stein)." *The Literature of the United States*. Penguin Books, 1961, pp. 213–38.

Daigrepont, Lloyd M. "The Cult of Passion in 'The Age of Innocence.'" *American Literary Realism*, vol. 40, no. 1, 2007, pp. 1–15. *JSTOR*, www.jstor.org/stable/27747269. Accessed Apr. 3, 2021.

Davis, Sophia. "Military Landscapes and Secret Science: The Case of Orford Ness." *Cultural Geographies*, vol. 15, no. 1, 2008, pp. 143–49. *JSTOR*, www.jstor.org/stable/44251197. Accessed Oct. 1, 2020.

Dawdy, Shannon Lee. "Clockpunk Anthropology and the Ruins of Modernity." *Current Anthropology*, vol. 51, no. 6, 2010, pp. 761–93. *JSTOR*, www.jstor.org/stable/10.1086/657626. Accessed Apr. 2, 2020.

Day, Brian J. "The Moral Intuition of Ruskin's 'Storm-Cloud.'" *Studies in English Literature, 1500-1900*, vol. 45, no. 4, 2005, pp. 917–33. *JSTOR*, www.jstor.org/stable/3844621. Accessed May 28, 2021.

De Quincey, Thomas. "The Palimpsest of the Human Brain." 1845. *Quotidiana*, edited by Patrick Madden. Dec. 01, 2006. Feb. 01, 2020. http://essays.quotidiana.org/dequincey/palimpsest_of_the_human_brain/.

Dean, Sharon L. *Constance Fenimore Woolson and Edith Wharton: Perspectives on Landscape and Art*. University of Tennessee Press, 2002.

DeJean, Joan. *How Paris Became Paris: The Invention of the Modern City*. Bloomsbury USA, 2014.

Dekkers, Midas. *The Way of All Flesh: The Romance of Ruins*. Farrar, Straus and Giroux, 2000.

DeSilvey, Caitlin. *Curated Decay: Heritage Beyond Saving*. University of Minnesota Press, 2017.

DeSilvey, Caitlin. "Observed Decay: Telling Stories with Mutable Things." *Journal of Material Culture*, vol. 11, no. 3, Nov. 2006, pp. 318–38, doi:10.1177/1359183506068808.

DeSilvey, Caitlin and Tim Edensor. "Reckoning with Ruins." *Progress in Human Geography*, vol. 37, no. 4, Aug. 2013, pp. 465–85, doi:10.1177/0309132512462271.

Dewey, John. *Art as Experience*. 1934. Perigree Books, 1980.

Dewey, John. *Experience and Nature*. 1929. Dover Publications, 1958.

Diderot, Denis. *Ruines et Paysages: Salons De 1767*. Edited by Else Marie Bukdahl et al., Hermann, 1995.

Dillon, Brian. "Fragments from a History of Ruin: Picking Through the Wreckage." *CABINET* /, 2006, www.cabinetmagazine.org/issues/20/dillon.php.

Dillon, Brian. "Introduction." *Ruins*, edited by Brian Dillon, Whitechapel Gallery, 2011, pp. 10–19.

Dillon, Brian. *Ruin Lust: Artists' Fascination with Ruins, from Turner to the Present Day*. Tate Publishing, 2014.

Dillon, Sarah. "Introduction: The Palimpsest." *The Palimpsest Literature, Criticism, Theory*. Continuum, 2007, pp. 1–9. Continuum Literary Studies Series.

Dini, Rachele. *Consumerism, Waste, and Re-Use in TWENTIETH-CENTURY Fiction: Legacies of the Avant-Garde*. Palgrave Macmillan, 2016.

Dixon Hunt, John. *Greater Perfections: The Practice of Garden Theory*. University of Pennsylvania Press, 2000.

Dixon Hunt, John. "Introduction: Reading and Writing the Site." *Gardens and the Picturesque: Studies in the History of Landscape Architecture*. MIT Press, 1992.

Douglas, Mary. "Introduction." *Purity and Danger*. Routledge, 1966, pp. 1–6.

Downing Lay, Charles. *A Garden Book for Autumn and Winter*. Duffield & Co., 1924.

Drizou, Myrto. "Edith Wharton's Odyssey." *The New Edith Wharton Studies*, edited by Jennifer Haytock and Laura Rattray, Cambridge University Press, 2019, pp. 65–79. Twenty-First-Century Critical Revisions.

Dubowitz, Dan. *Wastelands*. Dewi Lewis Publishing, 2010.

Duffy, Cian. *The Landscapes of the Sublime, 1700–1930: Classic Ground*. Palgrave Macmillan, 2013.

Duncan, James and Derek Gregory, editors. *Writes of Passage: Reading Travel Writing*. Routledge, 1999.

Dyman, Jenni. "'A Bottle of Perrier' and 'Mr. Jones'." *Lurking Feminism: The Ghost Stories of Edith Wharton*. Peter Lang, 1996, pp. 115–38.

Edenson, Tim. "Walking Through Ruins." *Ways of Walking: Ethnography and Practice on Foot*, edited by Tim Ingold and Jo Lee Vergunst, Ashgate, 2008, pp. 123–42.

Edensor, Tim. "The Ghosts of Industrial Ruins: Ordering and Disordering Memory in Excessive Space." *Environment and Planning D: Society and Space*, vol. 23, no. 6, Dec. 2005, pp. 829–49, doi:10.1068/d58j.

Edensor, Tim. "Waste Matter - The Debris of Industrial Ruins and the Disordering of the Material World." *Journal of Material Culture*, vol. 10, no. 3, Nov. 2005, pp. 311–32, doi:10.1177/1359183505057346.

Edensor, Tim et al. "Obliterating Informal Space: The London Olympics and the Lea Valley: A Photo Essay." *Space and Culture*, vol. 11, no. 3, Aug. 2008, pp. 285–93, doi:10.1177/1206331208319152.

Eisenberg, Evan. *Ecology of Eden*. Vintage Books, 1999.

Elkin, Lauren. *Flâneuse: Women Walk the City in Paris, New York, Tokyo, Venice and London*. Vintage, 2017.

Emmert, Scott D. "Drawing-Room Naturalism in Edith Wharton's Early Short Stories." *Journal of the Short Story in English*, vol. 39, Autumn 2002, pp. 57–71. http://jsse.revues.org/index271.html#text

Empson, William. *Some Versions of Pastoral*. Chatto & Windus, 1935.

Estok, Simon C. "Theorizing in a Space of Ambivalent Openness: Ecocriticism and Ecophobia." *ISLE: Interdisciplinary Studies in Literature and Environment*, vol. 16, issue 2, Spring 2009, pp. 203–25. https://doi.org/10.1093/isle/isp010

Ettin, Andrew V. *Literature and the Pastoral*. Yale University Press, 1984.

Evans, Tamara S. "Edith Wharton and Poetic Realism: An Impasse." *The German Quarterly*, vol. 65, no. 3/4, 1992, pp. 361–68. *JSTOR*, www.jstor.org/stable/407594. Accessed Aug. 16, 2020.

Falk, Cynthia G. "'The Intolerable Ugliness of New York': Architecture and Society in Edith Wharton's The Age of Innocence." *American Studies*, vol. 42, no. 2, 2001, pp. 19–43. *JSTOR*, www.jstor.org/stable/40643250. Accessed Apr. 11, 2021.

Farley, Paul and Michael Symmons Roberts. *Edgelands: Journeys into England's True Wilderness.* Vintage, 2012.

Farrand, Beatrix. *Beatrix Farrand's Plant Book for Dumbarton Oaks.* Edited by Diane Kostial McGuire, Dumbarton Oaks, Trustees for Harvard University, 1980.

Farrand, Beatrix. "City Parks." *Municipal Affairs, a Quarterly Magazine, III,* 1899, pp. 687–90.

Feldman, James W. "Introduction: Stories in the Wilderness." *Storied Wilderness: Rewilding the Apostle Islands.* University of Washington Press, 2011, pp. 3–21.

Fenimore Cooper, James. "American and European Scenery Compared." *The Homebook of the Picturesque, or American Scenery, Art, and Literature.* George Putnam, 1852, pp. 51–70.

Ferri, Sabrina. *Ruins Past: Modernity in Italy, 1744–1836.* Oxford University Press, 2015.

Finlay, Alec, editor. *Ian Hamilton Finlay Selections.* University of California Press, 2011.

Finney, Gail. *The Counterfeit Idyll: The Garden Ideal and Social Reality in Nineteenth-Century Fiction.* M. Niemeyer, 1984.

Finoki, Bryan. "The Anatomy of Ruins." *Triple Canopy,* 2009, www.canopycanopycanopy .com/contents/the_anatomy_of_ruins.

Fisher, Mark. *The Weird and the Eerie.* Repeater Books, 2016.

Fiskio, Janet. "Unsettling Ecocriticism: Rethinking Agrarianism, Place, and Citizenship." *American Literature,* vol. 84, 2012, pp. 301–25.

Flaubert, Gustave. *Selected Letters.* Penguin Classics, 1987.

Fleissner, Jennifer L. "The Biological Clock: Edith Wharton, Naturalism, and the Temporality of Womanhood." *American Literature,* vol. 78, no. 3, 2006, pp. 519–48.

Foster, E. M. *A Room with a View.* Edited by Oliver Stallybrass, Edward Arnold, 1977.

Francis, Mark and Randolph T. Hester, editors. *The Meaning of Gardens: Idea, Place and Action.* MIT Press, 1990.

Freire, Jorge. *Edith Wharton: Una mujer rebelde en la edad de la inocencia.* Alrevés, 2015.

Frijda, Nico. *The Laws of Emotion.* Lawrence Erlbaum, 2007.

Frost, Robert. *The Poetry of Robert Frost.* Edited by Edward Connery Lathem, Henry Holt and Company, 2002.

Fryer, Judith. "Book II: Edith Wharton." *Felicitous Space: The Imaginative Structures of Edith Wharton and Willa Cather.* University of North Carolina Press, 1986, pp. 54–199.

Gabrys, Jennifer. *Digital Rubbish: A Natural History of Electronics.* University of Michigan Press, 2011.

Gabrys, Jennifer. "Sink: The Dirt of Systems." *Environment and Planning D: Society and Space,* vol. 27, no. 4, Aug. 2009, pp. 666–81, doi:10.1068/d5708.

Gamboni, Dario. *The Destruction of Art: Iconoclasm and Vandalism since the French Revolution.* Yale University Press, 1997.

Gans, Deborah and Claire Weisz. *Extreme Sites: The Greening of Brownfield.* Academy Press, 2004.

Garrard, Greg. *Ecocriticism.* Routledge, 2010. The New Critical Idiom.

Garrard, Greg. "Radical Pastoral?" *Studies in Romanticism,* vol. 35, no. 3, 1996, pp. 449–65. *JSTOR,* www.jstor.org/stable/25601184. Accessed May 27, 2021.

Garrett, Bradley L. "Urban Explorers: Quests for Myth, Mystery and Meaning." *Geography Compass,* vol. 4, no. 10, Oct. 2010, pp. 1448–61, doi:10.1111/j.1749-8198.2010.00389.x.

Giesecke, Annette and Naomi Jacobs, editors. *Earth Perfect? Nature, Utopia and the Garden.* Black Dog, 2012.

Gifford, Terry. *Pastoral.* Routledge, 1999. The New Critical Idiom.

Gifford, Terry. *Pastoral.* Routledge, 2019. The New Critical Idiom.

Ginsberg, Robert. *The Aesthetics of Ruins*. Rodopi, 2004.

Goldsmith, Meredith and Emily J. Orlando, editors. *Edith Wharton and Cosmopolitanism*. University Press of Florida, 2016.

Goldstein, Laurence. *Ruins and Empire: The Evolution of a Theme in Augustan and Romantic Literature*. University of Pittsburgh Press, 1977.

González-Ruibal, Alfredo. "Time to Destroy: An Archaeology of Supermodernity." *Current Anthropology*, vol. 49, no. 2, 2008, pp. 247–79. *JSTOR*, www.jstor.org/stable/10.1086/526099. Accessed Apr. 1, 2020.

Goodbody, Axel and Kate Rigby. *Ecocritical Theory: New European Approaches*. University of Virginia Press, 2011.

Goodman, Susan. "Edith Wharton's 'Sketch of an Essay on Walt Whitman'." *Walt Whitman Quarterly Review*, vol. 10, Summer 1992, pp. 3–9. https://doi.org/10.13008/2153-3695.134

Gordillo, Gastón. "Ships Stranded in the Forest: Debris of Progress on a Phantom River." *Current Anthropology*, vol. 52, no. 2, 2011, pp. 141–67. *JSTOR*, www.jstor.org/stable/10.1086/658909. Accessed Apr. 2, 2020.

Graham, Wade. *American Eden: From Monticello to Central Park to Our Backyards*. HarperCollins, 2011.

Grandin, Greg. *Fordlandia: The Rise and Fall of Henry Ford's Forgotten Jungle City*. Metropolitan Books, 2009.

Greenaway, Kate. *Language of Flowers*. Gramercy Publishing Company, 1978.

Greene, Graham. "'Short Stories.'" *Edith Wharton: The Contemporary Reviews*, edited by James W. Tuttleton et al., Cambridge University Press, 1992, p. 537.

Greene, Graham. "'Short Stories.'" *Edith Wharton: The Contemporary Reviews*, edited by James W. Tuttleton et al., Cambridge University Press, 1992, p. 542.

Greenleaf Whittier, John. "Prelude", "Among the Hills." *The Poetic Works of John Greenleaf Whittier*, vol. 1, Houghton Mifflin, 1892. 4 vols.

Greg, W. W. *Pastoral Poetry and Pastoral Drama*. Russell & Russell, 1959.

Grieco, Margaret and John Urry, editors. *Mobilities: New Perspectives on Transport and Society*. Routledge, 2012.

Groth, Jacqueline and Eric Corijn. "Reclaiming Urbanity: Indeterminate Spaces, Informal Actors and Urban Agenda Setting." *Urban Studies*, vol. 42, no. 3, 2005, pp. 503–26. *JSTOR*, www.jstor.org/stable/43198269. Accessed Oct. 2, 2020.

Gutzwiller, Kathryn J. *Theocritus' Pastoral Analogies: The Formation of a Genre*. Wisconsin University Press, 1991.

Haila, Yrjo and Chuck Dyke, editors. *How Nature Speaks: The Dynamics of the Human Ecological Condition*. Duke University Press, 2006.

Hanley, Keith and John K. Walton, *Constructing Cultural Tourism: John Ruskin and the Tourist Gaze*. Channel View Publications, 2010.

Hanson, David et al. *Waste Land: Meditations on a Ravaged Landscape*. Aperture, 1997.

Harbison, Robert. *Ruins and Fragments: Tales of Loss and Rediscovery*. Reaktion Books, 2015.

Hardy, Thomas. "The Revisitation." *The Complete Poems of Thomas Hardy*. Macmillan, 1982.

Harries, Elizabeth Wanning. *The Unfinished Manner: Essays on the Fragment in the Later Eighteenth Century*. University Press of Virginia, 1994.

Harris, Alexandra. *Romantic Moderns: English Writers, Artists and the Imagination from Virginia Woolf to John Piper*. Thames & Hudson, 2010.

Harrison, Carolyn and Gail Davies. "Conserving Biodiversity that Matters: Practitioners' Perspectives on Brownfield Development and Urban Nature Conservation in

London." *Journal of Environmental Management*, vol. 65, no. 1, 2002, pp. 95–108, doi:10.1006/jema.2002.0539

Harrison, Robert Pogue. *Gardens: An Essay on the Human Condition*. University of Chicago Press, 2008.

Hawkins, Gay and Stephen Muecke, editors. *Culture and Waste: The Creation and Destruction of Value*. Rowman & Littlefield, 2003.

Hawkins, H. Gregory. "Turn Your Trash into… Rubbish, Art and Politics. Richard Wentworth's Geographical Imagination." *Social & Cultural Geography*, vol. 11, no. 8, 2010, pp. 805–27. https://doi.org/10.1080/14649365.2010.522719.

Hawthorne, Nathaniel. *The Blithedale Romance*. Edited by Seymour Gross and Rosalie Murphy, W. W. Norton, 1978. Norton Critical Edition.

Hawthorne, Nathaniel. "Letters and Journals, 1841." *The Blithedale Romance*, edited by Seymour Gross and Rosalie Murphy, W. W. Norton, 1978. Norton Critical Edition.

Hawthorne, Nathaniel. *The Marble Faun. Novels: 'Fanshawe', 'The Scarlet Letter', 'The House of the Seven Gables', 'The Blithedale Romance', 'The Marble Faun'*. Library of America, 1983, pp. 849–1242.

Haycock, Jennifer. "'Unmediated Bonding Between Men': The Accumulation of Men in the Short Stories'." *Edith Wharton and the Conversations of Literary Modernism*. Palgrave Macmillan, 2008, pp. 75–100.

Hayman, John. *John Ruskin and Switzerland*. Wilfred Laurier University Press, 1990.

Haytock, Jennifer. "The Dogs of 'Kerfol': Animals, Authorship, and Wharton." *Journal of the Short Story in English*, vol. 58, June 1, 2012, pp. 175–86.

Head, Dominic. *An Introduction to Modern British Fiction 1950–2000*. Cambridge University Press, 2002.

Heckscher, Morrison H. *Creating Central Park*. Metropolitan Museum of Art, 2008.

Hedrick, U. P. *A History of Horticulture in America to 1860*. Timber Press, 1988.

Heidegger, Martin. *Country Path Conversations*. Translated by Bret W. Davis, Indiana University Press, 2016.

Heinberg, Richard. *Memories and Visions of Paradise: Exploring the Universal Myth of a Lost Golden Age*. Quest Books, 1995.

Heise, Ursula K. *Sense of Place and Sense of Planet: The Environmental Imagination of the Global*. Oxford University Press, 2008.

Hell, Julia. *The Conquest of Ruins: The Third Reich and the Fall of Rome*. University of Chicago Press, 2019.

Hendry, Michael. "Two Greek Syllables in Wharton's 'The Pelican'." *Notes and Queries*, vol. 255, no. 2, 2010, pp. 224–25.

Heringman, Noah. *Romantic Rocks, Aesthetic Geology*. Cornell University Press, 2004.

Hess, Scott. "Postmodern Pastoral, Advertising, and the Masque of Technology." *Interdisciplinary Studies in Literature and Environment*, vol. 11, no. 1, 2004, pp. 71–100. *JSTOR*, www.jstor.org/stable/44086226. Accessed May 24, 2021.

Hess, Scott. *William Wordsworth and the Ecology of Authorship: The Roots of Environmentalism in Nineteenth Century Culture*. University of Virginia Press, 2012.

Higgins, Thomas. *The Crooked Elm, Or, Life by the Wayside*. Whittemore, Niles and Hall, 1858.

High, Steven C. and David W. Lewis. *Corporate Wasteland: The Landscape and Memory of Deindustrialization*. Cornell University Press, 2007.

Hiltner, Ken. "General Introduction." *Ecocriticism: The Essential Reader*, edited by Ken Hiltner, Routledge, 2015, pp. xii–xvi.

Hinchliffe, Steve, et al. "Urban Wild Things: A Cosmopolitical Experiment." *Environment and Planning D: Society and Space*, vol. 23, no. 5, Oct. 2005, pp. 643–58, doi:10.1068/d351t.

Hiss, Tony. *The Experience of Place: A new way of looking and dealing with our radically changing cities and countryside*. Random House, 1990.

Hochman, Barbara. "The Good, the Bad, and the Literary: Edith Wharton's 'Bunner Sisters' and the Social Contexts of Reading." *Studies in American Naturalism*, vol. 1, no. 1/2, 2006, pp. 128–43. *JSTOR*, www.jstor.org/stable/23431279. Accessed May 28, 2021.

Holloway, Lewis and Moya Kneafsey, editors. *Geographies of Rural Cultures and Societies*. Ashgate, 2004.

The Holy Bible: New International Version. Hodder & Stoughton, 2000.

Hoyles, Martin. *The Story of Gardening*. Journeyman Press, 1991.

Hutchinson, Stuart. "Unpackaging Edith Wharton: 'Ethan Frome' and 'Summer.'" *The Cambridge Quarterly*, vol. 27, no. 3, 1998, pp. 219–32. *JSTOR*, www.jstor.org/stable/42967926 Accessed Aug. 14, 2020.

Huyssen, Andreas. "Introduction." *Present Pasts: Urban Palimpsests and the Politics of Memory*. Standford University Press, 2003, pp. 1–10.

Huyssen, Andreas. "Nostalgia for Ruins." *Grey Room*, no. 23, 2006, pp. 6–21. www.jstor.org/stable/20442718. Accessed Feb. 13, 2020.

Hyde Bailey, Liberty. *The Outlook to Nature*. The Macmillan Company, 1905.

Illingworth, John. "Ruskin and Gardening." *Garden History*, vol. 22, no. 2, 1994, pp. 218–33. *JSTOR*, www.jstor.org/stable/1587029. Accessed Feb. 22, 2021.

Ireton, Sean and Caroline Schaumann. *Heights of Reflection: Mountains in the German Imagination from the Middle Ages to the Twenty-First Century*. Bowdell & Brewer, 2012.

Jackson, J. B. *The Necessity for Ruins*. University of Massachusetts Press, 1980.

Jackson, Peter et al. *Transnational Spaces*. Routledge, 2004.

Jackson Downing, Andrew. *Rural Essays*. G. P. Putnam, 1853.

Jackson Downing, Andrew. *A Treatise on the Theory and Practice of Landscape Gardening Adapted to North America*. Wiley and Putnam, 1841.

James, Henry. *The American Scene*. Chapman and Hall, 1907.

James, Henry. *The Italian Hours*. Harper, 1909.

Janowitz, Anne. *England's Ruins: Poetic Purpose and the National Landscape*. Blackwell, 1990.

Jehlen, Myra. *American Incarnation: The Individual, the Nation, the Continent*. Harvard University Press, 1986.

Jenkins, Jennifer, editor. *Remaking the Landscape: The Changing Face of Britain*. Profile Books, 2002.

Jones, Hannah. "Exploring the Creative Possibilities of Awkward Space in the City." *Landscape and Urban Planning*, vol. 83, no. 1, Nov. 12, 2007, pp. 70–76, doi:10.1016/j.landurbplan.2007.05.007.

Jones, Karen R. and John Wills. *The Invention of the Park: Recreational Landscapes from the Garden of Eden to Disney's Magic Kingdom*. Polity Press, 2005.

Jorgensen, Anna and Marian Tylecote. "Ambivalent Landscapes—Wilderness in the Urban Interstices." *Landscape Research*, vol. 32, no. 4, Aug. 2, 2007, pp. 443–62, doi:10.1080/01426390701449802.

Joslin, Katherine. "'Embattled tendencies'." *Special Relationships*, edited by Janet Beer and Bridget Bennett, Manchester University Press, 2018. https://doi.org/10.7765/9781526137654.00015. Web. May 28, 2021.

Kant, Immanuel. *Observations on the Feeling of the Beautiful and Sublime and Other Writings.* Edited by Patrick R. Frierson and Paul Guyer, Cambridge University Press, 2011.

Kant, Immanuel. *Political Writings.* Translated by H. B. Nisbet, edited by Hans Reiss, Cambridge University Press, 1991.

Kaplan, Amy. *The Social Construction of American Realism.* University of Chicago Press, 1988.

Keetley, Dawn and Matthew Wynn Sivils. "Introduction: Approaches to the Ecogothic." *Ecogothic in Nineteenth-Century American Literature*, edited by Dawn Keetley and Matthew Wynn Sivils, Routledge, 2018, pp. 1–20.

Kemp, Wolfgang and Joyce Rheuban. "Images of Decay: Photography in the Picturesque Tradition." vol. 54, Oct. 1990, p. 102. https://doi.org/10.2307/778671.

Kennedy, Greg. "Chapter 1: Waste." *An Ontology of Trash: The Disposable and Its Problematic Nature.* SUNY Press, 2007, pp. 1–22.

Kermode, Frank. *English Pastoral Poetry: From the Beginnings to Marvell.* George G. Harrap, 1952.

Kerridge, Richard. "Ecothrillers: Environmental Cliffhangers." *The Green Studies Reader: From Romanticism to Ecocriticism*, edited by Laurence Coupe, Routledge, 2000, pp. 242–52.

Klages, Mary. *Woeful Afflictions: Disability and Sentimentality in Victorian America.* University of Pennsylvania Press, 1999.

Knights, Pamela. *The Cambridge Introduction to Edith Wharton.* Cambridge University Press, 2009.

Koolhaas, Rem. *Delirious New York: A Retroactive Manifesto for Manhattan.* Monacelli Press, 1994.

Kornasky, Linda. "On 'Listen[Ing] to Spectres Too': Wharton's 'Bunner Sisters' and Ideologies of Sexual Selection." *American Literary Realism, 1870-1910*, vol. 30, no. 1, 1997, pp. 47–58. *JSTOR*, www.jstor.org/stable/27746714. Accessed May 28, 2021.

Krupar, Shiloh R. "Alien Still Life: Distilling the Toxic Logics of the Rocky Flats National Wildlife Refuge." *Environment and Planning D: Society and Space*, vol. 29, no. 2, Apr. 2011, pp. 268–90, doi:10.1068/d12809.

Krupar, Shiloh R. "Where Eagles Dare: An Ethno-Fable with Personal Landfill." *Environment and Planning D: Society and Space*, vol. 25, no. 2, Apr. 2007, pp. 194–212, doi:10.1068/d4505.

Lahusen, Thomas. "Decay or Endurance? The Ruins of Socialism." *Slavic Review*, vol. 65, no. 4, 2006, pp. 736–46. *JSTOR*, www.jstor.org/stable/4148452. Accessed Apr. 2, 2020.

"Landscapes of Waste." *Companion Encyclopedia of Geography: From Local to Global*, by Ian Douglas et al., Taylor & Francis, 2007, pp. 703–21.

Laqueur, Thomas W. *The Work of the Dead: A Cultural History of Mortal Remains.* Princeton University Press, 2015.

Lazare, Félix and Louis Lazare. *Dictionnaire Administratif et Historique des Rues de Paris et de ses Monuments.* Paris, 1844.

Lazzaro, Claudia. *The Italian Renaissance Garden: from the Conventions of Planting, Design, and Ornament to the Grand Gardens of Sixteenth-Century Central Italy.* Yale University Press, 1990.

Leask, Nigel. *Curiosity and the Aesthetics of Travel Writing, 1700–1800.* Oxford University Press, 2002.

Lee, Hermione. *Edith Wharton.* Vintage Books, 2008.

Lee, Hermione. "Introduction." *Ethan Frome; Summer; Bunner Sisters*, by Edith Wharton, Everyman's Library, 2008, pp. Ix–xxiv.

Lee, Vernon. *Genius Loci: Notes on Places*. Leopold Classic Library, 1898.

Lee, Vernon. *Hauntings and Other Fantastic Tales*. Edited by Catherine Maxwell and Patricia Pulham, Broadview Press, 2006.

Leed, Eric J. *The Mind of the Traveller: From Gilgamesh to Global Tourism*. Basic Books, 1991.

Lefebvre, Henri. *La production de l'espace*. Anthropos, 2000.

Lefebvre, Henri. *The Production of Space*. Translated by Donald Nicholson-Smith, Blackwell, 1991.

Leopardi, Giacomo. *Canti*. Mondadori, 1987.

Lévesque, Luc. *The "terrain vague" as Material - Some Observations*. House Boat, 2002.

Levine, Jessica. *Delicate Pursuit: Discretion in Henry James and Edith Wharton*. Routledge, 2013.

Lewis, Richard Warrington Baldwin. *Edith Wharton: A Biography*. Harper & Row, 1975.

Lidoff, Joan. "Another Sleeping Beauty: Narcissism in The House of Mirth." *American Quarterly*, vol. 32, no. 5, 1980, pp. 519–39. *JSTOR*, www.jstor.org/stable/2712411. Accessed May 28, 2021.

Lindner, Christoph. *Imagining New York City: Literature, Urbanism, and the Visual Arts, 1890–1940*. Oxford University Press, 2015.

Lorimer, Jamie. "Living Roofs and Brownfield Wildlife: Towards a Fluid Biogeography of UK Nature Conservation." *Environment and Planning A: Economy and Space*, vol. 40, no. 9, Sept. 2008, pp. 2042–60, doi:10.1068/a39261.

Loudon, John Claudius. *Encyclopedia of Architecture*. Appleton & Co., 1839.

Loughrey, Bryan. *The Pastoral Mode: A Casebook*. Macmillan, 1984.

Loukaki, Argyro. *Living Ruins, Value Conflicts*. Ashgate, 2008.

Love, Glen A. "Ecocriticism and Science: Toward Consilience?" *New Literary History*, vol. 30, no. 3, 1999, pp. 561–76. www.jstor.org/stable/20057555. Accessed Apr. 14, 2021.

Lovejoy, Arthur O. "The First Gothic Revival and the Return to Nature." *Modern Language Notes*, vol. 47, no. 7, 1932, pp. 419–46. *JSTOR*, www.jstor.org/stable/2913411. Accessed Dec. 11, 2020.

Lovejoy, Arthur O. "'Nature' as Aesthetic Norm." *Modern Language Notes*, vol. 42, no. 7, 1927, pp. 444–50. *JSTOR*, www.jstor.org/stable/2913933. Accessed Dec. 10, 2020.

Lutz, Tom. *Cosmopolitan Vistas: American Regionalism and Literary Value*. Cornell University Press, 2004.

Luzzi, Joseph. *Romantic Europe and the Ghost of Italy*. Yale University Press, 2008.

Lynch, Kevin and Michael Southworth. "The Waste of Place." *Wasting Away*. Sierra Club Books, 1990, pp. 81–117.

Lynn, Robin and Francis Morrone. *Guide to New York City Urban Landscapes*. W.W. Norton & Company, 2013.

Mabey, Richard. *The Unofficial Countryside*. Dovecote, 2010.

Macaulay, Rose. *The Pleasure of Ruins*. Walker and Company, 1966.

MacFarlane, Robert. *Mountains of the Mind*. Pantheon Books, 2003.

MacKian, Sara. *Everyday Spirituality: Social and Spatial Worlds of Enchantment*. Palgrave Macmillan, 2012.

Maclean, Gerald, Donna Landry, and Joseph P. Ward, editors. *The Country and the City Revisited: England and the Politics of Culture, 1550–1850*. Cambridge University Press, 1999.

Makowsky, Veronica and Lynn Z. Bloom. "Edith Wharton's Tentative Embrace of Charity: Class and Character in *Summer*." *American Literary Realism*, vol. 32, 2000, pp. 220–33.

Mansfield, Katherine. *Katherine Mansfield Notebooks: Complete Edition*. Edited by Margaret Scott, University of Minnesota Press, 2002.

Manzulli, Mia. "Edith Wharton's Gardens as a Legacy to Alice Walker." *Edith Wharton Review*, vol. 11, no. 2, 1994, pp. 9–16. *JSTOR*, www.jstor.org/stable/43512844. Accessed Mar. 19, 2021.

Manzulli, Mia. "'Garden Talks': The Correspondence of Edith Wharton and Beatrix Farrand." *A Forward Glance: New Essays on Edith Wharton*, edited by Clare Colquitt, Susan Goodman, and Candace Waid, Associated University Presses, 1999.

Marinelli, Peter V. *Pastoral*. Methuen, 1971. The Critical Idiom.

Marx, Leo. "American Literary Culture and the Fatalistic View of Technology." *The Pilot and the Passenger: Essays on Literature, Technology, and Culture in the United States*, edited by Leo Marx, Oxford University Press, 1988, pp. 179–207.

Marx, Leo. "Does Pastoralism Have a Future?" *The Pastoral Landscape*, edited by John Dixon Hunt, Washington National Gallery of Art, 1992.

Marx, Leo. *The Machine in the Garden: Technology and the Pastoral Ideal in America*. Oxford University Press, 1967.

Mason, Randall. *The Once and Future New York: Historic Preservation and the Modern City*. University of Minnesota Press, 2009.

Matless, David. "Nature, the Modern and the Mystic: Tales from Early Twentieth Century Geography." *Transactions of the Institute of British Geographers*, vol. 16, no. 3, 1991, pp. 272–86. *JSTOR*, www.jstor.org/stable/622948. Accessed May 28, 2021.

Mazel, David. *Mountaineering Women: Stories By Early Climbers*. Texas A&M University Press, 1994.

McDowell, Margaret B. "Edith Wharton's Ghost Stories." *Criticism*, vol. 12, no. 2, 1970, pp. 133–52.

McFarland, Thomas. "Introduction: Fragmented Modalities and the Criteria of Romanticism." *Romanticism and the Forms of Ruin*. Princeton University Press, 1981.

McKay, George. *Radical Gardening: Politics, Idealism and Rebellion in the Garden*. Frances Lincoln, 2011.

McKibben, Bill. *The End of Nature*. Viking, 1990.

McLean, Teresa. *Medieval English Gardens*. Dover Publications, 1980.

McMaster, Anne. "Beginning with the Same Ending: Virginia Woolf and Edith Wharton." *Virginia Woolf: Texts and Contexts: Selected Papers from the Fifth Annual Conference on Virginia Woolf*, edited by Beth Rigel Daugherty and Eileen Barrett, Pace University Press, 1996.

McNamara, Kevin R. and Timothy Gray. "Some Versions of Urban Pastoral." *The Cambridge Companion to the City in Literature*, edited by Kevin R. McNamara, Cambridge University Press, Cambridge, 2014, pp. 245–60. Cambridge Companions to Literature.

McNeillie, Andrew. *The Essays of Virginia Woolf*. Vol. 1. 1904-1912. Harcourt, 1986.

Meeker, Joseph. *The Comedy of Survival: Literary Ecology and a Play Ethic*. 3rd ed., University of Arizona Press, 1980.

Mellor, Leo. *Reading the Ruins: Modernism, Bombsites and British Culture*. Cambridge University Press, 2011.

Merchant, Carolyn. *Reinventing Eden: The Fate of Nature in Western Culture*. 2nd ed., Routledge, 2013.

Mickey, Thomas. *America's Romance with the English Garden*. Ohio University Press, 2013.

Mikkelsen, Ann Marie. *Pastoral, Pragmatism, and Twentieth-Century American Poetry*. Palgrave Macmillan, 2011.

Miller, Mara. *The Garden as Art*. SUNY Press, 1993.

Miller, Perry. *Nature's Nation*. Harvard University Press, 1967.

Mills, Sara. *Discourses of Difference: An Analysis of Women's Travel and Colonialism*. Routledge, 1991.

Monteiro, George. "Suicide and the New England Conscience: Notes on Edith Wharton, Robinson, and Frost." *American Literary Realism*, vol. 50, no. 2, 2018, pp. 145–51. *JSTOR*, www.jstor.org/stable/10.5406/amerlitereal.50.2.0145. Accessed Mar. 1, 2021.

Montgomery, Maureen E. "Leisured Lives." *Edith Wharton in Context*, edited by Laura Rattray, Cambridge University Press, 2012, pp. 234–42.

Moore, Charles W. et al. *The Poetics of Gardens*. The MIT Press, 2000.

Moore, Gregory C. G. and Helen Fordham. "The Victorian Effort to Exclude the Amateur 'Public Intellectual' from Economics: The Case of Stephen Versus Ruskin." *History of Economics Review*, vol. 66, no. 1, 2017, pp. 19–43.

Moore, Sarah A. "Garbage Matters: Concepts in New Geographies of Waste." *Progress in Human Geography*, vol. 36, no. 6, Dec. 2012, pp. 780–99, doi:10.1177/0309132512437077.

Morgan, Colleen. "Book review, *Ruins of Modernity*." *Visual Studies*, vol. 26, no. 1, 2011, p. 84.

Morris Copeland, Robert. *Country Life: A Handbook of Agriculture, Horticulture, and Landscape Gardening*. 2nd ed., Orange Judd and Co., 1867.

Morse Earle, Alice. "Introduction" to Horace Walpole, *Essay on Modern Gardening* (reprint of 1785 edn). Kirgate Press, 1904.

Moser, Walter. "The Accumulation of Waste." *Waste-Site Stories: The Recycling of Memory*, edited by Brian Neville and Johanne Villeneuve, SUNY Press, 2002, pp. 85–106.

Muir, John. *Our National Parks*. University of California Press, 1991.

Nash, Roderick. *Wilderness and the American Mind*. Yale University Press, 1982.

Nicolson, Marjorie Hope. *Mountain Gloom and Mountain Glory: The Development of the Aesthetics of the Infinite*. Cornell University Press, 1959.

Nietzsche, Friedrich. *Thus Spoke Zarathustra: A Book for Everyone and None*. Translated by Graham Parkes, Oxford World's Classics, 2008.

Nietzsche, Friedrich. *The Will to Power*. Translated by Walter Kaufmann, Random House, 1967.

Nowlin, Michael E. "Edith Wharton as Critic, Traveler, and War Hero." *Studies in the Novel*, vol. 30, no. 3, 1998, pp. 444–51. *JSTOR*, www.jstor.org/stable/29533282. Accessed Nov. 2, 2020.

Noyce, Wilfrid. *Scholar Mountaineers: Pioneers of Parnassus*. Roy, 1950.

O'Brien, Dan editor. *Gardening: Philosophy for Everyone*. Wiley-Blackwell, 2010.

O'Nan, Stewart. *Wish You Were Here*. Grove Press, 2002.

Oakes, Timothy and Patricia Price. *The Cultural Geography Reader*. Routledge, 2008.

"The Oaten Flute." *The Oaten Flute: Essays on Pastoral Poetry and the Pastoral Ideal*, by Renato Poggioli, Harvard University Press, 1975, pp. 1–41.

Ohler, Paul. "Sexual Violence and Ghostly Justice in 'The Lady's Maid's Bell' and 'Kerfol.'" *Edith Wharton Review*, vol. 32, no. 1–2, 2016, pp. 40–56. *JSTOR*, www.jstor.org/stable/10.5325/editwharrevi.32.1-2.0040. Accessed Apr. 1, 2021.

Olin-Ammentorp, Julie. *Edith Wharton, Willa Cather, and the Place of Culture*. University of Nebraska Press, 2019.

Olin-Ammentorp, Julie. "Wharton and World War I." *Edith Wharton in Context*, edited by Laura Rattray, Cambridge University Press, Cambridge, 2012, pp. 293–301. Literature in Context.

Olmsted, Frederick Law. *Writings on Landscape, Culture, and Society*. Edited by Charles E. Beveridge, Library of America, 2015.

Olmsted, Frederick Law and Theodora Kimball. *Forty Years of Landscape Architecture: Central Park*. MIT Press, 1973.

Orlando, Emily J. *Edith Wharton and the Visual Arts*. University of Alabama Press, 2007.

Orlando, Francesco. *Obsolete Objects in the Literary Imagination: Ruins, Relics, Rarities, Rubbish, Uninhabited Places, and Hidden Treasures*. Yale University Press, 2008.

Orne Jewett, Sarah. *Country By-Ways*. Houghton, Mifflin and Company, 1881.

Outka, Paul. *Race and Nature from Transcendentalism to the Harlem Renaissance*. Palgrave Macmillan, 2008.

Page, Max. *The Creative Destruction of Manhattan, 1900–1940*. University of Chicago Press, 1999.

"palimpsest, n. and adj." *OED Online*, Oxford University Press, March 2020. www.oed.com/view/Entry/136319. Accessed Apr. 1, 2020.

Park, Mungo. *Travels in the Interior Districts of Africa; Performed in the Years 1795, 1796, and 1797*. London, 1799.

Parsons, Glenn and Allen Carlson. *Functional Beauty*. Clarendon Press, 2008.

Peel, Robin. "Wharton and Italy." *Edith Wharton in Context*, edited by Laura Rattray, Cambridge University Press, Cambridge, 2012, pp. 285–92. Literature in Context.

Penrose, Sefryn, editor. *Images of Change: An Archaeology of England's Contemporary Landscape*. English Heritage, 2008.

Perez, Gilberto. "Introduction: Film and Physics." *The Material Ghost: Films and Their Medium*. The Johns Hopkins University Press, 2000, pp. 1–28.

Perrault, Charles and Alfred Edwin Johnson. *Perrault's Fairy Tales*. Dover Publications, 1969.

Phillips, Dana. *The Truth of Ecology*. Oxford University Press, 2003.

Pierrot, Jean. *The Decadent Imagination, 1800–1900*. Translated by D. Cottman, Chicago: Chicago University Press, 1981.

Piggott, Stuart. *Ancient Britons and the Antiquarian Imagination: Ideas from the Renaissance to the Regency*. Thames and Hudson, 1989.

Piggott, Stuart. *Ruins in a Landscape: Essays in Antiquarianism*. Edinburgh University Press, 1976.

Pile, Steve. "Emotions and Affect in Recent Human Geography." *Transactions of the Institute of British Geographers*, vol. 35, no. 1, 2010, pp. 5–20. *JSTOR*, www.jstor.org/stable/40647285. Accessed May 28, 2021.

Piper, John. *British Romantic Artists*. Collins, 1946.

Pite, Ralph. "How Green Were the Romantics?" *Studies in Romanticism*, vol. 35, no. 3, 1996, pp. 357–73. *JSTOR*, www.jstor.org/stable/25601179. Accessed May 25, 2021.

Pollan, Michael. *Second Nature: A Gardener's Education*. Grove Press, 1991.

Pope, Alexander. "Discourse on Pastoral Poetry." *Essays on Poetry and Criticism*, edited by E. Aubra and Aubrey Williams, Methuen & Co., 1961.

Pusca, Anca. "Industrial and Human Ruins of Postcommunist Europe." *Space and Culture*, vol. 13, no. 3, Aug. 2010, pp. 239–55, doi:10.1177/1206331210365255.

Qviström, Mattias. "Landscapes out of Order: Studying the Inner Urban Fringe beyond the Rural - Urban Divide." *Geografiska Annaler. Series B, Human Geography*, vol. 89, no. 3, 2007, pp. 269–82. *JSTOR*, www.jstor.org/stable/4621585. Accessed Jan. 28, 2021.

Qviström, Mattias. "A Waste of Time? On Spatial Planning and 'Wastelands' at the City Edge of Malmo (Sweden)." *Urban Forestry & Urban Greening*, vol. 7, no. 3, Aug. 1, 2008, pp. 157–69, doi:10.1016/j.ufug.2007.03.004.

Ramsden, George. *Edith Wharton's Library*. Stone Trough Books, 1999.

Randel, Fred V. "The Mountaintops of English Romanticism." *Texas Studies in Literature and Language*, vol. 23, no. 3, 1981, pp. 294–323. *JSTOR*, www.jstor.org/stable/40754651. Accessed Nov. 13, 2020.

Restuccia, Frances L. "The Name of the Lily: Edith Wharton's Feminism(s)." *Contemporary Literature*, vol. 28, no. 2, 1987, pp. 223–38. *JSTOR*, www.jstor.org/stable/1208389. Accessed Nov. 30, 2020.

Rich, Charlotte. "Fictions of Colonial Anxiety: Edith Wharton's 'The Seed of the Faith' and 'A Bottle of Perrier'." *Journal of the Short Story in English* [Online], vol. 43, Autumn 2004, Online since August 5, 2008, connection on April 30, 2019, pp. 1–12.

Ring, Jim. *How the English Made the Alps*. Faber & Faber, 2011.

Robinson, Roxana. "Introduction." *The New York Stories of Edith Wharton*. New York Review of Books, 2007, pp. vii–xxviii.

Rose, Alan Henry. "'Such Depths of Sad Initiation': Edith Wharton and New England." *The New England Quarterly*, vol. 50, no. 3, 1977, pp. 423–39. *JSTOR*, www.jstor.org/stable/364277. Accessed Oct. 2, 2020.

Rosenmeyer, T. G. *The Green Cabinet: Theocritus and the European Pastoral Lyric*. University of California Press, 1969.

Rosenzweig, Roy and Elizabeth Blackmar. *The Park and the People: A History of Central Park*. Cornell University Press, 1992.

Rosowski, Susan J., editor. *Willa Cather's Ecological Imagination*. University of Nebraska Press, 2003.

Ross, Stephanie. *What Gardens Mean*. University of Chicago Press, 1998.

Rossi, Peter H. Rossi. *Down and Out in America: The Origins of Homelessness*. University of Chicago Press, 1989.

Roth, Michael S. et al., editors. *Irresistible Decay: Ruins Reclaimed*. Getty Research Institute for the History of Art & the Humanities, 1998.

Roy, Anjali Gera. *Imperialism and Sikh Migration: The Komagata Maru Incident*. Routledge, 2018.

Ruff, Allan R. *An Author and a Gardener: The Gardens and Friendship of Edith Wharton and Lawrence Johnston*. Windgather Press, 2014.

Ruskin, John. *Little Masterpieces*. Doubleday and McClure, 1898.

Ruskin, John. *Modern Painters, Part V: Of Mountain Beauty, Volume IV*. Smith, Elder and Co., 1904, p. 319.

Ruskin, John. *The Complete Works of John Ruskin*, vol. 5. Edited by E. T. Cook and Alexander Wedderburn, George Allen, 1903.

Ruskin, John. *The Complete Works of John Ruskin*, vol. 6. Edited by E. T. Cook and Alexander Wedderburn, George Allen, 1903.

Ruskin, John. *The Complete Works of John Ruskin*, vol. 39. Edited by E. T. Cook and Alexander Wedderburn, George Allen, 1903.

Ruskin, John. *Praeterita*. Vol. 1, George Allen, 1907.

Ruskin, John. *Praeterita and Dilecta*. Edited by E. T. Cook and Alexander Wedderburn, George Allen, 1908.

Ruskin, John. *The Seven Lamps of Architecture*. Dover Publications, 2017.

Ryle, Martin. "The Past, the Future and the Golden Age: Some Contemporary Versions of Pastoral." *The Pleasures and Politics of Consuming Differently*, edited by Kate Soper, Martin Ryle, and Lyn Thomas, Palgrave Macmillan, 2011.

Sacks, Oliver. "Why We Need Gardens." *Everything in Its Place: First Loves and Last Tales*. Picador, 2020, pp. 243–47.

Saguaro, Shelley. *Garden Plots: The Politics and Poetics of Gardens.* Ashgate Publishing, 2006.

Said, Edward W. *Orientalism.* Penguin, 2003.

Sales, Roger. *English Literature in History 1780–1830: Pastoral and Politics.* St. Martin's Press, 1983.

São Bento Cadima, Margarida. "The Production of Space in Colson Whitehead's Sag Harbor and Edith Wharton's Summer." *RSA Journal Rivista Di Studi Americani*, vol. 30, 2019, pp. 163–78.

Saunders, Judith. "Literary Influences." *Edith Wharton in Context*, edited by Laura Rattray, Cambridge University Press, 2012, pp. 325–34.

Scanlan, John. *On Garbage.* Reaktion Books, 2005.

Schiller, Friedrich. *On the Naive and Sentimental in Literature.* Carcanet New Press, 1981.

Schlegel, Friedrich. *Friedrich Schlegel's Lucinde and the Fragments.* Translated by Peter Firchow, University of Minnesota Press, 1971.

Schönle, Andreas. "Ruins and History: Observations on Russian Approaches to Destruction and Decay." *Slavic Review*, vol. 65, no. 4, 2006, pp. 649–69. *JSTOR*, www .jstor.org/stable/4148448. Accessed Mar. 15, 2020.

Schuyler, David. *New Urban Landscape: The Redefinition of City Form in Nineteenth-Century America.* Johns Hopkins University Press, 1988.

Scobey, David. *Empire City: The Making and Meaning of the New York City Landscape.* Temple University Press, 2002.

Scroggins, Mark. "Review: *Constructing Cultural Tourism.*" *Journal of Tourism History*, vol. 3, no. 3, 2011, pp. 333.

Serres, Michel. *The Natural Contract.* Translated by Elizabeth MacArthur and William Paulson, University of Michigan Press, 1995.

Shackford, Martha Hale. "A Definition of the Pastoral Idyll." *PMLA*, vol. 19, no. 4, 1904, pp. 583–92. *JSTOR*, www.jstor.org/stable/456511. Accessed May 27, 2021.

Shanks, Michael. *The Archaeological Imagination.* Left Coast Press, 2016.

Shelley, Percy Bysshe. "Preface." *Revolt of Islam; a Poem, in Twelve Cantos.* C. and J. Ollier, 1818.

Shanks, Michael et al. "The Perfume of Garbage: Modernity and the Archaeological." *Modernism/modernity*, vol. 11 no. 1, 2004, pp. 61–83. *Project MUSE*, doi:10.1353/ mod.2004.0027.

Shaw, Philip. *The Sublime.* Routledge, 2006.

Shoard, Marion. "Edgelands of Promise." *Landscapes*, vol. 1, no. 2, 2000, pp. 74–93, doi:10. 1179/lan.2000.1.2.74.

Showalter, Elaine. "The Death of the Lady (Novelist): Wharton's *House of Mirth.*" *Representations*, no. 9, 1985, pp. 133–49. *JSTOR*, www.jstor.org/stable/3043768. Accessed Apr. 1, 2020.

Signe Morrison, Susan. *The Literature of Waste: Material Ecopoetics and Ethical Matter.* Palgrave Macmillan, 2015.

Simmel, Georg. "The Alpine Journey." *Theory, Culture and Society*, vol. 8, no. 3, Aug. 1991, pp. 95–98, doi:10.1177/026327691008003006.

Simmel, Georg. "The Ruin," translated by David Kettler. *The Hudson Review*, vol. 11, no. 3, Autumn 1958, pp. 379–85.

Simmel, Georg. "Two Essays." *The Hudson Review*, vol. 11, no. 3, 1958, pp. 371–85. *JSTOR*, www.jstor.org/stable/3848614. Accessed Dec. 2, 2020.

Simonson, Martin et al., editors. *A Contested West: New Readings of Place in Western American Literature.* Portal Editions, 2013.

Singley, Carol J. *Edith Wharton: Matters of Mind and Spirit*. Cambridge University Press, 1995.

Singley, Carol J. "'Gothic Borrowings and Innovations in Edith Wharton's 'A Bottle of Perrier'." *Edith Wharton: New Critical Essays*, edited by Alfred Bendixen and Annette Zilversmit, Garland Publishing, 1992, pp. 271–90.

Skillern, Rhonda. "Becoming a 'Good Girl': Law, Language, and Ritual in Edith Wharton's *Summer*." *The Cambridge Companion to Edith Wharton*, edited by Millicent Bell, Cambridge University Press, 1995, pp. 117–36.

Skoie, Mathilde and Sonia Bjornstad Velaquez. *Pastoral and the Humanities: Arcadia Re-Inscribed*. Bristol Phoenix, 2006.

Skulkind, Jeanne, editor. *Moments of Being: Virginia Woolf, Unpublished Autobiographical Writings*. Harcourt, 1976.

Slotkin, Louis. *Regeneration through Violence: The Mythology of the American Frontier, 1600–1860*. Harper Perennial, 1996.

Smith, Henry Nash. *Virgin Land: The American West as Symbol and Myth*. Harvard University Press, 1950.

Smith, Jos. *The New Nature Writing: Rethinking the Literature of Place*. Bloomsbury, 2017.

Smith, Sidonie. *Moving Lives: Twentieth-Century Women's Travel Writing*, University of Minnesota Press, 2001.

Smith, Vanessa. "Piracy and Exchange: Stevenson's Pacific Fiction." *Robert Louis Stevenson*, edited by Harold Bloom, Chelsea House Publishers, 2005, pp. 261–306.

Snyder, Gary. *The Practice of the Wild*. Counterpoint, 1990.

Somers, Renée. *Edith Wharton as Spatial Activist and Analyst*. Routledge, 2005.

Somers-Hall, Henry. "The Concept of Ruin: Sartre and the Existential City." *Urbis Research Forum Review*, vol. 1, 2009, pp. 17–19.

Sontag, Susan. *Notes on 'Camp'*. Penguin Books, 2018.

Spann, Edward K. *The New Metropolis: New York City, 1840-1857*. Columbia University Press, 1981.

Springer, Carolyn. *The Marble Wilderness: Ruins and Representation in Italian Romanticism, 1775–1850*. Cambridge University Press, 1987.

Steinmetz, George. "Detroit: A Tale of Two Crises." *Environment and Planning D: Society and Space*, vol. 27, no. 5, Oct. 2009, pp. 761–70, doi:10.1068/d2705ed.

Steinmetz, George. "Harrowed Landscapes: White Ruingazers in Namibia and Detroit and the Cultivation of Memory." *Visual Studies*, vol. 23, no. 3, Dec. 2008, pp. 211–37.

Stephen, Leslie. "John Ruskin" [1900]. *The National Review*. In *Studies of a Biographer*, vol. 3, Duckworth, 1902, pp. 83–118.

Stephen, Leslie. "Mr. Ruskin's *Fors Clavigera*." *Saturday Review*, vol. 31, no. 7, 1871, pp. 13–14.

Stephen, Leslie. "Mr. Ruskin's Recent Writings." *Fraser's Magazine*, vol. 9, no. 54, 1874, pp. 688–701.

Stephen, Leslie. "The Regrets of a Mountaineer." *The Playground of Europe*, by Leslie Stephen, Longmans, Green and Co., 1871, pp. 263–98.

Stephen, Leslie. "A Substitute for the Alps." *The National Review*, vol. 23, no. 136, June 1894, pp. 460–67.

Sterling, Charlee M. "Introduction." *Irony in the Short Stories of Edith Wharton*. The E. Mellen Press, 2005, pp. 1–28.

Stewart, Kathleen. *A Space on the Side of the Road: Cultural Poetics in an "Other" America*. Princeton University Press, 1996.

Stewart, Susan. *On Longing: Narratives of the Miniature, the Gigantic, the Souvenir, the Collection.* Duke University Press, 1993.

Stewart, Susan. *The Ruins Lesson: Meaning and Material in Western Culture.* University of Chicago Press, 2020.

Stoler, Ann Laura, editor. *Haunted by Empire: Geographies of Intimacy in North American History.* Duke University Press, 2006.

Stoler, Ann Laura. *Imperial Debris: On Ruins and Ruination.* Duke University Press, 2013.

Strong, Roy. *Garden Party: Collected Writings 1979–99.* Frances Lincoln, 2000.

Stuart Davies, David. "Introduction." *Ghost Stories of Edith Wharton,* by Edith Wharton, Wordsworth Editions, 2009, pp. vii–xii.

Sweeney, Susan Elizabeth. "Edith Wharton's Case of Roman Fever." *Wretched Exotic: Essays on Edith Wharton in Europe,* edited by Katherine Joslin and Alan Price, Peter Lang, 1996, pp. 313–31. XXIV American Literature.

Sweet, Rosemary. *Cities and the Grand Tour: The British in Italy, C.1690-1820.* Cambridge University Press, 2012.

Tally, Robert T. "Review of Bertrand Westphal, *La Géocritique: Réel, fiction, espace.*" *L'Esprit Créateur: The International Quarterly of French and Francophone Studies,* vol. 49, no. 3, 2009, p. 134.

Taylor, Dorceta. "Central Park as a Model for Social Control: Urban Parks, Social Class and Leisure Behavior in Nineteenth-Century America." *Journal of Leisure Research,* vol. 16, no. 2, 1999, pp. 420–77.

Thill, Brian. *Waste.* Bloomsbury Academic, 2015.

Thomas, Sophie. "The Fragment." *Romanticism: An Oxford Guide,* edited by Nicholas Roe, Oxford University Press, 2005, pp. 502–19.

Thomas, Sophie. *Romanticism and Visual Culture.* Routledge, 2010.

Thompson, Michael. "The Filth in the Way." *Rubbish Theory: The Creation and Destruction of Value.* Pluto, 2017, pp. 1–12.

Thrift, Nigel J. *Spatial Formations.* Sage, 1996.

Toliver, Harold E. *Pastoral Forms and Attitudes.* University of California Press, 1971.

Totten, Gary. "Imagining the American West in Wharton's Short Fiction." *Journal of the Short Story in English,* vol. 58, 2012, pp. 143–58.

Totten, Gary. "'Inhospitable Splendour': Spectacles of Consumer Culture and Race in Wharton's 'Summer.'" *Twentieth Century Literature,* vol. 58, no. 1, 2012, pp. 60–89. *JSTOR,* www.jstor.org/stable/41698769. Accessed Oct. 1, 2020.

Totten, Gary. "Women, Art, and the Natural World in Edith Wharton's Works." *The New Edith Wharton Studies,* edited by Jennifer Haytock and Laura Rattray, Cambridge University Press, Cambridge, 2019, pp. 175–88. Twenty-First-Century Critical Revisions.

Towheed, Shafquat and E. G. C. King, editors. *Reading and the First World War: New Directions in Book History.* Palgrave Macmillan, 2015.

Trigg, Dylan. "The Place of Trauma: Memory, Hauntings, and the Temporality of Ruins." *Memory Studies,* vol. 2, no. 1, Jan. 2009, pp. 87–101, doi:10.1177/1750698008097397.

Trotter, David. *Cooking with Mud: The Idea of Mess in Nineteenth-Century Art and Fiction.* Oxford University Press, 2000.

Trumpener, Katie and James M. Nyce. "The Recovered Fragments: Archaeological and Anthropological Perspectives in Edith Wharton's The Age of Innocence." *Literary Anthropology: A New Interdisciplinary Approach to People, Signs, and Literature,* edited by Fernando Poyatos, John Benjamins Publishing Company, 1988, pp. 161–69.

Twain, Mark. *A Tramp Abroad.* American Publishing Co., 1880.

Tylor, Edward Burnett. *Primitive Culture.* John Murray, 1871.

Tynan, Aidan. *The Desert in Modern Literature and Philosophy: Wasteland Aesthetics*. Edinburgh University Press, 2020.

Tyrrell, Ian R. *Transnational Nation United States History in Global Perspective since 1789*. Palgrave Macmillan, 2015.

Urry, John. *Consuming Places*. Routledge, 1995.

Urry, John. *The Tourist Gaze: Leisure and Travel in Contemporary Societies*. Sage, 1990.

Van der Hoorn, Mélanie. "Exorcizing Remains: Architectural Fragments as Intermediaries between History and Individual Experience." *Journal of Material Culture*, vol. 8, no. 2, July 2003, pp. 189–213, doi:10.1177/13591835030082004.

Veblen, Thorstein. *Theory of the Leisure Class*. Oxford University Press, 2007.

"Velarium, n." *OED Online*. Oxford University Press, March 2020. www.oed.com/view/Entry/221954. Accessed Apr. 14, 2020.

Vergara, Camilo José. *American Ruins*. Monacelli Press, 1999.

Vincent, Patrick. "The Moral of Landscape: John Ruskin and John Muir in the Swiss Alps." *Literature, Ethics, Morality: American Studies Perspectives*, edited by Ridvan Askin and Philipp Schweighauser, Tubingen, 2015.

Viney, William. *Waste: A Philosophy of Things*. Bloomsbury Academic, 2014.

Vlach, John Michael. *Back of the Big House: The Cultural Landscape of the Plantation*. exhibition, 1995.

"Voiceful, adj." *OED Online*. Oxford University Press, December 2019. www.oed.com/view/Entry/224337. Accessed Feb. 20, 2020.

Von Rosk, Nancy. "Spectacular Homes and Pastoral Theatres: Gender, Urbanity and Domesticity in the House of Mirth." *Studies in the Novel*, vol. 33, no. 3, 2001, pp. 322–50. JSTOR, www.jstor.org/stable/29533458. Accessed May 24, 2021.

Waid, Candace. "Pomegranate Seeds: Letters from the Underworld (The Touchstone and Ghosts)." *Edith Wharton's Letters from the Underworld: Fictions of Women and Writing*. The University of North Carolina Press, 1991, pp. 173–203.

Waid, Candace. "The Woman behind the Door." *Edith Wharton's Letters from the Underworld: Fictions of Women and Writing*. The University of North Carolina Press, 1991, pp. 85–126.

Warn, David and Oliver Zunz, editors. *The Landscape of Modernity: Essays on New York City, 1900–1940*. Russel Sage Foundation, 1992.

Weingarten, Karen. "Between the Town and the Mountain: Abortion and the Politics of Life in Edith Wharton's *Summer*." *Canadian Review of American Studies/Revue canadienne d'études americaines*, vol. 40, no. 3, 2010, pp. 352–72, doi: 10.3138/cras.40.3.351

Weiss, Allen. *Mirrors of Infinity: The French Formal Garden and 17th-Century Metaphysics*. Princeton Architectural Press, 1995.

Westphal, Bertrand. *Geocriticism: Real and Fictional Spaces*. Translated by Robert T. Tally, Palgrave Macmillan, 2011.

Westphal, Bertrand. *La géocritique: Reel, Fiction, Espace*. Paris: Les Éditions de Minuit, 2007.

Wheeler, Michael. *Ruskin's God*. Cambridge University Press, 1999.

White, Barbara A. "Introduction." *Wharton's New England: Seven Stories and Ethan Frome*, edited by Barbara A. White, University Press of New England, 1995, pp. vii–xxviii.

White, Barbara A. "Wharton's Telling of the Short Story: Theory and Practice." *Edith Wharton: A Study of the Short Fiction*. Twayne Publishers, 1991, pp. 3–26. Twayne's Studies in Short Fiction.

White, Barbara A. "Young Gentlemen Narrators, Ghosts, and Married Couples in the Middle Stories." *Edith Wharton: A Study of the Short Fiction*. Twayne Publishers, 1991, pp. 57–82. Twayne's Studies in Short Fiction.

Whitehead, Sarah. "Demeter Forgiven: Wharton's Use of the Persephone Myth in Her Short Stories." *Edith Wharton Review*, vol. 26, no. 1, 2010, pp. 17–25. *JSTOR*, www.jstor .org/stable/43513029. Accessed Mar. 11, 2021.

Whitehouse, Tanya. *How Ruins Acquire Aesthetic Value: Modern Ruins, Ruin Porn, and the Ruin Tradition*. Palgrave Macmillan, 2018.

Wilford, Justin. "Out of Rubble: Natural Disaster and the Materiality of the House." *Environment and Planning D: Society and Space*, vol. 26, no. 4, Aug. 2008, pp. 647–62, doi:10.1068/d4207.

Williams, David. "Underworld, Underground, Underhistory: Towards a Counterhistory of Waste and Wastelands." *Performance Research*, vol. 15, no. 4, Dec. 2010, pp. 131–40.

Williams, Raymond. *The Country and the City*. Oxford University Press, 1973.

Wilson, Edmund. "Justice to Edith Wharton." *The Wound and the Bow*. Houghton Mifflin Company, 1941, pp. 195–213.

Wilson, Edward O. *In Search of Nature*. Island Press, 1996.

Wilson-Jordan, Jacqueline. "Materializing the Word: The Woman Writer and the Struggle for Authority in 'Mr. Jones.'" *Memorial Boxes and Guarded Interiors: Edith Wharton and Material Culture*, edited by Gary Totten, University of Alabama Press, 2007, pp. 63–82. Studies in American Realism and Naturalism.

Wood, Gillian D'Arcy. *The Shock of the Real: Romanticism and Visual Culture, 1760–1860*. Palgrave, 2001.

Woodward, Christopher. *In Ruins*. Chatto & Windus, 2001.

Woolf, Virginia. "American Fiction." *The Moment and Other Essays*. Harcourt, 1948, pp. 113–27.

Woolf, Virginia. "The Symbol." *A Haunted House: The Complete Shorter Fiction*, edited by Susan Dick, Vintage, 2003.

Wren Atkinson, Jennifer. *Gardenland: Nature, Fantasy, and Everyday Practice*. University of Georgia Press, 2018.

Wright, Janet Stobbs. "Law, Justice, and Female Revenge in 'Kerfol', by Edith Wharton, and 'Trifles' and 'A Jury of her Peers', by Susan Glaspell." *Atlantis*, vol. 24, no. 1, 2002, pp. 225–43. *JSTOR*, www.jstor.org/stable/41055055. Accessed Apr. 2, 2021.

Wylie, Alison. *Thinking from Things: Essays in the Philosophy of Archaeology*. University of California Press, 2002.

Yablon, Nick. "Introduction: Of Light Bulbs and Bathtubs: Excavating the Modern City." *Untimely Ruins: An Archaeology of American Urban Modernity, 1819–1919*. The University of Chicago Press, 2010, pp. 1–17.

Yeazell, Ruth Bernard. "The Conspicuous Wasting of Lily Bart." *ELH*, vol. 59, no. 3, 1992, pp. 713–34. *JSTOR*, www.jstor.org/stable/2873449. Accessed Nov. 1, 2018.

Young, John H. *Our Deportment, or, The Manners, Conduct and Dress of the Most Refined Society: Including Forms for Letters, Invitations, Etc. Also Valuable Suggestions on Home Culture and Training*. F. B. Dickerson & Co., 1879.

Zetzel, Susanna S. "The Garden in the Machine: The Construction of Nature in Olmsted's Central Park." *Prospects*, vol. 14, 1989, pp. 291–339, doi:10.1017/S0361233300005779.

Zilversmit, Annette. "Edith Wharton's Last Ghosts." *College Literature*, vol. 14, no. 3, 1987, pp. 296–309. *JSTOR*, www.jstor.org/stable/25111756. Accessed Apr. 11, 2021.

Zucker, Paul. "Ruins. An Aesthetic Hybrid." *The Journal of Aesthetics and Art Criticism*, vol. 20, no. 2, 1961, pp. 119–30, doi:10.2307/427461. Accessed Mar. 13, 2020.

INDEX

9 781839 988431